INSTINCT IN MAN

INSTINCT IN MAN

A CONTRIBUTION TO THE
PSYCHOLOGY OF EDUCATION

BY

JAMES DREVER, M.A., B.Sc., D.Phil.

Combe Lecturer on Psychology in the University of Edinburgh

SECOND EDITION

Cambridge :
at the University Press
1921

CAMBRIDGE
UNIVERSITY PRESS

University Printing House, Cambridge CB2 8BS, United Kingdom

Cambridge University Press is part of the University of Cambridge.

It furthers the University's mission by disseminating knowledge in the pursuit of education, learning and research at the highest international levels of excellence.

www.cambridge.org
Information on this title: www.cambridge.org/9781107511767

© Cambridge University Press 1921

First edition 1917
Second edition 1921
First published 1921
First paperback edition 2015

A catalogue record for this publication is available from the British Library

ISBN 978-1-107-51176-7 Paperback

PREFATORY NOTE

THE following essay was originally submitted and approved as a thesis for the Doctorate in Philosophy of the University of Edinburgh. Certain slight changes, chiefly in the direction of compressing the historical portions, have since been introduced, but nothing material has been either added or subtracted.

The essential portions of the essay are those represented by chapters V to XI. The short discussions of the 'Sentiments' and the 'Appetites' in chapters IX and XI were added mainly for the sake of completeness, and in order to show the relation of the 'instincts' to mental development and a developed mental life. Originally it was intended to treat this development more fully, but considerations of space forbade, and the discussions in question represent all that is left of that part of the original design. It was also intended to deal in some detail with the investigations and theories of Jung, Freud, and their followers, at least in their educational bearings. Ultimately, however, it was decided to leave this topic for another occasion. Hence, in the work which follows, only the merest suggestions of the relations of these theories to some of the more important points in the discussion will be found.

The historical sketch of views on 'Instinct' in modern times, in chapters II and III, is largely of the nature of an Introduction, and its main purpose is to justify the general sense in which 'Instinct' is used throughout. It is possibly too long for an Introduction, as it is undoubtedly too short for a real history, and no claim to originality of views or treatment is put forward. Nevertheless it is no mere compilation. There has hitherto been no attempt, so far as the writer knows, to deal adequately

with this part of the history of psychology. Hence, though
not claiming consideration as such a history, this section of the
essay may at least claim to indicate the main lines upon which
a real historical discussion of Instinct must proceed. The
object of the essay will explain the reason for the selection
made, as regards the works of the older psychologists to be
specially emphasized. A fairly full account is given of one
aspect of Malebranche's psychology, and from a point of view
seldom previously taken up. There is no English translation
of Malebranche's *Recherche de la Vérité* later than 1700. Consequently his psychology is almost unknown in England, and
seems to have been forgotten in France. This is, we believe,
very unfortunate, for Malebranche must take high rank as a
psychologist. The controversies regarding 'instinct,' of the
later 18th century, and the older 'Vitalism' have not been
considered sufficiently important for our present-day discussions of Instinct, to deserve more than passing mention.

It may perhaps prevent misunderstanding if we state here,
clearly and concisely, our attitude towards one important aspect
of biology and its theories of the origin of Instinct. While
it must be acknowledged that the controversy between Dar-
winians and Lamarckians as to the transmission of acquired
characteristics is by no means settled in favour of the former,
yet the definite adoption of the Darwinian point of view appears
to simplify the treatment of the psychology of Instinct, however it may be as regards its biology. Consequently it has
been deemed advisable to speak throughout as if the theory of
natural selection were the established and orthodox biological
account of the mode in which instincts have been evolved. The
difficulties which this theory involves do not seem, for the
present at any rate, to be psychological difficulties. If and
when they do so present themselves, it may perhaps be necessary
to revise and modify some portions of our treatment, but our
descriptive psychology of Instinct cannot be affected.

The only other point requiring to be noticed is with respect
to the use made of literature, especially of foreign literature.
Wherever a standard translation was available, that has been
utilized, but the originals have also, in the majority of cases,

been consulted, and the originals of all quotations from Malebranche are given in the footnotes. Further the views of no writer have been mentioned, except merely incidentally, without direct recourse being had to the writer's own original works. A full bibliography of practically all the books consulted and used has been appended.

The author desires to acknowledge a Grant, not exceeding £50, in the form of a guarantee against possible loss in the publication of this work, from the Carnegie Trust for the Universities of Scotland.

J. D.

EDINBURGH.
1st July, 1917.

PREFATORY NOTE TO SECOND EDITION

THE gratifying reception which this essay has met with has encouraged the author to allow the second edition to go to press practically unchanged as far as the body of the work is concerned. A few footnotes have been added, and some typographical errors corrected, but otherwise no change has been made there. The only significant difference between this and the first edition is the new appendix on "The Emotional Phase of Affective Experience" which takes the place of the appendix on "The 'Joy' Emotions." This gives the gist of a paper read before a general meeting of the British Psychological Society on the 19th of June, 1920.

The indebtedness of the author to Stout, MacDougall, Lloyd Morgan, Shand, Mitchell, Hobhouse, and other psychologists of the present day—especially the first two—was so obvious that it did not seem necessary to make special mention of the fact in the preface to the first edition. Lest this should seem somewhat ungracious, the author takes this opportunity of recording his deep sense of the debt which he owes to these writers. He would also express his regret if he has at any time interpreted anyone in a sense different from that intended by the original author.

J. D.

EDINBURGH.
30th August, 1920.

CONTENTS

CHAPTER I

INTRODUCTION

Our purpose is to attempt to give a psychological account of Instinct in Man, and thereafter to study, still in the main from the psychological point of view, the relation of Instinct to Emotion, with special reference to human emotions, and the part which Instinct plays in that phase of human development to which we give the name Education. We must, therefore, first of all get a clear idea of what is involved in a 'psychological account.' That we shall make our aim in the present chapter, and we shall also endeavour to arrive at what might be called a working notion of Instinct from the psychological point of view, as a preliminary to the more detailed study of Instinct with the object of attaining a scientific view of it within the universe of discourse of psychology.

To determine clearly what is implied in 'psychological account' is by no means an easy matter. The text-book of psychology is not always to be relied upon as a safe guide in this respect. Owing to the peculiar relation of psychology to the development of the "philosophy of the human mind[1]" the text-book of psychology often contains a good deal that is philosophy rather than psychology. On the other hand, some of the more recent developments in psychology have been in close association with developments in physiology and in

---

[1] This name is characteristically given by philosophers of the Scottish School to their philosophy, which included psychology, epistemology, and ethics, but it may with equal fitness be applied to the whole development of philosophy from Locke to Mill, exclusive of the German philosophical thought of that period. The very great importance of this "philosophy of the human mind" for the development of psychology will be indicated later.

biology, and, as a consequence, the more recent text-books of psychology contain a good deal that is physiology or biology rather than psychology. No doubt most of these divergences from the strict letter of the 'psychological account' could be easily and completely justified from the standpoint of the text-books in question. Nevertheless our concern at present being with the psychological as such, we cannot take any standpoint except the purely psychological.

In the case of a subject like Instinct we should naturally expect a more serious intrusion into psychology on the part of physiology or biology, than on the part of philosophy. Accordingly we may begin by trying to mark off the 'psychological account' from the physiological and the biological. If that is adequately done, the main difficulty will be overcome, and the lesser difficulty from the side of philosophy can be easily met.

The phenomena of animal behaviour which we group together under the term 'instinctive' seem to be primarily the concern of the biologist rather than of the psychologist. In a certain sense biology may of course be regarded as inclusive of psychology, just as it is inclusive of physiology. But that is only the general, and, more especially, the theoretical sense of biology. The concrete and practical activities of the biologist delimit a sphere of work different from the sphere of both psychologist and physiologist, and the actual methods of biology are the methods of neither psychology nor physiology. Hence, at the present stage of development of the sciences which study living organisms and their behaviour, it will probably conduce to clearness both of thought and of exposition, as it will almost certainly conduce to the progress of the respective sciences themselves, if we distinguish somewhat sharply between them.

Biology we may take as the science which studies the general phenomena of life and the behaviour of living organisms objectively. It is concerned, in the first instance, with the behaviour of living organisms and the bearing of that behaviour on the conservation of the individual and the perpetuation of the race. It is concerned, secondly, with the conditions which determine that behaviour in their general objective aspect, that is, so far as these conditions depend upon the general structure of the organism, its relation to its environment, the operation of hereditary transmission, spontaneous variation, and natural selection. It is concerned, in the third place, with the results which follow from that behaviour, again in their general objective aspect, that is, so far as these results determine general structure, relation to environment, the operation of heredity, variation, and natural selection.

Physiology is concerned primarily with the objective study of the properties, processes, and functions of living matter, so far as these determine the behaviour of living organisms, but always with the aim—and this is very important—of ultimately expressing the behaviour of living organisms in terms of physical processes and physical laws. This aim is the inevitable aim of the physiologist as such. If it were realized, then physiology would necessarily become a part of physics, and biology as a separate science would apparently disappear. So long, however, as the phenomena of life refuse to be expressed in terms of physics, physiology as such and biology as such will exist as independent sciences working side by side. But of this we must be perfectly clear. The physiologist is quite within his rights, is in truth doing his duty as physiologist, in pushing the physical explanation of the phenomena of living matter as far as it will go. That some physiologists do not believe that the physical explanation will ever cover all the phenomena of living matter does not alter the essential aim of physiology in the least. Nor does the fact that many physiologists are also biologists, and that most biologists are physiologists, alter the relation between the sciences as such.

What then is the field of psychology as such? Psychology, as such, is primarily concerned with the study of experience as experience, and with the interpretation of the behaviour of living organisms in terms of experience. It finds common ground with the other sciences in its attempting to understand behaviour, the behaviour of living organisms, but for psychology the understanding of behaviour means interpreting it in psychological terms. The characteristic field of psychology is the inner world which in some way 'corresponds' to the external manifestations of activity, which we term behaviour. This field cannot be studied objectively, in the sense in which we speak of objective methods of study as regards physiology. Hence, while both physiologist and psychologist may attempt to explain the same facts of behaviour, the two explanations must necessarily be in very different terms.

This peculiarity of psychology—for this characteristic marks it off from all the physical and natural sciences—is at once its strength and its weakness. It is the strength of psychology, because the psychologist has a more direct relation to his subject matter in his own experience than physicist, physiologist, or biologist can have to his. It is the weakness of psychology because this direct relation is limited to the psychologist's own individual experience, and all knowledge of the experience of other persons and other living organisms is indirect, depending upon inference which becomes less and less reliable the greater the interval, in experience and possibilities of experience, that separates the psychologist from the living organism whose behaviour he seeks to interpret. This weakness places psychology in a very doubtful position, when compared with the natural and physical sciences, and it must be conceded that, where an objective explanation is possible and attainable, and where it is at the same time adequate, it will always, and rightly, have the preference. There is all the more reason in this for the psychologist to assert the rights of his science in its own proper field, if he puts forward any serious claim for the recognition of psychology as a science.

The strength of the psychologist's position, we have said, arises from the fact that he knows his subject matter directly, as far as his own experience is concerned. On the one hand, this fact implies a quite unique command over the organon of interpretation which he employs. On the other hand, if rightly regarded, this direct knowledge of experience entitles the psychologist to assert the independence of his science, no matter how far physiology may push its physical explanation. His explanation is in terms of experience, in psychical terms, and as such lies beyond the reach of any physical explanation. For consider physiology as so advanced as to enable an individual to observe the physical processes taking place in his own brain, which correspond to the experiences he is having[1]. Obviously there will still be a psychical series as well as a physical series, and the impossibility of the two series coinciding will be more apparent than ever.

This might not be very significant for the ultimate scientific explanation of things, were it not that the psychologist finds in the psychical series important factors, which have, and can have, no analogue in the physical series, as, for example, conscious purpose. It may be argued, therefore, that psychology will always preserve biology from being swallowed up by physiology. Further it must be maintained that it is the duty of the psychologist, as of the physiologist in his case, to push the psychical explanation as far as it will go, in the explanation of behaviour not fully and adequately explained by the physiologist in physical terms. This does not appear to have been sufficiently emphasized in the past, but recent work in biology, like that of Jennings[2] in the study of the behaviour of lower organisms, seems to indicate the possibility of an increased recognition of the psychological explanation in the future. In any case there is no mistaking the duty of the psychologist as a psychologist.

This is a matter of such fundamental importance for psychology as a science, that we may be excused for dwelling on it for a little, and trying to see to what conclusions our principle will lead us. With the development of the sciences in question one of two ultimate conditions will come to prevail. There are only the two alternatives. Either the physical explanation of the physiologist will stop at a point, at which the psychical explanation of the psychologist begins, the fields being divided, as it were, by a knife-edge, and biology having, as far as the behaviour of living organisms is concerned, no longer an independent field, that is a field that has not been invaded and subdued by either physiologist or psychologist;

---

[1] Cf. Verworn's account of Du Bois Reymond's 'astronomical knowledge of the brain' in *Allgemeine Physiologie*, p. 32, 1903.

[2] See *Contributions to the Study of the Behaviour of Lower Organisms.* Carnegie Institution of Washington, Publication No. 16. Also McDougall, *Body and Mind,* chap. xix.

or there will be intermediate between the points at which the respective explanations stop a field of vital phenomena, which will belong to the biologist as such by right of occupation, and, by right of conquest, to neither physiologist nor psychologist.

If we consider, for example, the behaviour of living organisms, so low in the scale as the protozoa and metazoa, we shall be able to make this clearer. The physiologist had until quite recently explained the behaviour of these organisms in physical terms by the conception of 'tropism[1].' Within the last ten years almost conclusive evidence has been brought forward, that tropism does not explain their behaviour. Accordingly Jennings, by whom a great deal of valuable work has been done in this field, now puts forward a conception of 'physiological state[2].' At the same time as he employs this conception and term, he acknowledges that there may be a possible explanation in psychological terms[3]. Here is then our point, in what might be called its lowest terms. The psychological explanation of the behaviour of these organisms must be attempted by the psychologist, until it is shown to break down, or until it becomes unnecessary. For the physiologist the object is still to interpret the 'physiological state' in physical terms. Jennings, as biologist, is concerned with this factor, in the conditions determining behaviour, simply as such, and, though his using the term 'physiological state' seems to indicate a leaning towards physiology rather than psychology for the ultimate explanation, his concern is not so much with the ultimate explanation as with the mode in which and the extent to which this factor determines behaviour. For him it is simply a 'vital' phenomenon.

The characteristic weakness of psychology must undoubtedly give a preference to the physiological explanation, when one is forthcoming, and that, even where a psychological explanation seems to cover the facts more completely and adequately, because of the inferential nature of the psychological explanation along its whole course, if we may speak in that way, and the many factors rendering such inference doubtful and difficult

[1] See Jennings, *Behaviour of Lower Organisms*, Paper No. 4.
[2] Jennings, Paper No. 5.　　　　　[3] Jennings, Paper No. 7.

under the particular circumstances. Nevertheless the psychologist is justified in maintaining his psychical explanation, until the whole mass of the phenomena in question, and every detail, are explicable without it, that is to say, until there is nothing left for the psychologist as such to explain.

Leaving biology out of account, let us see how the general principle affects the relations of physiology and psychology. A large and very influential group of psychologists at the present day have virtually abandoned the standpoint of psychology and adopted that of physiology, by conceding that a really scientific explanation of experience, or of mental process, in psychical terms is impossible, because the principle of conservation of energy in the physical world and the necessity imposed upon the physicist, of looking for a causal explanation of a physical process in physical processes, excludes any scientific explanation of behaviour except in physical terms.

" If I move my lips to say yes or no, it is a physical movement, and the whole endless chain of its causes must have gone on in the physical world. Thus the physicist, however far he may be from the actual demonstration of the details, must postulate that those lips were moved to a yes, because the brain processes made it necessary, and these brain processes depended upon the inborn disposition of the nervous system, and the trillions of influences which have reached it since birth[1]."

This is of course true for the physicist, but how it is true for the psychologist is not so clear. With the psychologist this point of view leads either to epiphenomenalism or to some form of the hypothesis of psycho-physical parallelism, which, when we come to consider behaviour, must also become epiphenomenalism, if the whole causal explanation of the behaviour is to be sought in preceding physical process.

Apart from the difficulties which the hypothesis of psycho-physical parallelism involves[2], it is, as a hypothesis, in the extraordinary position of explaining nothing. The physiologist naturally takes the view, that, if it amuses the psychologist to

---

[1] Münsterberg, *Psychology and the Teacher*, p. 104.
[2] See James, *Principles of Psychology*, vol. I, chap. v, and more recently Sturt, *Principles of Understanding*, chap. II, and McDougall, *Body and Mind*, chaps. XI–XIV.

dignify his study with the name of science, he is in the meantime welcome to the amusement, but the processes he is studying make, on his own confession, no difference to the facts, and can have no bearing whatever, ultimately, on the scientific explanation of animal behaviour. As we have seen this is in any case the view which the physiologist as physiologist is bound to take, at least until he has determined the limits beyond which it is impossible for his explanation to carry him. The hypothesis of psycho-physical parallelism is therefore nothing to the physiologist. It is not his hypothesis; it explains nothing for him; he can and does ignore it. On the other hand, the psychologist, so long as he restricts himself to the explanation of behaviour in terms of experience and mental process, does not require the hypothesis. It is only when he wishes to relate his results to the results and the claims of the physiologist, that the need arises for some hypothesis to express and explain this relation. The hypothesis of psycho-physical parallelism expresses this relation as an eternally incomprehensible mystery, and explains it not at all.

The steps by which modern psychology has reached the position, where such a hypothesis becomes possible, are more or less clear. First of all an intellectualistic bias has caused certain important aspects of experience to fall into the background. That rendered possible the mechanical psychology of associationism. Then the experimental and objective methods of the new experimental psychology, bringing physiologist and psychologist together, as regards methods of approach to their subject-matter, have also modified the view of the psychologist regarding the nature of that subject-matter, until sensations, images, memories, emotions have come to present themselves as simply the psychical analogues of certain physiological processes.

Not that the psychologist may not legitimately study the processes in the nervous system, which are correlated with experience, and which mediate between experience and behaviour. He will occupy every little hill of knowledge which enables him to get a better view of his own field, but for him, so far as he is psychologist, "everything has to be found by the direct method, and whatever is suspected from other discovery must be verified by it[1]." McDougall from the physiological side comes very near to the true point of view when he says[2]: "The physiological psychologist must recognize that all the objective methods of psychological study presuppose the results of the subjective or introspective method, and can only be fruitful in so far as they are based upon an accurate introspective analysis of mental processes. He must recognize too that introspective psychology is in a much more advanced condition than neurology."

This is very near the right point of view, but it is still the point of view of the psychological physiologist rather than of the psychologist as such. What requires to be emphasized is, that the indirect explanation of experience in terms of nervous structure and nervous process is no psychological explanation at all, but a physiological one, and that all kinds of errors will creep into psychology unless this fact is clearly recognized. Not only do objective methods presuppose the introspective method, but the results obtained by objective methods are only valid for psychology, when, and in so far as, they can be interpreted in terms of experience. The order of procedure is: introspection, objective study, and then again introspection for the psychological interpretation. What is, as such, incapable of being so interpreted belongs to physiology, not psychology. There is thus a legitimate and an illegitimate physiological psychology, and the hypothesis of psycho-physical parallelism is the undoubted, the unmistakeable offspring of the illegitimate. May we not regard it as at the same time the *reductio ad absurdum* of such a physiological psychology?

There appears to be no necessity for psychology to take the line of thought which leads to psycho-physical parallelism, unless we are prepared to admit that psychology is essentially a branch of physiology. It seems quite gratuitous to assume that causation is a principle applying only to the physical[3],

[1] Mitchell, *Structure and Growth of the Mind*, p. 447.
[2] McDougall, *Physiological Psychology*, p. 13.
[3] See James, *Principles of Psychology*, vol. I, p. 136 f. for a powerful statement on this point.

that the conservation of physical energy is a necessary postulate of psychologist, as of physiologist and physicist, that experience as dynamic cannot be studied scientifically, and that therefore the psychologist must be content with the description of an experience which is epiphenomenal, which is static, and which is merely an abstraction from the reality of life. Are there no effects, even in the physical world, which obstinately refuse to be explained apart from human purpose and endeavour? The mere asking of the question seems sufficient to refute a mechanical psychology, developing from physiological psychology, and resting on the hypothesis of psycho-physical parallelism. It is impossible to discuss the psychology of interest and motive, of emotion and volition, without the conviction being forced upon us that no physiological explanation can ever *explain* these phenomena.

The James-Lange theory of the emotions, which might be regarded as an approach to a physiological explanation in this part of the field of experience, has been definitely rejected even by leading physiologists[1]. Jennings' investigations of the behaviour of lower organisms, already cited, show that the physiological explanation is inadequate to explain behaviour even in such cases. On the other hand, the physiologist must admit that, so long as the psychologist restricts himself to the direct explanation of experience, that is, in terms of experience, there is no gap in his explanation where the work of the physiologist becomes necessary to complete it, while the physiological explanation of experience is far from complete, and its gaps must be filled by the psychologist.

The general position is that the psychologist may sometimes find the indirect explanation of experience in physiological terms useful, just as he may sometimes find the indirect explanation in biological terms useful, but the usefulness, in both cases, is mainly in making clear the relation of experience to behaviour, or of behaviour to experience, where it is not a mere usefulness of analogy. But the psychologist, so far as he is a psychologist, must rely upon, and stand by, his own method, and his own explanation.

[1] Sherrington, *Integrative Action of the Nervous System*, p. 256 ff.

The relation of biology to psychology seems also in need of being cleared up, but, in this case, the main difficulty arises from the fact, that, as against the psychologist, the biologist tends to think as a physiologist. So far as the results of physiological or psychological investigation bear upon the problems of the biologist, he will of course utilize the results obtained by the other sciences, but his problems and his methods are the problems and methods of neither physiology nor psychology, and their results merely supplement his own analysis. That is to say, where biological analysis leaves off in the study of behaviour on the one side, physiological analysis begins, where it leaves off on the other side psychological analysis begins.

In what follows we shall not as a rule require to distinguish the physiological account of Instinct from the biological, and may call both biological. Since the biologist, like the physiologist, studies the behaviour of living organisms from the objective point of view, the biological explanation is continuous with the physiological, in a way in which it cannot be continuous with the psychological. Hence the biologist always tends to talk in physiological terms, rather than psychological, even where he is dealing with phenomena, the physiological explanation of which derives its whole meaning from the investigations of the psychologist. This fact seems to make it still more incumbent on the psychologist to assert the rights of the psychical explanation, or at least to develop the psychical explanation, instead of merely accepting the biological, seeing that, in the present state of biological science, the scales are so heavily weighted against psychology. He will, at any rate, avoid a good deal of confusion by keeping the two accounts separate.

We are still left with the relation of psychology to philosophy. The general principle to be applied here is, that psychology is no more concerned with the ultimate nature and meaning of reality than is any other science. All that psychology is concerned with, is the description and orderly arrangement, or scientific explanation, of the facts of experience from the inner or subjective side, and the relation of these facts of experience to the observed behaviour of living organisms, but not at all with the ultimate meaning of these facts, or of experience, or of life. The psychologist may find it necessary to frame hypotheses, which go beyond the facts themselves, in order to account for the facts psychologically. For example, the psychologist may find it necessary to talk of a mind or soul which experiences, in order to account for the facts of experience[1]. With the ultimate nature of the mind or soul philosophy is of course concerned, but the psychologist is concerned with the soul merely as a conceptual synthesis of certain facts in the field he studies. Or the psychologist may require some hypothesis to cover the facts involved in psychical changes determining or apparently determining physical. Psycho-physical parallelism is such a hypothesis. In so far as this is taken as a statement of the real nature of a certain relation, it concerns the philosopher, but for psychology it might be a mere conceptual synthesis. That this particular hypothesis has no value at all for psychology, and that any value it has must be for philosophy, does not affect the argument in the least. Psychology makes no statement regarding the ultimate nature of the facts it studies, nor the ultimate reality expressed by its hypotheses. Its aim is merely to bring scientific order into a certain field of phenomena; its account and its hypotheses are valid only for the facts they cover, and with reference to the aim of the science itself.

On the other hand a philosophy, developed without regard to the conclusions of psychology, or of the physical sciences, and taking no account of their hypotheses, could hardly hope to satisfy the human reason. For each science is the result of the working of the human reason in a particular limited field, and its validity within its own field cannot be ignored by a philosophy that claims validity in all fields. Thus the conclusions and the hypotheses of psychology, as of other sciences, necessarily furnish problems for philosophy. Philosophy must begin, as it were, where psychology leaves off.

[1] E.g. McDougall in *Body and Mind.*

DEFINITION OF INSTINCT.

The argument has hitherto been very general, but we now come to its application. Is it possible to give a psychological account of Instinct? The answer to this question will depend on the meaning we assign to 'Instinct,' the way in which we define it. The definition of Instinct has recently led to considerable confusion in psychology, both animal and human. Some writers, Rutgers Marshall[1], Lloyd Morgan[2], Stout[3] among others, would restrict the term to the objective, that is, generally, the biological sense. Rutgers Marshall is especially emphatic. "The word Instinct should properly be used in an objective sense, and in an objective sense only." It is the tendency of the clearest writers to avoid its use "with subjective connotation." He finds it difficult to see how the word can be used except in an objective sense[4]. Nearly all modern definitions of Instinct are in objective terms, that is in terms of behaviour, and many psychologists are content to accept this usage, but whether they are justified in doing so is very questionable, as we shall see presently. At the outset, then, we are apparently faced with a definition of Instinct, which practically excludes it from the universe of discourse of psychology.

There is, however, another side of the argument. In general literature from Bacon[5] to the present day, and in popular speech, the word Instinct has had a subjective, though undeniably somewhat vague, signification. Thus the subjective and psychological sense of the word is by far the older, and, in spite of what Rutgers Marshall says, the established sense in our own and modern languages. Further it is true to the root meaning. Now psychology has employed the word in this sense, though again, it must be confessed, often rather vaguely, since before Descartes. Lord Herbert of Cherbury, in his *De Veritate*, published in 1624, in enumerating the human

[1] Rutgers Marshall, *Instinct and Reason*, p. 85.
[2] Lloyd Morgan, *Instinct and Experience*, p. 104 et passim.
[3] *British Journal of Psychology*, vol. III, p. 243.
[4] *Instinct and Reason*, loc. cit. See also Karl Groos, *Die Spiele der Tiere*, English translation by E. Baldwin, p. 62.
[5] "Man, upon the instinct of an advancement formal and essential, is carried to seek an advancement local." *Advancement of Learning*, book II.

faculties, begins with *Instinctus Naturalis*[1]. This Natural
Instinct has a double sense throughout Lord Herbert's work.
It is first of all the original source of the motive forces urging
towards self-preservation both animals and man, and urging
man also towards those things which will secure his happiness[2].
In the second place it is the source of what he calls *Notitiae
Communes*, which are sacred principles, guaranteed by Nature
herself, possessing the six distinguishing characteristics of
priority, independence, universality, certainty, necessity, im-
mediacy[3]. Descartes' 'innate ideas' took the place of Lord
Herbert's 'notitiae communes,' and that part of the connotation of the word Instinct was only occasionally and
incidentally included by subsequent psychologists. But, as
we shall see later, nearly every psychologist since Descartes
has employed the word Instinct, and in a sense generally
corresponding to the first of Lord Herbert's senses.

Moreover, even the biologist has discovered that he cannot
define Instinct, for the purposes of biology, in purely objective
terms. He cannot define Instinct without introducing into the
definition psychological terms, and thus virtually conceding
that Instinct must have a psychological aspect and a psychological sense.

Thus Romanes holds that the only point, "wherein instinct
can be consistently separated from reflex action" is in regard
to its mental constituent, and he would define Instinct as
"mental action (whether in animals or human beings), directed
towards the accomplishing of adaptive movement antecedent
to individual experience, without necessary knowledge of the
relation between the means employed and the ends attained,
but similarly performed under the same appropriate circumstances by all the individuals of the same species[4]."

---

[1] "Quod igitur in omnium est ore, tanquam verum accipimus, neque enim
sine Providentia illa Universali momenta actionum disponente fieri potest quod
ubique fit, denique, si quicquam intra nos Instinctus Naturalis potest, hoc
potest certe, qui cum in Elementis, plantis, irrationaliter, hoc est sine discursu,
operetur; cur non in nobis idem praestiterit, praesertim in iis quae ad nostram
spectant conservationem; cum in homine et plura desiderentur, et in illo
demum reliqua perficiantur animantia?" *De Veritate*, p. 3.

[2] *De Veritate*, p. 81.   [3] *De Veritate*, p. 76.

[4] Romanes, *Animal Intelligence*, p. 15.

Darwin[1], while not attempting a definition of Instinct, finds it necessary to speak of "mental actions" and frequently to use terms descriptive of psychical phenomena in his descriptions of instincts. He also uses the expression "instinct impels." A. R. Wallace maintains[2] that "much of the mystery of instinct arises from the persistent refusal to recognize the agency of imitation, memory, observation, and reason as often forming part of it."

We may consider, therefore, that the psychologist is quite within his rights in discussing Instinct. That even the biologist is forced to concede. The next question is: how are we to define Instinct for the purpose of psychological discussion? The psychologist must preserve as far as possible the continuity of psychological thought, and understand by Instinct what the psychologists of the past have understood by it. Subject to this condition, the psychologist of the present day nevertheless finds himself at a great advantage, as compared with the older psychologists, on account of the data placed at his disposal by the biologist. Two courses seem to be open to the psychologist. He may take his departure from the notion of conscious impulse, as G. H. Schneider, for example, does[3], and define Instinct as "conscious impulse towards actions tending to the preservation of the individual or the maintenance of the race without conscious foresight of the end, and prior to individual experience of the means." Or he may make the nature of the experience which accompanies instinctive behaviour his point of departure, and define Instinct in some such terms as McDougall employs.

Of these alternatives the second seems the preferable one. A psychology of Instinct, starting from the notion of conscious impulse, is in serious difficulties at the very outset, and is almost compelled to follow the biological account instead of developing a psychological account. If, on the other hand, we start from 'instinct experience,' we necessarily start with a

---

[1] Darwin, *Origin of Species*, chap. VII. See also posthumous essay appended to Romanes, *Mental Evolution in Animals*.
[2] A. R. Wallace, *Darwinism*, p. 442.
[3] Schneider, *Der menschliche Wille*, p. 109: "Instinct ist das psychische Streben nach Arterhaltung ohne Bewusstsein des Zweckes von diesem Streben."

psychological account of this experience, and explain our biological facts from the psychological point of view throughout.

McDougall defines[1] not Instinct but 'an instinct,' and he defines this as "an inherited or innate psycho-physical disposition which determines its possessor to perceive, and to pay attention to, objects of a certain class, to experience an emotional excitement of a particular quality upon perceiving such an object, and to act in regard to it in a particular manner, or, at least, to experience an impulse to such action."

The inclusion in the definition of the notion of a 'psycho-physical disposition' is of questionable value, and seems to smack a little of the old Faculty Psychology, or of Herbartianism. Otherwise this is evidently the kind of definition from which the psychologist must start. It is in psychological terms. It attempts to characterize the kind of experience, which accompanies and underlies instinctive behaviour, finding it necessary to describe this experience as involving cognitive, affective, and conative elements. Whether McDougall's description of 'instinct experience' is right or wrong, or partly right and partly wrong, we shall proceed to enquire later. At any rate it is a psychological definition, bringing Instinct into the psychological universe of discourse, and making a discussion of Instinct by the psychologist possible. It is also, beyond question, in line with the original sense, both popular and psychological, of the word 'instinct' as a 'prompting from within' arising from the natural constitution of men and animals, and determining the behaviour of man or animal, sometimes independently of what is popularly opposed to it, and popularly called 'intelligence' or 'reason.'

There is, however, another definition of Instinct, which has been largely employed in psychological works during the last half-century, and which may be regarded as a definition intended to satisfy both the biologist and the psychologist. In this case Instinct is defined in objective terms, that is, in terms of action or behaviour. James affords a simple example of this kind of definition, when he defines Instinct as "the faculty of acting

[1] McDougall, *Social Psychology*, p. 29.

in such a way as to produce certain ends, without foresight of the ends, and without previous education in the performance[1]." A more complex definition of this kind is that given by Lloyd Morgan. He defines instinctive behaviour—avoiding the definition of Instinct itself altogether—as "comprising those complex groups of coordinated acts, which, though they contribute to experience, are, on their first occurrence, not determined by individual experience: which are adaptive and tend to the well-being of the individual and the preservation of the race; which are due to the cooperation of external and internal stimuli; which are similarly performed by all members of the same more or less restricted group of animals; but which are subject to variation, and to subsequent modification under the guidance of individual experience[2]."

We shall return later to a discussion of Lloyd Morgan's views regarding the nature of Instinct and 'instinct experience,' as we find these expressed in his most recent works. For the present we are merely concerned with this definition as a possible definition for the psychologist to adopt. Lloyd Morgan is by no means alone in discussing the psychology of Instinct on this basis. Hobhouse, in an important discussion of Instinct[3], practically subscribes to his views[4], and, while regarding Instinct as simply "the response of inherited structure to stimulus[5]," proceeds to a psychological discussion of instinctive behaviour on lines, which are almost identical with Lloyd Morgan's.

We may attempt to make a definition of Instinct which will be acceptable to both biologist and psychologist, but the result may be a definition satisfactory to neither, a definition that can find a place in neither science as such. From the biological point of view 'internal stimuli,' if that means more than stimuli coming from within the physical organism, can mean nothing[6]. The clause 'though they contribute to experience' is equally meaningless. From the psychological point of

---

[1] James, *Principles of Psychology*, vol. II, p. 383.
[2] Art. 'Instinct' in *Encyclopaedia Britannica*, 11th ed. The same definition may be found elsewhere in Lloyd Morgan's works on Comparative Psychology.
[3] Hobhouse, *Mind in Evolution*, chap. IV.
[4] Op. cit., p. 46, footnote. [5] Op. cit., p. 53.
[6] In a private letter Professor Lloyd Morgan informs me that this is exactly what he means.

view, the definition merely mentions the fact that there are psychological phenomena connected with the objective manifestations of instinctive behaviour, but makes no attempt to specify the character of these psychological phenomena. The definition might easily be made satisfactory to the biologist, because it is mainly a definition in biological terms. But to the psychologist it could never be made satisfactory, for it is a definition which is essentially in objective terms, in terms of behaviour as such, and no attempt whatever is made to describe the experience which underlies that behaviour. To admit that the behaviour is conscious is to admit that it comes within the purview of the psychologist, to attempt to define it without defining the nature of that consciousness is to give a definition which, by no stretch of imagination can be called psychological.

The definition of Instinct given by Lloyd Morgan is an example of a tendency which has recently appeared in psychology to extend the limits of the science in such a way as to cause it to lose its own identity. One direction in which this tendency shows itself is the definition of psychology as "the positive science of the behaviour of living things[1]." But to define psychology in this way is hopelessly to confuse the fields of physiology, psychology, and biology. It is essential to specify the point of view from which psychology approaches the study of the behaviour of living organisms. It is true that practically we do study psychology in order to understand the behaviour of animals, of other people, or of ourselves, the ultimate controlling end being the modifying of our own behaviour or that of others in order to attain our ends. But it is equally true that the mere study of behaviour would never give us the insight into the meaning of behaviour that we require. The fact is that, in order to understand behaviour as we wish to understand it, we must interpret it in psychological terms. We are able to do so, because we bring with us to the observation of behaviour a psychological knowledge of the experience underlying it, which is necessary for its interpretation. This is the case, either when we are observing behaviour, in order to verify psychological conclusions already reached, or

---

[1] McDougall, *Psychology, the Study of Behaviour*, p. 19.

psychological hypotheses, already provisionally formed,—for it must be conceded that the behaviour of animals, and of other persons, may become a secondary source of the data of psychology—or when we are observing the behaviour of animals or of other human beings in order to understand the experience underlying the behaviour, and thus the behaviour itself, so that we may have definite and sure guidance in our own actions with respect to these others, animals or human beings as the case may be.

The study of behaviour as behaviour, apart from this point of view, can only result in an explanation in historical and descriptive terms, and is undoubtedly the province of the biologist. The psychologist takes as his province the study of experience, in order that he may give an explanation of behaviour in terms of experience, and by so doing understand it psychologically, and put himself in a position to enable others also, if necessary, to understand it psychologically. In the same way the physiologist takes as his province the study of the life processes in nerve, muscle, and living tissue generally, in order that he in turn may give a physiological explanation of these processes, and understand behaviour physiologically. This is the conclusion to which we have already come.

But note the results which follow from a confusion of the different points of view. Instinct is a biological phenomenon, and we can give an account of Instinct in biological terms. So long as our universe of discourse is biological such a definition is quite in place. But Instinct is also a psychological phenomenon, and presumably it may also be defined in psychological terms. If we take Instinct, as biologically regarded and described, over into the universe of discourse of psychology, confusion is bound to arise. In psychology we describe and explain phenomena of experience, and we talk of perception, of interest, of intelligence, of reason, defining these in terms of experience, and on the whole finding little difficulty in understanding the various phenomena subsumed under each, and the modifications of behaviour produced by the various kinds of experience so described. But there enters upon the scene a biological *dramatis persona*, Instinct biologically defined. We are nonplussed. Instinct refuses to enter into any relation with perception, or interest, or intelligence, or reason. All kinds of insoluble problems arise. We meet expressions like "Instinct suffused with intelligence[1]," "intelligence arising within the sphere of instinct[2]" in our psychological reading, and can attach no definite psychological meaning to them. They *have* no definite meaning. And all the trouble of this sort has arisen because we are not consistently adhering to one universe of discourse.

In the discussion that follows we shall understand Instinct in some such sense as McDougall understands it, attempting to reach a more definite position later, as regards the real nature of 'instinct experience,' and to formulate a more adequate definition. In the meantime, and provisionally, we understand by Instinct an innate impelling force guiding cognition, accompanied by interest or emotion, and at least partly determining action. We are quite in agreement with McDougall's protest against using the term Instinct to denote exclusively instinctive action[3]. At the same time that appears quite consistent with his own definition of psychology. Natural inclination or propensity would best express in a general way the essential element in what we mean for the present to call Instinct. Until we come to a clearer psychological under-standing of Instinct, we may take natural inclination or propensity as the topic under discussion.

In what follows we shall first of all trace the general historical development of psychological views regarding Instinct in this sense. In the second place we shall attempt to give a satisfactory psychological account of the nature of Instinct. Lastly we shall attempt to trace its relations to other elements and aspects of experience, and more especially to some of the more important phenomena of development and education.

[1] Hobhouse, *Mind in Evolution*, p. 77.
[2] Hobhouse, op. cit., p. 79.
[3] *British Journal of Psychology*, vol. III, p. 253.

CHAPTER II

DESCRIPTIVE PSYCHOLOGY OF NATURAL INCLINATION
OR INSTINCT FROM HOBBES TO DUGALD STEWART

Three distinct influences may be traced in the psychology of the present day: in the first place the influence of Locke, Hume, and the Scottish school of philosophy, which, though sometimes identified with Associationism, is really much wider, in the second place the influence of German psychology, mainly Kantian and post-Kantian, in the third place the influence of modern physiology and biology. In considering the historical development of modern views regarding Instinct, we shall find it convenient to keep these lines of influence separate, and we shall begin with the line of influence which is the most distinctively psychological, that through Hume and the Scottish School.

The tendency of recent psychology to interpret the active side of experience in terms which are essentially non-psychological has had for its counterpart, among those psychologists who stood by the older introspective method, a tendency to concentrate attention on the cognitive side of experience, and either to ignore feeling, motive, and volition altogether, or to attempt an interpretation of these in cognitive terms, with some slight recognition of pleasure-pain, at any rate as hedonic tone. The field of psychology was not always so circumscribed. The older psychologists took the whole of human experience as they found it, and, with such scientific procedure and method as their philosophical leanings would permit, endeavoured to give some account of the affective and active aspects of experience as, and in terms of, affection and action. It is because they did so, and because the measure of success which attended their

efforts was by no means negligible, that we find it profitable
to discuss, in connection with our present topic, the development
of introspective psychology prior to the raising of the various
evolution problems by modern biology.

A start may fittingly be made with the psychology of
Thomas Hobbes[1], not because Hobbes was the first to give us
a psychology of feelings, emotions, and volitions, or of natural
inclinations and propensities, but rather because he sums up
to a considerable extent previous results, at the same time
making a relatively marked advance from the vagueness and
crudity of previous treatment.

Hobbes occupies in the psychology of natural propensities,
inclinations, and behaviour a position somewhat analogous to
that which Hume occupies in the psychology of perception.
"The main stream of English ethics begins with Hobbes and
the replies that Hobbes provoked[2]."

The stimulus under which Hobbes undertook a psychological
analysis of human nature may be found in the then current
conception of the Law of Nature, upon which, it was maintained
by writers like Grotius[3], the whole structure of society and
civilization was based.　According to Grotius, Natural Law "is
a part of divine law that follows necessarily from the essential
nature of man[4]."　Hobbes attempted to discover what was the
essential nature of man.　He found it necessary to deny that
man is naturally a social animal, and to assert the primacy of
man's egoistic tendencies.　This became the great point at
issue between Hobbes and his critics, and led to the development, in England and Scotland, of a descriptive psychology of
the active side of human nature.

What is for us the most interesting part of the psychology
is to be found mainly in the sixth and succeeding chapters of
the *Leviathan*[5].　The sixth chapter itself is devoted to a discussion "Of the Interiour Beginnings of Voluntary Motions,

---

[1] 1588–1679.　The chief works of Hobbes germane to the present discussion
are: *Human Nature* (1650, 2nd ed. 1651), and *Leviathan* (1651).

[2] Sidgwick, *History of Ethics*, p. 159.

[3] 1583–1645.

[4] Sidgwick, op. cit., p. 161.

[5] There are numerous editions.　Our references by page will be to that
published in 'Everyman Library.'

commonly called the Passions." What Hobbes calls 'voluntary' or 'animal motion' is distinguished from 'vital motion' by the fact that it is always determined by a preceding thought[1]. Before the external phase of the movement itself, in walking, speaking, striking, and the like, there is an internal phase which he calls 'endeavour,' "the small beginnings of motion[2]." Of 'endeavour' there are two kinds, 'endeavour' towards, which is appetite or desire, 'endeavour' fromwards which is aversion[3].

Hobbes draws a distinction between appetites and aversions which are innate, and appetites and aversions for particular things which arise from experience[4], but in his subsequent discussion he does not attempt to develop this distinction. Instead he proceeds to classify human emotions and sentiments on the basis of the wider distinction between appetite and aversion, and extracts the ethical distinction between good and evil from the same psychological source[5].

In the light of later thought three points in the discussion are notable. In the first place Hobbes assigns similar inclinations and emotions to animals. "The alternate succession," he says, "of appetites and aversions, hopes and fears, is no less in other living creatures than in man[6]." In the second place curiosity is assigned a peculiar position among emotions, since, according to his view, it is "found in no other living creature but man[7]," and "this singular passion" is, after reason, a second mark distinguishing man from the lower animals. In the third place he confuses in a very peculiar way pleasure and pain which determine appetite and aversion with appetite and aversion themselves. This confusion appears more particularly in his *Human Nature*, where he defines pleasure as motion which helps 'vital motion,' and pain as the reverse[8], and concludes that "since all delight is appetite...there can be no contentment but in proceeding....Felicity therefore, by which we mean continual delight, consisteth not in having prospered, but in prospering[9]."

The "cardinal doctrine in moral psychology[10]," which

---

[1] *Leviathan*, p. 23.   [2] p. 23.   [3] p. 23.   [4] p. 24.
[5] p. 24.   [6] p. 26.   [7] p. 26.
[8] Molesworth, *The English Works of Thomas Hobbes*, vol. IV, p. 31.
[9] Molesworth, vol. IV, p. 33.   [10] Sidgwick, op. cit., p. 164.

Hobbes reaches as a result of his psychological analysis of human nature, is that all man's desires are essentially directed towards his own preservation and happiness, and what are apparently unselfish emotions are analysed and explained in terms of this self-regarding tendency. It was on the ground of this psychological egoism that Hobbes was attacked later by Shaftesbury, Butler, and Hutcheson but the attack was made with weapons forged by a more acute psychologist than any of them.

The rise of Cartesianism gave a great impulse to the development of modern descriptive and analytic psychology. Though the main tendency of this new psychology and philosophy was to concentrate attention on the purely cognitive and intellectual aspects of mind, culminating in what Schopenhauer has called —and rightly from the psychological point of view—the "mad sophistry of Hegel[1]," yet Descartes[2] himself, and Malebranche more particularly among his immediate followers, attempted to give some account also of the feeling elements in human nature, of man's natural inclinations, emotions, and passions.

Descartes' treatment of human inclinations and passions must be regarded as a very subordinate part of his work, and as not at all representing the real direction of his interests. Nevertheless it is significant and suggestive. He starts with the two principles, that the sole function of the mind is thought, and that thoughts are of two kinds, 'actions of the soul' and 'passions.' The 'actions of the soul' are our desires. 'Passions' are "kinds of perception or forms of knowledge which are found in us"; the soul does not make them what they are, but receives them "from the things which are represented by them[3]."

From this wide use of the word 'passion' Descartes immediately passes on to the narrower and more usual application. The perceptions 'found in us' are again of two kinds, the one kind being merely the perceptions of our desires, which appear therefore as both actions and passions of the soul, the second

---

[1] *Die Welt als Wille und Vorstellung.* Trans. by Haldane and Kemp, vol. II, p. 31.
[2] 1596–1650.
[3] *Passions of the Soul,* part I, art. XVII. Translation by Haldane and Ross, vol. I.

kind having the body, not the soul, as their çause[1]. Among
the latter three kinds must be distinguished: (*a*) perceptions
which relate to objects without us, that is sensations[2], (*b*) perceptions which relate to our own body, such as "hunger, thirst,
and other natural appetites[3]," (*c*) perceptions which relate to
our soul itself, such as "the feelings of joy, anger, and other
such sensations, which are sometimes excited in us by the
objects which move our nerves, and sometimes also by other
causes[4]." These last are the passions, in the ordinary restricted
sense.

The account given of the passions is in the main physiological,
that is, in terms of movements of the 'animal spirits[5].' But
Descartes attempts a classification of them in terms of the
"diverse ways in which they are significant for us[6]," distinguishing six primary emotions, wonder, love, hatred, desire, joy, and
sadness, of which all the other emotions—and he describes
about forty—are modifications or combinations[7]. In several
notable passages, also, he emphasizes their function to "incline
and dispose the soul to desire the things for which they prepare
the body[8]." "The objects which move the senses do not
excite diverse passions in us, because of all the diversities which
are in them, but only because of the diverse ways in which they
may harm or help us, or in general be of some importance to
us; and the customary mode of action of all the passions
is simply this, that they dispose the soul to desire those
things, which Nature tells us are of use, and to persist in
this desire, and also bring about that same agitation of spirits,
which customarily causes them to dispose the body to the
movement which serves for the carrying into effect of these
things[9]."

This is really the closest approximation to a psychological
theory of Instinct that we find in Descartes. With his views

---

[1] Art. XIX.
[2] Art. XXIII.
[3] Art. XXIV.   Translations are generally by Haldane and Ross.
[4] Art. XXV.
[5] See arts. XXVII, XXX, XLVI, etc.   Also Meditation VI.
[6] *Passions of the Soul*, part I, art. XVII.
[7] Op. cit., part II, art. LXIX.
[8] Part I, art. XL.   [9] Part II, art. LII.

regarding the relation of soul and body, and his apparent[1]
belief that animals are mere complex machines, we need not
feel surprise to find him stop at this point.

How are we to estimate this portion of the work of Descartes?
A modern writer[2] has said of Descartes' treatment of the
emotions that it is difficult "to find any treatment of the
emotions much superior to it in originality, thoroughness, and
suggestiveness." This is a remarkably high estimate, and
scarcely justified by the facts. In some respects Hobbes'
discussion of the emotions is more definite. Both Hobbes
and Descartes are considerably in the debt of previous writers.
But we do find in Descartes an interesting anticipation of the
James-Lange theory, a very clear recognition of the function
of the emotions, and connected with that some indications of
a theory with regard to the expression of the emotions. We
also find in Descartes, as in Hobbes, an early attempt at a
psychological classification of the emotions, but Descartes'
basis is wider than that of Hobbes. Lastly, though Descartes
does not apparently use the word 'Instinct' there is a quite
definite assertion of the part which Nature plays in determining the fundamental passions and desires of man, which
can be regarded as the germ of a theory of Instinct.

In our opinion, however, the greatest service rendered by
Descartes in this psychological field was the extent to which he
paved the way for Malebranche[3], who gives us by far the best
discussion of natural tendencies, inclinations, and passions,
prior to the biological discussions of the nineteenth century,
and the biologico-psychological discussions of the twentieth.
Founding upon the psychology of Descartes, both of the
intellectual processes and of the feelings and inclinations,
Malebranche carries us far beyond that psychology in the latter
field. Again and again he surprises by his knowledge of human
nature, and his acute analysis of the various factors on the
emotional and active side. To remember him only as a
Cartesian is to remember him for what is probably the less

---

[1] It is not very certain what the real views of Descartes were in this connection. Note the words "nor *perhaps* any thought" in art. L, of part I.
[2] Irons, quoted by Ribot in *Psychology of the Emotions*, p. 111, footnote.
[3] 1638–1715.

important and less valuable part of his work. As a psychologist of human tendencies and emotions he takes exceedingly high rank.

Malebranche follows Descartes in the general lines of his psychology as of his philosophy. Understanding is opposed to Will, while sense, imagination, and the pure understanding are distinguished on the cognitive side of mental life, and inclinations and passions on the active side. Understanding and the inclinations are further considered as belonging to the mind as such, while the others belong to the mind only when and because it is united with a body.

In his chief philosophical work, *De la Recherche de la Vérité*[1] Malebranche uses the word 'Instinct' with moderate frequency, but can hardly be considered as using it in an exact and definite sense. Sometimes it means for him 'natural inclination' or propensity; at other times it appears to mean some kind of innate knowledge, '*connaissance d'instinct*[2].' Thus he says: "Pleasure is an instinct of nature, or to speak more precisely it is an impression of God himself, who inclines us towards some good[3]." Again, we are obeying God's voice, when we yield to "the instinct of nature, which moves us to the satisfying of our senses and our passions[4]." God "moves us to the good of the body only by instinct[5]." On the other hand we find him asserting that we are persuaded by "the instinct of sensation" that our souls are united to our bodies, 'instinct of sensation' being in this passage opposed to 'light of reason[6].' He also points out that God in his grace has added 'instinct' to 'illumination[7].'

Book IV, in which the natural inclinations are discussed,

---

[1] First published in 1674. As there is not, so far as we are aware, any modern English version of the *Recherche*—there are contemporary English versions by Sault and by Taylor—our references will always be to the text itself (Garnier ed.).

[2] p. 511.

[3] p. 43. "Le plaisir est un instinct de la nature, ou pour parler plus clairement, c'est une impression de Dieu même, qui nous incline vers quelque bien."

[4] p. 499. "C'est obéir à sa voix que de se rendre à cet instinct de la nature, qui nous porte à satisfaire nos sens et nos passions."

[5] p. 500. "Il nous porte au bien du corps seulement par instinct."

[6] p. 509. "C'est par l'instinct du sentiment que je suis persuadé que mon âme est unie à mon corps, ou que mon corps fait partie de mon être; je n'en ai point d'évidence." [7] p. 511.

strange to say, does not afford us a single instance of the use of the word 'instinct.' It opens with the thesis that the understanding receives its directions from the will, and that the mind must have inclinations, just as bodies have motions. Further the essential principle of all natural inclinations, and therefore of all will, is that they are directed towards 'good in general[1].' At the same time, he says, we must recognize that there are also natural inclinations towards particular goods.

Malebranche's psychological classification of the natural tendencies and the emotions commences with his division of the natural inclinations into three groups. The first group is of those inclinations included in, or derived from, the inclination towards 'good in general.' In this group is classified curiosity or the inclination towards novelty, which he derives from the inclination towards good in general. Curiosity is the vain striving of imperfect humanity to satisfy an inclination, which the circumstances in which man is placed make it impossible to satisfy. The second group comprises the inclinations towards particular goods which have to do with our own preservation and welfare, i.e. self-regarding tendencies. In the third group we have the inclinations towards particular goods which have to do with the welfare of others, i.e. the social tendencies.

The most important part of the fourth book is probably the discussion of the principal natural inclinations in the second group, included by Malebranche under self-love[2], that is 'love of greatness' and 'love of pleasure.' Taking the discussion of the 'love of greatness' in the fourth book along with the discussion of the 'contagion of the imagination[3]' in the third part of the second book, we get a very interesting and very complete psychological study of what, following Ribot and McDougall, we now call the 'self-feelings,' together with associated phenomena, more especially those dependent upon suggestibility and imitation.

Whatever tends to make us superior to others, such as learning, or virtue, or honours, or riches, "seems to make us in a certain way independent. All those that are our inferiors

---

[1] "Le bien en général."   [2] "L'amour propre."
[3] "Communication contagieuse des imaginations fortes."

reverence and fear us, are always prepared to execute what
we please for our welfare, and are afraid of offending us or
resisting our desires[1]."

Moreover, men desire not only to possess learning or riches,
but also to have the reputation of possessing them. For it is
the reputation of being rich, learned, virtuous, that "produces
in the imagination of those around us, or those with whom we
come into closest contact, a disposition very advantageous to
us." It "prostrates them at our feet," and "inspires them
with all the motions that tend to the preservation of our being,
and the augmentation of our greatness[2]."

Closely associated with these phenomena of 'self-feeling' are
the phenomena of 'contagion of the imagination,' that is, the
phenomena we classify under the heads of imitation and
suggestibility. This 'contagion of the imagination,' Malebranche says, is best seen in children with respect to their
parents, in servants with respect to their masters and mistresses,
or in courtiers with respect to their princes and kings, and it
is shown generally in all inferiors with respect to their superiors[3].

Malebranche illustrates by taking the case of courtiers and
kings, but most of the phenomena he cites are quite general.
The religion of a prince makes the religion, the reason of a
prince the reason of his subjects, and especially his courtiers.
Hence "the sentiments of a prince, his passions, his sports, his
words, and generally everything he does, will be in fashion."
When the tyrant Dionysius applied himself to the study of
geometry, on Plato's arrival in Syracuse, according to Plutarch
geometry immediately became the study of the whole court,

---

[1] Book IV, chap. VI. p. 403. "Toutes les choses, qui nous donnent une
certaine élévation au-dessus des autres, en nous rendant plus parfaits, comme
la science et la vertu, ou bien qui nous donnent quelque autorité sur eux, en
nous rendant plus puissants, comme les dignités et les richesses, semblent nous
rendre en quelque sorte indépendants. Tous ceux qui sont au-dessous de nous,
nous révèrent et nous craignent, ils sont toujours prêts à faire ce qui nous plaît
pour notre conservation, et ils n'osent nous nuire ni nous résister dans nos
désirs."

[2] Book IV, chap. VI, p. 404. "La réputation d'être riche, savant, vertueux,
produit dans l'imagination de ceux qui nous environnent, ou qui nous touchent
de plus près, des dispositions très commodes pour nous. Elle les abat à nos
pieds: elle les agite en notre faveur: elle leur inspire tous les mouvements qui
tendent à la conservation de notre être, et à l'augmentation de notre grandeur."

[3] Book II, part III, chap. II.

and the king's palace was filled with dust owing to the drawing of figures in it[1].

As regards children, their imitativeness and suggestibility are heightened by the narrowness of their experience, and the influence of their parents' example increased by mutual affection. The parents' sentiments and opinions are to the child the only principles of virtue and reason. Hence "the boy walks, and talks, and carries himself in the same way as his father, the girl imitates her mother in gait, discourse, and dress. If the mother lisps, her daughter lisps also; if the mother has any 'odd fling with the head,' the daughter shows the same; in short children imitate their parents in everything, even in bodily defects, face, and expression, as well as in their errors and vices[2]."

Finally, to complete his treatment of suggestion, Malebranche points out that suggestion may arise from other circumstances, in addition to the prestige of the source, as, for example, the manner in which, or the degree of conviction with which, any statement is made. Later he adds as an additional factor public opinion. "We live by opinion; we esteem and love what is esteemed and loved in the world[3]."

The second aspect of self-love is the 'love of pleasure.' Malebranche is quite conscious of the difficulties involved in this part of his treatment, and makes a strenuous effort, not without some success, to overcome these difficulties. The general principle he applies is one laid down in his first book: "Le plaisir et la douleur sont les caractères naturels et incontestables du bien et du mal[4]." This he interprets in the fourth book, pointing out that, though pleasure is "a good, and actually makes the enjoyer happy while and so long as he enjoys it," yet, after all, it is "but the seasoning whereby the

[1] Book II, part III, p. 245. "Si Denis le Tyran s'applique à la géométrie à l'arrivée de Platon dans Syracuse, la géométrie devient aussitôt à la mode, et le palais de ce roi, dit Plutarque, se remplit incontinent de poussière par le grand nombre de ceux qui tracent des figures."
[2] Book II, part III, p. 242. "Un jeune garçon marche, parle, et fait les mêmes gestes que son père. Une fille de même s'habille comme sa mère, marche comme elle, parle comme elle; si sa mère grasseye, la fille grasseye; si la mère a quelque tour de tête irrégulier, la fille le prend. Enfin les enfants imitent les parents en toutes choses, jusque dans leurs défauts et dans leurs grimaces, aussi bien que dans leurs erreurs et dans leurs vices."
[3] p. 280.
[4] Book I, chap. v, p. 46.

soul relishes her good[1]." That is to say, God has attached pleasure to certain objects, which man ought to seek, and pain to other objects, which he ought to avoid, in the interests of self-preservation. Both pleasure and pain are positive; pleasure is not the mere absence of pain, nor is pain the mere absence of pleasure[2]. But they must not, on the other hand, be regarded as the real object of the natural inclination, but rather as attached to it. The chief difficulties and inconsistencies, that arise on this theory, Malebranche attributes to the results of the Fall.

After discussing the two natural inclinations, curiosity and self-love, or rather the two groups of natural inclinations falling under these heads, Malebranche passes on to a discussion of the third group, natural inclinations tending towards the welfare and preservation of other creatures. He points out that the various inclinations of this group are always accompanied by passions, and must therefore come up later for consideration in that connection. The most notable part of this preliminary discussion is the very clear recognition of that tendency which McDougall has called 'primitive passive sympathy.'

We rejoice, he says, in the joy of others, we suffer by the evils that befall them. The rise or fall of beings of the same species as ourselves seems to augment or diminish our own being, and all the more so, if they are our friends, or nearly related to us[3]. Then comes a remarkable passage[4]. "Upon the sense of some sudden surprising evil," which he finds too strong for him, a man raises a cry for help. This cry "forced out involuntarily by the disposition of the machine," falls on the ears of those near enough to render assistance. "It pierces them and makes them understand it, let them be of what quality or nation

---

[1] Book IV, p. 377. "Car c'est par le plaisir que l'âme goûte son bien."

[2] Book V, chap. III, p. 483.

[3] Book IV, chap. XIII, p. 459.

[4] p. 461. "A la vue de quelque mal qui surprend, ou que l'on sent comme insurmontable par ses propres forces, on jette, par exemple, un grand cri; ce cri poussé souvent sans qu'on y pense, et par la disposition de la machine, entre infailliblement dans les oreilles de ceux qui sont assez proches pour donner le secours dont on a besoin; il les pénètre ce cri, et se fait entendre à eux, de quelque nation et de quelque qualité qu'ils soient; car ce cri est de toutes les langues, et de toutes les conditions, comme en effet il en doit être; il agite le cerveau et change en un moment toute la disposition du corps de ceux qui en sont frappés, il les fait même courir au secours sans qu'ils y pensent."

soever." It is "a cry of all nations and all conditions," and it stirs with emotion all those who hear it, and makes them involuntarily rush to give help.

This communication of the emotions through sympathy is also described, and alluded to, in several passages in book v. Thus, in the third chapter, we read that, if a man's own strength appears insufficient to meet a certain situation, he "mechanically" utters certain words and cries, "and there is diffused over the face, and the rest of the body, such an air and expression as is capable of actuating others with the same passion, he himself is possessed with[1]." In the seventh chapter of the same book, where he is treating of wonder or admiration, Malebranche makes the very clear statement, that all the passions have their own appropriate expressive signs, which "mechanically" over-spread the countenance, and "mechanically" inspire others with the same emotions[2]. This is true also of wonder or admiration, which produces on our face an expression that "mechanically" arouses in others the same emotion, and causes their faces to take on precisely the same expression[3].

This description of the phenomena of 'primitive passive sympathy' is very notable. Equally notable is Malebranche's clear recognition of the social significance of these phenomena. Subsequent ethical writers laid great stress on sympathy, but none of them has given so clear and so adequate a psychological account of it as Malebranche. There is yet another interesting point in this chapter on wonder or admiration. After referring to admiration some of the phenomena we now refer rather to the original self tendencies, Malebranche indicates a theory of play, which to some extent anticipates the theory of Karl Groos. The Author of nature "regulates the phenomena of

---

[1] p. 484. "Que si les forces de l'homme ne lui suffisent pas dans le besoin qu'il en a, ces mêmes esprits sont distribués de telle manière, qu'ils lui font proférer machinalement certaines paroles et certains cris, et qu'ils répandent sur son visage et sur le reste de son corps, un certain air capable d'agiter les autres de la même passion dont il est ému."

[2] p. 525. "Toutes les passions...répandent machinalement sur le visage ...un air qui, par son impression, dispose machinalement tous ceux qui le voient à ces passions."

[3] p. 525. "L'admiration même...produit sur notre visage un air qui imprime machinalement l'admiration dans les autres; et qui agit même sur leur cerveau d'une manière si bien réglée, que les esprits qui y sont contenus, sont poussés dans les muscles de leur visage pour y former un air tout semblable au nôtre."

the soul with reference to the good of the body, and causes the young to be delighted with such exercises as invigorate the body. Thus, while the flesh and fibres of their nerves are yet soft, the channels, through which the animal spirits must necessarily flow to produce all sorts of motions, are worn and kept open[1]."

At the outset of his discussion of the passions or emotions in the fifth book, Malebranche makes clear the relation of these to the inclinations. Emotions are due, he says, following Descartes, to the fact that the soul is joined to a body, and they arise from the motions of the blood and animal spirits[2]. Nevertheless they are inseparable from the inclinations. Just as the essential principle of the inclinations is the love of good in general, so the essential principle of all the emotions is that they incline us "to love our own body and what is useful for its preservation[3]." One of the laws of the union of soul and body is that all inclinations of the soul should be accompanied by emotions. From this it follows, the principle just mentioned notwithstanding, that "we are united by our passions to whatever seems to be the good or evil of the mind, as well as to what we take for the good or evil of the body[4]." Interest is determined by all the passions, that is, they tend to make us apply our minds to objects, although this seems more particularly the function of 'admiration' or wonder, which stimulates the desire for knowledge and truth.

Though natural inclinations and passions are common to all men, yet they vary in strength in different individuals. There is also variety in the objects to which emotions attach themselves in different individuals. This is true both in regard to natural inclinations referring to the mind alone, and in regard to those referring to the body, as well as in regard to general passions. In particular passions there is an infinite variety,

---

[1] p. 530. "Cette disposition (qui excite à la chasse, à la danse, etc.) est fort ordinaire aux jeunes gens....Dieu, qui, comme Auteur de la nature, règle les plaisirs de l'âme par rapport au bien du corps, leur fait trouver du plaisir dans l'exercice, afin que leur corps se fortifie. Ainsi dans le temps que les chairs et les fibres des nerfs sont encore molles, les chemins par lesquels il est nécessaire que les esprits animaux s'écoulent pour produire toutes sortes de mouvements, se tracent et se conservent."

[2] Cf. Descartes, Lange, James, Ribot.

[3] p. 471.   [4] p. 481.

according to the relations that different objects may have to different individuals.

All emotions, apart from admiration, have seven characteristic marks[1]:

1.   A 'judgment' of the mind concerning some object.

2.   A determination of the will, towards the object, if it appears good, away from it, if it appears evil.

3.   The characteristic feeling[2] which attends the emotions, the primary feelings being love, hatred, desire, joy, sorrow.

4.   Changes in the course of "the blood and animal spirits" of such a nature as to dispose the body in a way "suitable to the ruling passion."

5.   A "sensible commotion of the soul," by which the soul participates in what affects the body.

6.   Secondary feelings[3] of love, hatred, joy, desire, sorrow, arising from the "concussion caused in the brain by the animal spirits."

7.   An internal satisfaction "which detains the soul in her passion," and which attends all the passions whatsoever and makes them pleasant, arising from the feeling that we are "in the best state we can be in reference to those things we perceive by our senses."

This summarizes practically the whole of Malebranche's theory of the emotions.   He illustrates the various points by hatred, and, in discussing hatred, makes some other points clear.   In the first place, he asserts, that the difference between hatred and love, is not in the motion of the will, which in both cases is towards good, but in the feelings, determined by these motions of the will.   The 'motions of the will' are natural causes of the "sentiments de l'esprit," and these in turn maintain the 'motions of the will.'   All this might happen, though a man had not a body.   In the second place, the organic effects produced are such as tend to the satisfaction of the inclination, that is, the realization of its end, and they in turn cause also in the mind the characteristic 'sentiments,' thus intensifying the primary 'sentiments,' and adapting them more particularly to the circumstances of the case.

[1] Book v, chap. III, p. 482.   [2] "sentiments."   [3] "sentiment de la passion."

The remainder of Malebranche's treatment of the emotions can be very briefly indicated. He goes on to consider in detail the individual emotions. The 'mother passions' are love and hate. These produce the 'general passions' desire, joy, and sorrow. All the other emotions are made up of these, more or less compounded and modified by circumstances, with the exception of admiration and the secondary emotions developed from it. Admiration is called an 'imperfect passion,' because it is not excited by either the idea or the sense of the good, but only by the novel. Its derived emotions are esteem, veneration, contempt, and disdain, according as the admired thing appears great or small, pride, haughtiness, valour, humility, timidity, and so on, when the object is ourselves or our own qualities. The whole classification is elaborate and interesting, but it contains little that is really new, little that is very different from the psychology of Descartes.

The really memorable part of Malebranche's work is his description of the phenomena we group under sympathy, imitation, and suggestibility, his assertion of the relation of the emotions to the natural inclinations on the one hand, and to organic resonance on the other, and his classification and analysis of natural inclinations in the three groups, curiosity, self-regard, social tendencies. But altogether his contribution to psychology is of the first importance.

Except for his somewhat elaborate descriptive psychology of the emotions, Spinoza[1] did not contribute very much to the development of the psychology of the instincts or natural inclinations of man. Strictly speaking, the notion of instinct or natural inclination has no place in his system of thought. All the elements of experience are for him cognitive elements. He understands by will "the faculty of affirming and denying," not the desire "by which the mind takes a liking or an aversion to anything[2]." "There is in the mind no volition...except that which the idea, in so far as it is an idea, involves[3]." "Will and intellect are one and the same thing[4]."

---

[1] 1632–1677.
[2] *Ethics*, book II, prop. XLVIII, note.
[3] Book II, prop. XLIX.   [4] Book II, prop. XLIX, Cor.

In view of such explicit statements, one finds it very difficult to understand how Spinoza can ever make the transition from knowing to acting, how he can ever give any psychological account of emotions and desires, save as 'inadequate ideas.' But for the introduction of a notion quite inconsistent with the idea of mathematical necessity, upon which his whole system is based, he could not have made the transition. That notion is the notion of 'conatus,' which first appears in the proposition: "Everything endeavours so far as it can to persist in its own being[1]." Later we find that the mind is also conscious of this 'conatus[2],' and, when it "has reference to the mind alone," 'conatus' is identified with will, when "it refers at one and the same time to mind and body," with appetite, and appetite operating consciously is desire[3].

Martineau points out that this 'conatus' is in its origin simply the Cartesian law of inertia. "This rule of physical inertia Spinoza had first made to do further duty as the principle of *life*, and now recognizes again in all the propensions and emotions of the mind[4]." The significance of this 'conatus' really lies in the fact that it shows the utter breakdown of a mechanical explanation of human experience, not merely the breakdown of a cognitive explanation. A further point of interest is its relation to the activity of the Leibnizian monads.

For the present we can consider this 'conatus' of Spinoza as corresponding to the 'instinct' of Malebranche. But 'conatus' is so obviously out of place in Spinoza's whole system of thought, that he employs the notion only when he cannot get on without it. In his discussion of the emotions he gets back to the cognitive as soon as he can, and as far as he can. The 'conatus' determines desire, and pleasure and pain, or joy and sorrow—his words are *laetitia* and *tristitia*—are, as it were, the guides of desire, in order to secure the end of self-conservation. These three—desire, joy, sorrow—are the primary feelings or emotions; all the other emotions are secondary modifications or combinations of these.

---

[1] *Ethics*, Book III, prop. VI.   [2] Book III, prop. IX.
[3] Book III, prop. IX, note.
[4] Martineau, *A Study of Spinoza*, p. 237.

Sympathy, or *imitatio affectuum,* is made to play a considerable part among the emotions, as later in Adam Smith, and the account given of sympathy also to some extent resembles Adam Smith's[1]. "By the fact that we imagine a thing, which is like ourselves, and which we have not regarded with any emotion, to be affected with any emotion, we also are affected with a like emotion[2]." This is McDougall's 'primitive passive sympathy,' but with Spinoza it is not, as with Malebranche, an immediate reaction on perception of the signs of an emotion, but apparently a secondary or derived emotion, though not to the same extent, as with Adam Smith.

It is interesting to find that McDougall's 'active sympathy' is also recognized by Spinoza. "Every one endeavours as much as he can to cause every one to love what he himself loves, and hate what he himself hates[3]."

There is one other point worthy of note in Spinoza's treatment of the emotions. That is his application of what has been called the 'law of transference,' traces of which are also to be found in Malebranche. This may be, and was later, regarded as a case of 'association of ideas[4].' With Spinoza it is made to explain cases where objects, originally indifferent, come to stimulate emotions, and, therefore, also the development of what, following Shand[5], we now call sentiments. "From the fact alone that we imagine anything, which has something similar to an object, which is wont to affect the mind with pleasure or pain, although that in which the thing is similar to the object be not the effecting cause of those emotions, nevertheless we shall hate or love it accordingly[6]."

The 'subjective note' with which modern philosophy opens in Descartes, "cogito ergo sum," has often been emphasized[7]. With the subjective character of the note psychology has less quarrel than with its intellectualism. Reid's name "the ideal system" or the "theory of ideas" is singularly appropriate for

---

[1] *Theory of Moral Sentiments.*
[2] Book III, prop. XXVII.
[3] Book III, prop. XXXI, Cor.
[4] Cf. Ribot, *Psychology of the Emotions,* part I, chap. XII.
[5] Stout, *Groundwork of Psychology,* chap. XVII.
[6] Book III, prop. XVI. See also props. XIV, XV, XVII.
[7] Seth, *Scottish Philosophy,* p. 19.

the Cartesian philosophy and its later developments. The character which justifies the name becomes specially evident in Locke, and, through Locke, has biassed practically all subsequent philosophy and psychology. Philosophy as a theory of knowing, psychology as an account of 'impressions' and 'ideas' have wellnigh held the whole field since Locke.

We say 'wellnigh' rather than 'entirely.' For the ethical empiricism, arising in this country after Locke, to some extent the Scottish school of philosophical thought, Rousseau, Schopenhauer, and a few others among Continental thinkers, continued the other aspect of psychological enquiries down to our own time, when a new interest has been stimulated by the results of biological and sociological investigations. The line of psychological development, which specially derives from Malebranche, rather than Descartes, has been hitherto largely ignored, except in so far as it has had a bearing on ethical theory. Nevertheless, from the purely psychological point of view, it is of great importance, and the future of philosophical thought proper may yet acknowledge its importance from the general philosophical point of view.

From our present point of view Locke[1] is of comparatively minor significance. Malebranche's psychology was really continued in the psychological enquiries of the English empiricists, who set themselves to answer the egoism of Hobbes in the ethical sphere, and more particularly in Shaftesbury[2], Butler[3], and Hutcheson[4]. The main ethical contention of all was that altruistic tendencies are as 'natural' as egoistic. Shaftesbury appears to accept the contention that our ends are always pleasures or the avoidance of pains[5], but Butler traverses this view, and maintains that pleasure is merely the result which follows from natural tendencies attaining their natural ends[6]. All these writers recognize 'instinct' in the sense in which we found it recognized by Malebranche, but the most elaborate and significant development of the psychology of Instinct was made by Hutcheson, and we shall here confine ourselves to the discussion of his views.

[1] 1632–1704.   [2] 1671–1713.   [3] 1692–1752.   [4] 1694–1747.
[5] See *An Enquiry concerning Virtue or Merit*, book II, part II.
[6] See *Sermon*, XI. Also Sidgwick, *History of Ethics*, p. 192.

To Hutcheson we owe first of all a clear statement regarding the nature of Instinct, and a clear recognition of its place in human experience and conduct. "We may further observe something in our nature," he says, "determining us very frequently to action, distinct from both sensation and desire, if by desire we mean a distinct inclination to something apprehended as good, either public or private, or as the means of avoiding evil, viz. a certain propensity of Instinct to objects and actions, without any conception of them as good, or as the means of preventing evil....Thus in anger, beside the intention of removing the uneasy sensation from the injury received; beside the desire of obtaining a reparation of it and security for the future, which are some sort of Goods, intended by men when they are calm, as well as during the passion, there is in the passionate person a propensity to occasion misery to the offended, even when there is no intention of any good to be obtained, or evil avoided, by this violence. And 'tis principally this propensity which we denote by the name Anger....This part of our constitution is as intelligible as many others universally observed and acknowledged; such as these, that danger of falling makes us stretch out our hands; noise makes us wink; that a child is determined to suck; many other animals to rise up and walk; some to run into water, before they can have any notion of good to be obtained or evil avoided by these means[1]."

We find that Hutcheson places Fear in the same category with Anger. He also recognizes what we call the gregarious instinct as of the same order, but he enumerates it among the 'appetites[2].' He makes an attempt to distinguish between 'Instinct,' 'Affection,' and 'Passion,' though the distinction is not consistently adhered to. The fundamental difference between Instinct (natural propensity) and Affection appears to be that the latter involves desire for a good, the former only 'uneasy sensations,' the latter is subsequent, the former prior to experience. Violent mental disturbance is the mark of the Passion, and that may arise in the case of both Instinct and Affection. In spite of this distinction, however, he often

---

[1] *Essay on the Nature and Conduct of the Passions,* section III.
[2] *Nature and Conduct of the Passions,* section IV.

confuses Affection and Instinct, sometimes using the words as
if they were synonymous. "In the calmest temper there must
remain affections or desire, some implanted instinct for which
we can give no reason; otherwise there could be no action of
any kind[1]."

Hutcheson also discusses the function of the instincts in
determining conduct, and their relation to Reason. His general
position is that "though we have instincts determining us to
desire ends, without supposing any previous reasoning, yet
'tis by the use of our reason that we find out the means of
attaining our ends[2]." Reason itself can never determine any
end. "No reason can excite to action previously to some end,
and no end can be proposed without some instinct or affection[3]."

The more systematic portion of Hutcheson's psychology is
associated with his classification of the 'natural powers' of the
human mind. These he arranges in six classes: (*a*) the external
senses, (*b*) the 'internal sense,' which determines the pleasures
arising from the perception of "regular, harmonious, uniform
objects, as also from grandeur and novelty," (*c*) the 'public
sense,' which determines us "to be pleased with the happiness
of others and to be uneasy at their misery," (*d*) the 'moral
sense,' which determines the perception of virtue and vice in
ourselves or others, (*e*) the 'sense of honour,' which makes us
pleased at the approbation of others and ashamed at their
condemnation, (*f*) the sense of the ridiculous. Desires and
aversions fall into similar classes[4].

It is in connection with the 'public sense' that he explicitly
recognizes the appetite which corresponds to our gregarious
instinct, and which he calls "desire for company." This
appetite, in the absence of company, determines a "fretfulness,
sullenness, and discontent," and it also apparently underlies
"benevolence and compassion," for these, he says, "presuppose
some such knowledge of other sensitive beings[5]."

Hutcheson goes on to define objects as good or evil according

---

[1] *Illustrations upon the Moral Sense*, section v
[2] Op. cit., section i.
[3] Op. cit., section v.
[4] *Nature and Conduct of the Passions*, section i.
[5] Op. cit., section iv.

as they cause or occasion, directly or indirectly, "grateful or ungrateful perceptions." Desires and aversions are determined by apprehended good and evil in this sense. They may be distinguished as primary or secondary, according as they are directed towards ends determined by 'natural propensities' or affections, or towards ends which merely serve as means for the attaining of primary ends. In the second category he would place such desires as the desire for wealth and power, and he employs the doctrine of 'association of ideas' to show how various particular secondary desires can arise from original or primary desires.

His distinction between calm and violent desires, which was later adopted by Hume, is possibly valuable for his ethics, but is not very significant for his psychology. His further division of desires into selfish and 'public' or benevolent leads him to a discussion of sympathy, which, after Malebranche's, is very disappointing.

Finally, though the distinction is somewhat obscured by his opening distinction between good and evil, Hutcheson, like Butler, carefully points out that desire is normally desire of an object, not of the pleasure or satisfaction to be obtained thereby. Desire, he says, is generally accompanied by an uneasy sensation, but the desire is not a desire simply to remove the uneasiness. Further there is a pleasant sensation attending the gratification of desire, in addition to the satisfaction obtained from the object itself of the desire, but "desire doth never arise from a view of obtaining that sensation of joy, connected with the success or gratification of the desire." In the case of the appetites, these are always characterized by the fact that there is a previous 'uneasy sensation' antecedently to "any opinion of good in the object" (that is, they are instincts according to the definition already given). The object is esteemed good because it allays this pain or uneasiness, but it is 'desired' prior to its being experienced as 'good[1].'

As far as the psychology of the instincts and emotions is concerned, Hume[2], Adam Smith[3], and others of the rising

---

[1] *Nature and Conduct of the Passions*, section IV.
[2] 1711-1776. [3] 1723-1790.

'Scottish School,' must be closely associated with Hutcheson, not only as regards their method of approach to ethics, which indeed was not original in Hutcheson, but also as regards a great number of their fundamental psychological doctrines. In some cases this is due to the influence of Descartes, Malebranche, and Locke on them all, but in many cases it is also direct borrowing from Hutcheson on the part of the others. They may reach different ethical conclusions, but their differences as regards the psychology of conduct are marvellously slight.

Neither Hume nor Adam Smith gives so systematic a psychology of the natural tendencies and emotions as Hutcheson, but both make valuable and interesting additions, Hume in his comparative discussions of animal psychology, and in his development of several points which Hutcheson did not sufficiently emphasize, Adam Smith in his elaborate discussion of sympathy. It is, however, somewhat notable that neither Hutcheson, Hume, nor Adam Smith, nor indeed any of the philosophers of the Scottish School, made a real psychological advance on Malebranche's treatment of sympathy, imitation, and suggestion; what advance they made was in the treatment of specific natural tendencies as distinct from these general tendencies.

In any history of the psychology of ethics, Hume must always occupy an important place, not merely for his careful and detailed analysis of the various psychological factors involved in human conduct, but still more for the vast influence which he exerted on the English associationist school. As regards his contributions to the psychology of Instinct, however, Hume's importance is by no means so great. He is throughout fettered by the account he has already[1] given of the elements of mind as 'impressions' and 'ideas.' There is a comparatively minor rôle for instincts to play. Most of Hume's difficulties, however great ingenuity he may display in surmounting them or getting round them, arise from this very source. They exist

---

[1] Hume comes to the psychology of conduct in book II of his *Treatise of Human Nature*, after he has already discussed the psychology of cognition in book I, and some of the conclusions he has already arrived at are of such a nature as inevitably to influence the whole subsequent development of his thought.

for Hume in a way they did not exist for Locke, since Locke almost wholly ignored the emotional side of human nature, in his psychology as in his educational theory, while Hume, under the influence of the teaching of Malebranche, Shaftesbury, and Hutcheson, frankly faced the problems presented by the emotions and affections, and attempted to find solutions of these problems, consistent with his intellectual psychology of impressions and ideas. His ingenuity is often exercised, and vainly exercised, to save his consistency.

Hume's conception of Instinct is nowhere very clear or definite. Its earliest appearance is in the first book of the *Treatise*, where he distinguishes those actions of animals which are due to intelligence from those due to instinct, but adds that reason itself "is nothing but a wonderful and unintelligible instinct in our souls[1]." The *Enquiry*, dealing with the same topics, gives a much clearer and more explicit statement:

"For, though animals learn many parts of their knowledge from observation, there are also many parts of it, which they derive from the original hand of Nature, which much exceed the share of capacity they possess on ordinary occasions, and in which they improve little or nothing by the longest practice and experience. These we denominate instincts, and are apt to admire as something very extraordinary and inexplicable by all the disquisitions of human understanding. But our wonder will perhaps cease or diminish, when we consider that the experimental reasoning itself, which we possess in common with beasts, and on which the whole conduct of life depends, is nothing but a species of instinct or mechanical power, that acts in us unknown to ourselves, and in its chief operations is not directed by any such relations or comparison of ideas, as are the proper objects of our intellectual faculties. Though the instinct be different, yet still it is an instinct, which teaches a man to avoid the fire, as much as that which teaches a bird, with such exactness, the art of incubation, and the whole economy and order of its nursery[2]."

In this passage 'instinct' seems to be used in two senses.

---

[1] *Treatise of Human Nature*, book I, part III, section XVI.
[2] *Enquiry concerning the Human Understanding*, section IX.

It is a kind of knowledge derived from "the original hand of Nature." On the other hand, it is a "mechanical power," which "acts in us." But most frequently the word is used in what appears to be a third sense, as equivalent to 'original impulse' or 'tendency.' For example: "The sentiment of justice is either derived from our reflecting on that tendency (the tendency to promote public utility), or, like hunger, thirst, and other appetites, resentment, love of life, attachment to offspring, and other passions, arises from a simple original instinct in the human breast, which Nature has implanted for like salutary purposes[1]."

In other words, Hume embodies all the different views, that have been held, or that can be held, with regard to the nature of Instinct, without apparently becoming conscious of any difficulty or inconsistency. Nevertheless it is in the third meaning that the term is generally used by him, that is, as equivalent to an original impulse or propensity, underlying in many cases emotional tendencies or passions, and this meaning becomes of considerable importance, when Hume goes on to treat of the passions.

In the *Natural History of Religion* Hume specifies two important characteristics of an instinct. In the first place, it is "absolutely universal in all nations and ages[2]." In the second place, it "has always a precise, determinate object, which it inflexibly pursues[3]."

Hume classifies emotions or passions into two groups, direct and indirect, as he calls them, but which might rather be called primary and secondary. Direct or primary passions are of two kinds, those founded upon experience of good and evil, for "the mind by an original instinct tends to unite itself with the good, and to avoid the evil[4]," and those arising from natural impulses or instincts, which "produce good and evil, and proceed not from them[5]." To the former group belong desire and aversion, to the latter "self-love, affection between the sexes, love of progeny, gratitude, resentment[6]."

[1] *Enquiry concerning the Principles of Morals*, section III, also appendix II.
[2] *The Natural History of Religion*, Introd.   [3] Loc. cit.
[4] *Treatise of Human Nature*, book II, part III, section IX.
[5] Op. cit., book II, part III, section IX.   [6] *Natural History of Religion*, Introd.

Pride and humility, love and hatred, are the typical indirect or secondary passions, which, though founded upon natural tendencies, always arise from a double relation of impressions and of ideas. Hope and fear, with their modifications, belong with desire and aversion, and these are the only direct passions to which Hume devotes much attention. Curiosity he treats separately, but apparently it also is a direct passion, though belonging to the second group.

Hume, like Hutcheson, holds that the ends of human action are dependent upon the sentiments and affections, and not on the intellectual functions. Hence reason is no motive for action, but has merely the function of directing the "impulse received from appetite or inclination[1]." The sole determining motives of the will are the passions, or ultimately Instinct, though this conclusion is nowhere, so far as we are aware, drawn explicitly. Passions, however, may be calm or violent, and it is when the motive is of the calm kind, that we are deceived into thinking that the motive is reason. "Reason is, and ought only to be, the slave of the passions[2]."

The only other aspect of his psychology, requiring some notice here, is the treatment of sympathy. Sympathy plays a very considerable part in the whole psychology of the emotions. It is defined as that propensity we have "to receive by communication" the "inclinations and sentiments" of others, and the first appeal to it is made in discussing the "love of fame[3]." Sympathy appears partly to cover what we call suggestibility, that is, the tendency to accept the opinions of certain others, but, in the case of opinions, Hume distinguishes between the effects of sympathy and those of 'authority,' so that we might say he recognizes both tendencies, though occasionally inclined to confuse their results.

Hume accounts for the communication of feeling through sympathy by supposing that the signs of the feeling give rise in others to the idea of the feeling, which, through its vividness, becomes an impression. He is thus very near to the position

---

[1] *Enquiry concerning the Principles of Morals*, appendix I.
[2] *Treatise of Human Nature*, book II, part III, section III.
[3] Op. cit., book II, part I, section XI.

that feeling is communicated directly on perceiving the signs of the feeling, that is to McDougall's 'primitive passive sympathy.' Upon this sympathy Hume bases the various phenomena, which we consider as arising rather from the gregarious instinct, including McDougall's 'active sympathy,' that is, the desire that others should share our feelings[1]. He is uncertain whether to base kindly feeling for others on sympathy or upon an original and specific instinct[2].

Adam Smith is notable in the history of psychology for his elaborate discussion of sympathy, and his attempt to base an ethical system on that tendency. Otherwise he makes no particular addition to the analysis of emotion and will by Hume and Hutcheson[3]. He differs somewhat from Hume in his account of the communication of feeling by sympathy. According to Adam Smith, we experience the feelings of others by imagining ourselves in their places. Perhaps too much should not be made of his use of the word 'imagine.' Nevertheless the use of that word undoubtedly suggests to him, as to the reader, a certain interpretation, which is, as certainly, a wrong reading of the facts.

"The mob, when they are gazing at a dancer on the slack rope, naturally writhe and twist and balance their own bodies, as they see him do, and as they feel that they must do, if in his situation[4]." "Sympathy does not arise so much from the view of the passion, as from that of the situation which excites it[5]." Both these statements show very clearly the direction of Adam Smith's thought regarding sympathy, and explain why he uses the word 'imagine.'

Active sympathy is also noted by Adam Smith, being distinguished as something more than the mere communication of feeling. "Nothing pleases us more than to observe in other men a fellow-feeling with all the emotions of our own breast; nor are we ever so much shocked as by the appearance of the

---

[1] *Treatise of Human Nature*, book II, part II, section IV.
[2] Loc. cit.
[3] This is perhaps not quite true, for there is a rather good analysis of 'surprise,' 'wonder,' 'admiration,' etc. at the beginning of his Essay on the 'History of Astronomy.'
[4] *Theory of Moral Sentiments*, part I, section I, chap. I.
[5] Loc. cit.

contrary[1]." "This correspondence of the sentiments of others with our own appears to be a cause of pleasure, and the want of it a cause of pain, which cannot be accounted for in this manner (i.e. by passive sympathy)[2]." When we have read a book so often that we no longer find entertainment in it, "we can still take pleasure in reading it to a companion[3]."

Adam Smith's whole theory of morals is founded upon the interaction of these two forms of sympathy. Our judgment of another is determined by the extent to which we can sympathize with the motives underlying his conduct, and our judgment of ourselves by the extent to which the 'impartial spectator' can sympathize with our motives. Apart from this aspect of his theory, Adam Smith agrees in the main with Hume, as regards the origin of the various emotions and passions, more especially those which rest directly upon instinct, as well as with respect to the analysis of the more complex emotional states[4].

Ten years after the publication of Adam Smith's *Theory of the Moral Sentiments*, Adam Ferguson[5] published his *Essay on the History of Civil Society*, which deserves mention here, if only for the clear statement with regard to the existence in man of a gregarious instinct. "Together with the parental affections," he says, "we may reckon a propensity, common to man and other animals, to mix with the herd, and, without reflection, to follow the crowd of his species[6]." "The track of a Laplander on the snowy shore gives joy to the heart of the lonely mariner."

Except for the first part of the book, which is devoted to a discussion of the general characteristics of human nature, Ferguson's Essay, though readable enough, is rather superficial. There is, however, this other very interesting and explicit statement: "Man, like the other animals, has certain instinctive propensities, which, prior to the perception of pleasure and pain, and prior to the experience of what is pernicious or useful,

---

[1] *Moral Sentiments*, part I, section I, chap. II.
[2] Loc. cit.   [3] Loc. cit.
[4] See especially Note to chap. V of section I, book I.
[5] 1723-1816. Adam Ferguson has the unique distinction of having filled three different professorial chairs in Edinburgh University, Natural Philosophy, Moral Philosophy, and Mathematics.
[6] *Essay on the History of Civil Society*, part I, section III.

lead him to perform many functions, which terminate in himself, or have a relation to his fellow-creatures. He has one set of dispositions which tend to his animal preservation, and to the continuance of his race; another which lead to society, and, by enlisting him on the side of one tribe or community, frequently engage him in wars and contentions with the rest of mankind[1]."

The line of psychological development from Malebranche through Hutcheson and Hume, like the line from Descartes through Locke and Hume, reached its final expression in the psychology underlying the philosophy of the Scottish School. But, whereas Reid[2] is by far the most important representative of the Scottish School in the one line of development—the psychology of cognition,—Dugald Stewart's[3] is the most interesting treatment of the psychology of conation.

To some extent Reid's *Common Sense* must be interpreted psychologically as a protest against the notion that the bare impression or idea represents the reality of our cognitive experience, and an assertion of the principle that living experience, even on its cognitive side, is determined by a 'given,' which is not in the impression or idea as such. It does not seem quite justifiable to interpret Reid's answer to Hume wholly in the light of the 'critical philosophy' of Kant. We must remember that Reid's philosophy of 'Common Sense' was developed—to use a phrase which Professor Pringle-Pattison uses similarly of Green—"within the shadow of, and with special reference to, the *Treatise of Human Nature*[4]." The *Treatise* is fundamentally and essentially a psychological analysis of experience, and Reid attacks it both as psychology and as epistemology.

Had Reid not been more concerned, because of Hume's conclusions, in showing that perception is perception of a real object, it is easy to see how his analysis of perception might have led him to a clear recognition of native or instinctive impulses. As it was, in discussing Instinct under that name, Reid

---

[1] *Essay on the History of Civil Society*, part I, section III.
[2] 1710–1796.   [3] 1753–1828.
[4] Seth, *Scottish Philosophy*, p. 125.

contributed comparatively little to psychology, owing largely
to the fact that he was considering Instinct from the outside.

Classifying the 'Active Powers,' Reid subdivides them into
three groups: Mechanical Principles of Action, Animal Principles, and Rational Principles. Instinct, with habit, is placed
under the first head, appetites, with desires and affections, under
the second[1]. He also uses the term 'instinct' in a vague,
popular sense, as determining that 'belief,' which underlies the
perception of real objects, and, therefore, is the ground of the
appeal to the principles of 'Common Sense.'

Apart from this very unsatisfactory treatment of Instinct,
under that name, some of Reid's positions are not without
considerable interest and significance for a psychology of the
determining motives of action. He recognizes that there are
two elements or constituents of human nature, which determine
human conduct, and which have been known by mankind in
all ages as 'passion' and 'reason.' Under 'passion' are com-
prehended "various principles of action similar to those we
observe in brute animals," called by the various names, appetites,
affections, passions, which words are not used definitely, but
"promiscuously[2]." Opposed to 'passion' is 'reason.' He gives
a wide meaning to 'reason,' so as to include the 'calm' passions,
which both Hutcheson and Hume had emphasized. 'Reason'
becomes, therefore, a motive force or principle of action. This
'reason' is the specific difference between the nature of man and
the nature of brutes[3]. It is "superior to every passion, and
able to give law to it[4]."

This illegitimate use of the term 'reason' was afterwards
rejected by Dugald Stewart, but it has at least this justification,
that principles and ideals, which we accept as representing a
law for us, do, by our acceptance, become real motive forces in
us. Reid's mistake lies in not making a psychological analysis
of these principles and ideals, as his predecessors, Hutcheson
and Hume, had done, and distinguishing in them what is
strictly reason and what is not. Throughout the third chapter

---

[1] *Essays on the Active Powers of Man.* Hamilton's edition of Reid's Works,
pp. 535, 547, 548.
[2] p. 535.   [3] p. 535.   [4] p. 536.

of the second essay on the 'Active Powers,' Reid continues this opposition of 'passion' and 'reason,' always meaning by 'passion' impulses of our 'animal nature,' what is common to man and the 'brute animals,' and what is characteristic of children "before the use of reason[1]."

Under Instinct, in its mechanical sense, Reid includes mainly what we prefer to call reflexes, such as the tendency to wink when anything threatens our eyes[2]. Rather strangely, however, he also includes imitation, and seems prepared to add 'instinctive' belief—apparently suggestibility—which, according to him, plays an important part in the education of the child. There are, in fact, according to Reid, two types of instinctive belief, the one corresponding to suggestibility, the other the belief "which children show, even in infancy, that an event, which they have observed in certain circumstances, will happen again in like circumstances[3]."

The discussion of the 'Animal Principles of Action' contains very little that is essentially new, but sums up and illustrates, in almost as full and comprehensive a manner as in Hume's *Treatise*, the psychology of the various natural tendencies in the human being. One point perhaps deserves to be noted. Reid differs from Adam Smith in his account of sympathy, deriving it from pity, and that in turn from kindly feeling or benevolent affection, wherein Adam Smith may be wrong, but Reid is certainly not right[4].

Dugald Stewart's psychology of what he calls the 'Instinctive Principles of Action' may be regarded as a summing up of the results reached by psychology so far, and as more representative, as regards this part of psychology, of the real conclusions at which the Scottish School had arrived, than the corresponding parts of Reid's psychology. The comprehensive and generally lucid statement by Dugald Stewart of the general position in psychology exerted very great influence, especially in France, during the early part of the nineteenth century, and we shall therefore close our discussion of this line of psychological development with an account of Stewart's psychology of

[1] p. 539.   [2] p. 547.   [3] p. 549.
[4] p. 565.   All the references are to Hamilton's edition of Reid's Works.

Instinct.   This we may regard as marking the high-water mark of the purely introspective psychology.

At the beginning of the second volume of his *Philosophy of the Human Mind*, Stewart states carefully the sense in which he intends to employ the word 'reason,' and to this sense he, in the main, adheres, both in that and in his other works.   "In the use which I make of the word 'reason,'" he says, "I employ it...to denote mainly the power by which we distinguish truth from falsehood, and combine means for the attainment of our ends[1]."   Consequently, when he classifies the 'Active Powers' into 'Instinctive or Implanted Propensities' and 'Rational and Governing Principles[2]' he is not necessarily attributing motive force to reason alone, as Reid did, or at least seemed to do.

The 'Instinctive Propensities' Stewart further classifies into appetites, desires, and affections, the 'Rational Principles' into self-love and the 'moral faculty.'   The relation of these to understanding or reason is not left for a moment in doubt. "Our active propensities are the motives which induce us to exert our intellectual powers; and our intellectual powers are the instruments by which we attain the ends recommended to us by our active propensities[3]."   The activity of reason "presupposes some determination of our nature," which will make the attainment of the ends, towards which our activity of reason is directed, desirable.   Not only so, but these active propensities also largely determine the direction and extent of the development of our intellectual powers, and hence "in accounting for the diversities of genius and of intellectual character among men, important lights may be derived from an examination of their active propensities[4]."

The appetites are distinguished by three characteristics, their originating from states of the body, their periodical and occasional, rather than constant, occurrence, and their feeling accompaniment of 'uneasiness,' which is "strong or weak in proportion to the strength or weakness of the appetite[5]."   The

[1] *Philosophy of the Human Mind*, vol. II, p. 11.
[2] *Philosophy of the Active and Moral Powers of Man*, vol. I, p. 12.
[3] Op. cit., vol. I, p. 2.
[4] Op. cit., vol. I, p. 6.
[5] Op. cit., vol. I, p. 15.

main and indubitably natural appetites are three, hunger, thirst, and sex. The corresponding impulses—and the same is true as regards the 'desires'—are "directed towards their respective objects," not to any pleasure that arises from their gratification. "The object of hunger is not happiness, but food, the object of curiosity not happiness, but knowledge[1]." Nevertheless, as a result of the experience of pleasure, the mere gratification of an appetite may become the end, and thus we may have the development of many acquired appetites, such as the appetite for tobacco, the appetite for intoxicants, and the like. "Occasional propensities to action and repose," which apply to the mind as well as the body, may be added to the appetites[2]. In animals there are also "instinctive impulses," in the form of antipathies against natural enemies, but Stewart doubts whether these natural antipathies show themselves in man.

The 'desires' differ from the appetites, in that they do not take their rise from states of the body, nor do they possess the characteristic of periodicity or occasional occurrence—that is, they are more or less permanent. Of natural 'desires,' five can be clearly distinguished, curiosity, the desire of society, the desire of esteem, ambition, and emulation[3].

Dugald Stewart's discussion of the desire for society, or the gregarious instinct, is of considerable interest. "We are led," he says, "by a natural and instinctive desire to associate with our species[4]," and this, apart from any perceived advantage to ourselves, and apart from any interest we may have in the happiness of others. Children show the instinct "long before the dawn of reason." The lower animals also clearly exhibit it[5]. In the light of this instinct, it is easy to show that Hobbes was in error in denying the original social nature of man. The tendency towards union among human beings cannot arise from any selfish need of the assistance of others, because it shows itself when men do not stand in need of such assistance, and it is where men "are most independent of each other, as

---

[1] *Active and Moral Powers of Man*, vol. I, p. 24.
[2] Op. cit., vol. I, p. 20.   [3] Op. cit., vol. I, p. 22.
[4] Op. cit., vol. I, p. 28.   [5] Op. cit., vol. I, p. 29.

to their animal wants, that the social principles operate with the greatest force[1]." "It is not the wants and necessities of man's animal being, which create his social principles, and produce an artificial and interested league, among individuals who are naturally solitary and hostile; but, determined by instinct to society, endowed with innumerable principles which have a reference to his fellow-creatures, he is placed by the conditions of his birth in that element where alone the perfection and happiness of his nature are to be found[2]." This is but a particular case of the "mutual adaptation" of nature, which is exhibited also in the case of all the animal instincts. "The lamb when it strikes with its forehead while yet unarmed proves that it is not its weapons, which determine its instincts, but that it has pre-existent instincts suited to its weapons[3]."

By the 'Desire of Esteem' Dugald Stewart means in the main what Ribot and McDougall call positive and negative self-feeling. Claiming this as "an original principle of our nature," he once more criticises those who would derive every principle of action from self-love, maintaining that the 'desire of esteem' shows itself too early to allow us to resolve it into a sense of the advantages which arise from the good opinion of others, and, citing also against such a view the desire of posthumous fame[4]. The importance of this original principle of action in the education of children is emphasized, and the part played by sensitiveness to the opinion of others, to public opinion, in the development of the moral life is fully recognized[5].

Ambition or the 'Desire of Power' covers several original tendencies of our nature, a fact of which Stewart is quite conscious, for he identifies it with the pleasure of activity, with the desire of being a cause—constructiveness[6]—and with the desire for property—acquisitiveness[7]—but the last, according to his view, is a derived, not an original principle. In discussing emulation or the 'Desire of Superiority,' he distinguishes this original principle very carefully from envy, which he regards as secondary and more complex.

---

[1] *Active and Moral Powers of Man*, vol. I, p. 33.
[2] Op. cit., vol. I, p. 34.   [3] Op. cit., vol. I, p. 35.   [4] Op. cit., vol. I, p. 42.
[5] Op. cit., vol. I, p. 55.   [6] Op. cit., vol. I, p. 60.   [7] Op. cit., vol. I, p. 63.

The Affections are "active principles whose real and ultimate object is the communication of either enjoyment or suffering to our fellow-creatures[1]." They may therefore be divided into benevolent affections and malevolent affections. Of the former, parental feeling is a typical example, of the latter, anger or resentment. Four of the benevolent affections are discussed in some detail, 'natural affection,' 'friendship,' 'patriotism,' and 'pity.' It is not suggested—in fact such a suggestion is explicitly deprecated—that these are all equally original and unanalysable principles of action. The probabilities are quite the other way. But, that they are all founded upon original and primary instinctive tendencies, cannot be doubted.

The treatment of pity is interesting, mainly because it involves the discussion of sympathy, which had already played so prominent a part in the psychology of morals. Adam Smith's analysis is examined and rejected. Stewart holds that looks, gestures, and tones of distress "speak in a moment from heart to heart[2]." The imagination is not involved at all. But what is involved, and how 'sympathetic induction' of feeling operates, is nowhere made clear. We are left with the impression that Stewart has no clear apprehension of sympathy as a direct communication of feeling, on perception of the signs of the feeling in others, however much occasional statements seem to point that way. In any case, 'sympathetic induction' of feeling does not appear to be appreciated in its wide significance at all, for Stewart is thinking only of sympathy in cases of pain and distress.

A 'principle of Imitation[3]' or 'Sympathetic Imitation[4]' is appealed to, in order to explain some of the examples of sympathy cited by Adam Smith, as, for example, the effects of the dancer's movements on the slack rope[5]. But Stewart explicitly declines to identify this 'sympathetic imitation' with sympathy[6]. The analysis of sympathy must therefore be regarded as psychologically far from complete, and that, even when

[1] *Active and Moral Powers of Man*, vol. I, p. 75.
[2] Op. cit., vol. I, p. 115.   [3] Op. cit., vol. I, p. 119.
[4] *Philosophy of the Human Mind*, vol. III, chap. II.
[5] See above, p. 46.
[6] *Active and Moral Powers of Man*, loc. cit.

Stewart had before his mind, from the very beginning, the very aspect of the phenomena, which can alone lead to a satisfactory analysis.

The 'malevolent affections' are treated rather summarily. Resentment, hatred, jealousy, envy, revenge, misanthropy, are enumerated, but the only one explicitly claimed as original and instinctive is the first, and anger or resentment alone receives full treatment. Two points are deserving of notice. In the first place Stewart accepts a distinction, originally drawn by Butler, between instinctive and deliberate resentment. He recognizes, that is to say, the fact that resentment operates both at the instinctive and at the rational level. In the second place he is misled by the system of morals, he is seeking to develop, into maintaining, with Reid, that the benevolent affections are always accompanied by agreeable, the malevolent by disagreeable feelings. He entirely overlooks that satisfaction which comes from the working out of any natural tendency whatsoever.

This somewhat lengthy discussion of the older psychology, so far as it referred to the instinctive tendencies and emotions, seemed to be necessary in view of the fact that claims have recently been made, that psychology had almost entirely neglected this field, till the development of biological science in the nineteenth century, and especially since Darwin, had compelled the psychologist to recognize an emotional, as well as an intellectual, aspect of human nature, and also the fact that the animal mind is more or less continuous with the human mind. McDougall, for example, maintains that a "comparative and evolutionary psychology" alone can provide a basis for the social sciences, and that this could not be developed before Darwin[1]. With no wish to detract from the value of the work done by Darwin, which will receive due recognition later, we cannot help pointing out that McDougall's criticism of the older psychology is misleading and unfair, and citing in evidence the psychological development from Malebranche to Dugald Stewart. Moreover, McDougall goes on to take up the position that

[1] McDougall, *Social Psychology*, p. 5.

an introspective psychology could never have given us the necessary insight into the instincts and emotions of man, at the same time suggesting, rather than asserting, that the old introspective psychology has to a large extent been superseded by the comparative study of animal and human behaviour. Again the psychological development we have just traced seems sufficient answer.

Dugald Stewart is as clear and emphatic as McDougall in pointing out the difficulties with which introspection must contend when it is directed to the investigation of our feelings and active tendencies[1]. In consequence of these difficulties introspective psychology will always have very distinct limitations in this field, so long as we rely on introspection alone. Its conclusions will always be somewhat vague and general, without the assistance of a comparative study of the behaviour of animals, without the study of various phenomena under experimental conditions, without the study of abnormal phenomena. But it is surely obvious that the comparative and evolutionary study of the behaviour of animals and human beings can give us no psychology at all, without such introspection—or retrospection—as we can undertake, even in face of the confessed difficulties involved, for the purpose of interpreting the observed facts of behaviour in terms of experience.

Dugald Stewart, as well as others of the older psychologists, quite realized the valuable data—though only secondary data—which the psychologist could receive from the objective study of human history and human conduct, as well as of the behaviour of the lower animals. In justice more especially to the psychology of the Scottish School, it is necessary that these facts should be recognized. As for the view that the animal mind is, to a certain extent, and in a certain sense, continuous with the human mind, that can hardly be regarded as a result of modern biological and evolutionary theories, for it is at least as old as Aristotle[2].

[1] *Active and Moral Powers of Man*, vol. I, p. 9.
[2] There are several very striking passages in Aristotle, but see especially the passage in *Historia Animalium* beginning: ἔνεστι γὰρ ἐν τοῖς πλείστοις καὶ τῶν ἄλλων ζῴων ἴχνη, τῶν περὶ τὴν ψυχὴν τρόπων, ἅπερ ἐπὶ τῶν ἀνθρώπων ἔχει φανερωτέρας τὰς διαφοράς (Bekker, p. 588, a 18).

CHAPTER III

PHILOSOPHICAL AND SCIENTIFIC VIEWS OF THE NATURE AND MEANING OF INSTINCT

We have considered the view of Instinct which a descriptive and purely introspective psychology had reached by the beginning of the nineteenth century. The views of Instinct which have prevailed in more recent times have been either philosophical, physiological, or biological, rather than psychological, though they have often professed to be psychological, and it remains for us to give some account of the development of these.

Recent philosophical views of Instinct have been the product in the main of German thought, more especially of German philosophical thought subsequent to Kant, but this philosophical development really has its source in Leibniz and Wolff, rather than in Kant himself. With respect to psychology, the main characteristic of the whole movement has been the deducing of a psychology from certain metaphysical principles, the psychological product of this method of procedure being best represented in the psychology of Herbart. We may say that one main difference between Scottish philosophy and German philosophy, and consequently between Scottish and German psychology—except experimental and recent—is that, in the former case, a system of metaphysics is deduced from the results of a psychological analysis, while, in the latter, a psychological theory is deduced from metaphysical principles.

It is true that Kant's Critical Philosophy on one side finds its beginning in the attempt to answer the contentions of Hume, and therefore in an examination of philosophical conclusions reached from a psychological starting-point. But, though Kant's philosophy may be said to start thus, his whole attitude, point of view, and method are determined to a much greater extent by Leibniz and Wolff, than by Locke and Hume. The intellectualistic bias of the Kantian philosophy might be regarded as a result of the influence of Locke and Hume. But the influence in this case is apparent rather than real. Wolff's influence was precisely in the same direction, and the bias was present even before Kant set himself to the solution of the problems raised by Hume.

It is by no means certain that future historians of philosophy will not regard Leibniz[1] as at least equally important with either Kant or Hegel. At all events the Leibnizian philosophy is the key, not only to the Kantian Criticism, and the post-Kantian Idealism, but to certain very characteristic features in the thought of Fichte, to the very interesting philosophical development connected with the names of Schopenhauer and von Hartmann, to certain aspects of Bergson's thought, and, in some measure to the Pluralism and Pragmatism of to-day.

The philosophy of Leibniz started in a reaction against the immobile pantheism of Spinoza. He asserted that real existence is, on the one hand, self-active power, on the other hand, individuality. That is, he finds reality in a plurality of self-active monads. With his philosophy as a whole we are not here concerned, but we must rather enquire how he works out a psychology on this basis, and particularly a psychology of the instincts and emotions.

Leibniz maintains that the human soul must be regarded as a monad, having the power of 'clear perception,' and by that power transcending the animal mind, though at the same time containing the animal mind. In virtue of the 'clear perceptions,' which we may identify with reason, the human mind brings to knowing certain innate principles, which are the forms of clear cognition. As containing the animal mind, however, the human soul has also 'confused perceptions'—sensations—and, not only so, but also 'obscure perceptions,' perceptions which are undistinguishable from one another, such as characterize plant life. But we must remember that all the perceptions manifest themselves as self-initiated effort.

[1] 1646–1716.

In this aspect, the 'obscure perceptions' correspond to unconscious impulse, the 'confused perceptions' to instincts, the 'clear perceptions' to rational will. Hence, "since all three grades stand in continuous connection, acts of will are originally formed in the obscure natural impulse[1]."

At the lowest level will is determined by an obscure feeling of discomfort or unrest; at the second level by pleasure and pain; at the highest level by distinct perceptions in the sense of rational knowledge. When he has reached this point, Leibniz becomes more or less intellectualistic, finding happiness and virtue in intellectual enlightenment, the good becoming the content of an enlightened will in precisely the same way as the true of a perfect understanding.

The parts of this psychology which are interesting to us, and which we would emphasize, are: in the first place, the central position assigned to self-activity, a self-activity realizing itself as perceptions of different degrees of distinctness on the cognitive side, as unconscious impulse, instinct, and will, on the conative: in the second place, the position assigned to 'obscure perceptions' and to unconscious impulse, with the relating of the latter to instinct and will, a clear anticipation of the doctrine of the 'unconscious,' or the 'subconscious,' which was destined to become so prominent later.

Under the direct influence of Leibniz, pragmatism immediately raised its head in the teaching of Thomasius[2], but the main development of the Leibnizian philosophy was through Wolff to Kant, a development almost solely on the intellectual side. For the history of psychology as such Wolff[3] is important, because he was the first to give the name 'psychology' real currency, because he interpreted Leibniz's 'pre-established harmony' pretty nearly in the sense of our psychophysical parallelism, and because he did a great deal to put psychology on a scientific footing, and to prepare the way for the work of Herbart, Fechner, and Wundt. As regards the psychology of Instinct he is not significant.

Kant[4] is, from the same point of view, scarcely more

---

[1] Erdmann, *History of Philosophy*, vol. II, p. 195.
[2] 1655–1728.   [3] 1679–1754.   [4] 1724–1804.

significant.   It is true that his answer to the empirical atomism
of Locke and Hume is conclusive as far as it goes, but that is
only so far as it is an analysis of the conditions of knowledge
as such[1]. Wherever the Critical Philosophy becomes a psychology it is at least as inadequate as that of Hume.   For, though
Kant maintains that experience involves more than a succession
of states, since it involves also a permanent identity, and that
the principles which constitute the form of experience are, as
it were, given by the mind to experience, the experience or
knowledge under discussion is abstract, not concrete, is experience or knowledge as such, not the experience or knowledge
which psychology investigates.

It is true that there is a kind of dynamic taking the place
of the static conception of Hume, but the dynamic is a logical
or dialectical dynamic, if we may use such a collocation of
terms, not the dynamic of living experience.   The inadequacy
of this conception does not make itself felt, so long as Kant's
aim is the solution of merely epistemological problems.   It
becomes immediately apparent when he turns to ethical
problems.   The synthetic unity of apperception then becomes
a self-determining principle, the dialectical a real dynamic, but
the transformation cannot be regarded as consistent with
Kantianism as such.

The notion of the Ego as self-determining activity became
the central principle of Fichte's[2] philosophy.   In his earlier
work, like Kant, Fichte concerned himself with the conditions
of knowledge, even maintaining that the philosopher as such
has nothing to do with apprehended objects or with the apprehending subject, leaving these to the psychologist[3].   As his
interest in ethics developed, and his ethical views focussed
and defined themselves, this standpoint gradually changed,
and he tended more and more to deduce a psychology from
his fundamental principles.   He gave up the use of the term
'Absolute Ego,' using rather the notion and sometimes the
term 'Life[4],' and occasionally expressing himself in a way

[1] Cf. Seth, *Hegelianism and Personality*, pp. 17 ff. and especially p. 31.
[2] 1762–1814.
[3] Erdmann, *History of Philosophy*, vol. II, p. 498.
[4] Seth, *Hegelianism and Personality*, p. 70.

that is strongly reminiscent of Bergson. "This Life is itself neither in space nor time; it is a mere force, pure force without substrate, which is not itself a phenomenon at all, and which cannot be perceived, but which lies at the basis of all possible phenomenal or perceived existence[1]."

With his strong conviction that the destination of man is to be found in action, not in pure thought, Fichte always tended towards the interpretation of this abstract 'Life' as real life, of its force as real force. Thus, in a final statement of his position, he says:

"I ascribe to myself a real active force—a force, which produces being, and which is quite different from the mere faculty of ideas. The ideas or plans, usually called ends or purposes, are not to be considered, like the ideas of cognition, as after-pictures of something given; they are rather fore-pictures, or exemplars of something which is to be produced. The real force, however, does not lie in them; it exists on its own account, and receives from them only its determinate direction, knowledge looking on, as it were, as a spectator of its action[2]."

In this aspect of his thought Fichte may be considered as a fore-runner of Schopenhauer, von Hartmann, Bergson, rather than of Hegel. "The Eternal Will is the creator of the world," he has said. He may not have meant this as a strictly philosophical principle, but Schopenhauer found in the same thought the basis for a new 'idealism,' the very antithesis of Hegelianism.

The influence of Schopenhauer[3], who gives us a more or less developed philosophy of Instinct, has, through von Hartmann, considerably affected present-day theories of Instinct in various directions. These two may be regarded as summing up the results of the attempt at a philosophical deduction of the psychology of Instinct.

For Schopenhauer, Kant's 'thing-in-itself' became Will, the word 'Will' denoting "that which is the inner nature of everything[4]." From the side of the intellect, the world is

---

[1] Seth, *Hegelianism and Personality*, p. 71, footnote.
[2] Seth, op. cit., p. 153.   [3] 1788–1860.
[4] Schopenhauer, *Die Welt als Wille und Vorstellung*. Translation by Haldane and Kemp, vol. I, p. 153.

only Idea[1]. Its inner reality, however, is teleological activity; it is Will. Understanding is the subjective correlative of the nature of matter as cause and effect[2]. The first example of understanding is the perception of the actual world, and "this is throughout knowledge of the cause from the effect[3]." The effect which is known immediately is the affection of the animal body, or sensation. Such effects being referred to their causes, the perceptions of objects arise. "At one stroke, the understanding, by means of its one simple function, changes the dull meaningless sensation into perception[4]." Such is Schopenhauer's psychology of perception.

All animals must be considered to have understanding since they perceive objects[5]. But the sphere of understanding, that is the scope of perception, varies enormously from the lowest to the highest. The difference between the mentality of man and of the lower animals is summed up in a striking passage, of which we cannot resist quoting at least the most important parts. It is reason, Schopenhauer says, that gives man "that thoughtfulness which distinguishes his consciousness so entirely from that of the lower animals, and through which his whole behaviour on earth is so different from that of his irrational fellow-creatures. He far surpasses them in power and also in suffering. They live in the present alone, he lives also in the future and the past. They satisfy the needs of the moment, he provides by the most ingenious preparations for the future, yea for days that he shall never see. They are entirely dependent on the impression of the moment, on the effect of the perceptible motive; he is determined by abstract conceptions independent of the present. Therefore he follows predetermined plans, he acts from maxims, without reference to his surroundings or the accidental impression of the moment. ...The brute on the other hand is determined by the present impression; only the fear of present compulsion can constrain its desires, until at last this fear has become custom, and as such continues to determine it; this is called training.

---

[1] Schopenhauer, *Die Welt als Wille und Vorstellung*, vol. I, p. 5.
[2] Op. cit., vol. I, p. 13.   [3] Op. cit., vol. I, p. 14.
[4] Op. cit., vol. I, p. 14.   [5] Op. cit., vol. I, p. 26.

The brute feels and perceives; man, in addition to this, thinks and knows; both will....The brute first knows death when it dies, but man draws consciously nearer to it every hour that he lives....Principally on this account man has philosophies and religions, though it is uncertain whether the qualities we admire most in his conduct...were ever the fruit of either of them[1]."

Schopenhauer makes his transition from the world as Idea to the world as Will, when he considers the real meaning of the perceived object. This transition, he says, could not be made at all if we were pure knowing subjects. But the body appears to us in two entirely different ways, to our understanding as perceived object, and as "objectified will" in our acts[2]. My body is therefore a condition of my knowledge of my will. "So far as I know my will specially as object, I know it as body[3]." This double knowledge, as Schopenhauer calls it, of the body can be used "as the key to the nature of every phenomenon[4]." What remains of any object when we set aside its idea is its reality, and that is Will. Moreover, the body being objectified will, "the parts of the body correspond to the principal desires through which the will manifests itself[5]."

Since every kind of "active and operating force in nature" is identified with will, we must conceive will as acting in inorganic nature, in the organic and vegetative changes of the animal body, in the "instinct and mechanical skill" of animals, as well as in our own self-conscious nature[6]. Individuality characterizes the higher manifestations of will, but the farther we go from man, the fainter do the traces of individuality become, until in the inorganic world they entirely disappear, except perhaps in the crystal alone[7]. In the fact that it is one and the same Will, that reveals itself in all forms, we have the explanation of the analogy that pervades nature, and of the harmony that underlies all, in spite of the perpetual conflict going on between the higher and the lower forms of 'objectified

[1] Schopenhauer, *Die Welt als Wille und Vorstellung*, vol. I, pp. 47–8.
[2] Op. cit., vol. I, p. 130.   [3] Op. cit., vol. I, p. 132.
[4] Op. cit., vol. I, p. 136.   [5] Op. cit., vol. I, p. 141.
[6] Op. cit., vol. I, p. 143.   [7] Op. cit., vol. I, p. 171.

will[1].' This harmony Schopenhauer speaks of as teleology, both inner and outer, the inner teleology being the relation of all the parts of an organism to one another, the outer, of the particular parts of organized nature to the rest, that is the other parts.

Such being the general lines of Schopenhauer's system of thought, what has he to say of Instinct from the point of view of the philosophy of Will? In the case of animal life, he says, the will may be set in motion in two ways, either from without or from within, through motivation or through instinct[2]. This contrast is not an absolute one, for the operation of a motive depends on an 'inner tendency,' that is, 'a definite quality of will, which we call the character.' The motive 'individualizes' this character for the concrete case. In the same way, Instinct "does not act entirely like a spring from within." Its action depends upon some external circumstance which determines it. Hence, even where such action is most mechanical, though it is primarily dependent on Instinct, it is yet 'subordinated to intellect.' The instinct "gives the universal, the rule; the intellect the particular, the application." "Instinct is a character which is only set in motion by a *quite specially determined* motive," while the character of will generally may be set in motion by very different motives[3]. Hence determination of action by Instinct only involves a limited sphere of knowledge, and as much intelligence as is necessary to apprehend the one special motive[4].

On the other hand, the difference between this mechanical tendency of instinct and ordinary organic processes in animals is, that, in the latter case, the will acts "perfectly blindly, in its primary condition[5]." The working for the future, the anticipation of an end, which we see both in the organic processes and in the instinctive activities of animals, might be brought under the conception of 'a knowledge *a priori*,' if knowledge 'lay at their foundation at all.' But this is not the case. "Their source lies deeper than the sphere of knowledge, in the will, as the thing-in-itself, which as such remains

[1] Schopenhauer, *Die Welt als Wille und Vorstellung*, vol. I, p. 201.
[2] Op. cit., vol. III, p. 96.   [3] Op. cit., vol. III, p. 97.
[4] Op. cit., vol. III, p. 98.   [5] Op. cit., vol. III, p. 101.

free even from the *forms* of knowledge; therefore with reference to it time has no significance[1]."

E. von Hartmann's[2] philosophy is not essentially different from Schopenhauer's, though it is an attempt to reconcile Schopenhauer with Schelling and Hegel. The reconciliation is effected by placing alongside of Schopenhauer's unconscious Will the unconscious Idea. For von Hartmann the Absolute, or, as he calls it, the Unconscious, is not only Will, but it is also Idea. "The unconscious Will of Nature *eo ipso* presupposes an unconscious Idea, as goal, content, or object of itself[3]."

Instinct is one of the most important and familiar manifestations of the Unconscious, both as Will and as Idea. Von Hartmann gives us two definitions of Instinct. It is "purposive action without consciousness of the purpose[4]," and it is "conscious willing of the means to an unconsciously willed end[5]." The second of these definitions is, however, merely an alternative statement and fuller explanation of the first.

Three possible accounts or explanations of Instinct, he says, are apparently available. We may explain it, "as a mere consequence of corporeal organization," or "as a cerebral or mental mechanism," or as "a result of unconscious mental activity[6]." He rejects the first and second views as inadequate, and incapable of accounting for the facts. Instinct must be regarded as conscious willing, as volition, not as mere mechanism, and conscious willing, conditioned by an unconscious purpose and not a mere unconscious mechanism.

There are two marks by which we can distinguish volition from the mechanism of reflex action. First of all there is emotion; secondly there is "consistency in carrying out the intention[7]." Both marks characterize the instinctive actions of animals. But conscious willing cannot itself explain Instinct. Instinct must also involve "unconscious ideation and volition," an unconscious purpose[8], because nothing else will explain the

---

[1] *Die Welt als Wille und Vorstellung*, vol. III, p. 104.
[2] 1842–1906.
[3] E. v. Hartmann, *Philosophy of the Unconscious* (translation by Coupland), vol. I, p. 39.
[4] Op. cit., vol. I, p. 79.   [5] Op. cit., vol. I, p. 88.
[6] Op. cit., vol. I, p. 79.   [7] Op. cit., vol. I, p. 61.
[8] Op. cit., vol. I, p. 88.

connection between the sensuous presentation as motive, and the "conscious will to some particular action." There must be some causal connection, and this causal connection does not arise from experience. The pleasure that follows has nothing to do with the will to act instinctively[1]. On the other hand, the derivation of the "willed end" from conscious rational activity is radically hopeless[2], when we think of the high grade of intelligence, that would be necessarily involved in such rational activity, to account for the results in the instinctive actions of the lowest organisms.

The unconscious knowledge, which underlies Instinct, is of the nature of "clairvoyance," and manifests itself as "clairvoyant intuition[3]." In the case of the human being this clairvoyant intuition is also present, but always with a "reverberation" in consciousness, and sometimes as "pure idea," without conscious will[4]. Clairvoyance may occur apart from Instinct. They are two distinct facts. But clairvoyance alone will explain the nature of Instinct-knowledge[5]. This clairvoyant intuition is "the characteristic attribute of the Unconscious[6]."

Summing up[7], von Hartmann finds that Instinct is not the result of conscious reflection, nor of corporeal, cerebral, or mental mechanisms, but of the conscious activity of the individual, "springing from his inmost nature and character"; that the end, towards which the activity is directed, is not conceived by an external mind, a Providence, but "unconsciously willed and imagined" by the individual, and the suitable means unconsciously chosen; and that the knowledge involved in this unconscious cognition, which is frequently such as could not be obtained from sense perception, is of the nature of clairvoyant intuition. It is necessary that the instinctive action itself should be vividly realized in consciousness, in order that the necessary accuracy of execution should be secured, but it is the execution only that is conscious.

[1] *Philosophy of the Unconscious*, vol. I, p. 87.
[2] Op. cit., vol. I, p. 93. [3] Op. cit., vol. I, p. 106.
[4] Op. cit., vol. I, p. 107. [5] Op. cit., vol. I, p. 114.
[6] Op. cit., vol. I, p. 114. [7] Op. cit., vol. I, p. 113.

Von Hartmann divides human instincts into two groups, those relating to physical, and those relating to psychical needs[1], and enumerates a great number, especially of those belonging to the first group. The capricious appetites of the sick, the "curative instincts" of children, the fear of falling, the instinct to suck, the distinguishing of "genuine from feigned friendship[2]," the fear of death, shame, disgust[3], love of dress on the part of girls[4], play[5], sympathy[6], gratitude and retaliation[7], maternal love[8], sexual love[9], may be cited as examples. He also anticipates in a rather significant way, and more fully than Malebranche, the view of play, which we attribute to Karl Groos, who indeed was considerably influenced by von Hartmann. Play appears as a "presaging instinct," which guides children and the young of animals to the exercise of the activities they will require in future, and thus "trains them in advance." Play is, therefore, "unconsciously subservient to the aims of the future life."

A fuller account is given of the clairvoyant intuition of Instinct in the second volume of the *Philosophy of the Unconscious*. Unconscious ideation, of which the unconscious knowledge of Instinct is a particular case, is of such a kind that the ordinary consciousness can form no conception of it, save negatively from what it is not. It is not affected by sickness or fatigue[10]; it has not the form of sensibility[11]; it does not hesitate, or doubt, or err[12]. The thought of the Unconscious is timeless and non-temporal; the "coming-to-manifestation" of its result is alone in time[13]. "Will and representation are united in inseparable unity[14]." On the other hand, conscious thought makes possible "the emancipation of the intellect from the will." While the apparent errors of Instinct are errors of consciousness, not of the Unconscious, it must also be remembered, that all progress depends upon the expansion of the sphere where consciousness prevails, because this makes

[1] *Philosophy of the Unconscious*, vol. I, p. 205.   [2] Op. cit., vol. I, p. 205.
[3] Op. cit., vol. I, p. 206.   [4] Op. cit., vol. I, p. 208.
[5] Op. cit., vol. I, p. 207.   [6] Op. cit., vol. I, p. 210.
[7] Op. cit., vol. I, p. 211.   [8] Op. cit., vol. I, p. 212.
[9] Op. cit., vol. I, 220.   [10] Op. cit., vol. II, p. 47.
[11] Op. cit., vol. II, p. 48.   [12] Op. cit., vol. II, pp. 50–51.
[13] Op. cit., vol. II, p. 51.   [14] Op. cit., vol. II, p. 55.

possible the "liberation of consciousness from the sway of passion and interest," that is of Will[1].

Lastly the function of Instinct in Nature, inclusive of human life, is threefold. "Every unconscious idea is accompanied by unconscious will, which represents the general will of self-preservation, and preservation of the species[2]." That is to say there are two main ends which instincts subserve, preservation of the self and preservation of the race. But there is a third end, especially important as regards humanity. That is the "perfection and ennoblement of the species[3]." The progress of the human race, individual, social, and national, the appreciation of the beautiful, the development of science and philosophy, the satisfaction of the deeper spiritual needs of the heart, all derive their driving force, their interest and will, from the Will and Idea of the Unconscious.

The main interest of this development of thought culminating in von Hartmann's philosophy of the "Unconscious" is perhaps philosophical rather than psychological. Philosophically it is an assertion of the ultimate psychical nature of Instinct, and of the impossibility of explaining, not merely the manifestations of Instinct, but Instinct itself in any but psychical terms. But, since this impossibility is asserted, not only of Instinct, but of all natural forces whatsoever, it is not clear how the assertion helps the psychologist very much. On the other hand, the notion of the 'unconscious,' as the 'subconscious,' has been a very fruitful one for abnormal psychology, and, through Freud and his school, by a kind of 'total reflection,' as it were, has, in recent times, affected other aspects of the psychology of Instinct. Apart from this, the notion of 'clairvoyant intuition,' as characteristic of Instinct-Knowledge, has received further emphasis in the thought of Bergson and his followers[4]. How far these two psychological deductions from philosophical principles ought to be permitted to modify our psychology of Instinct, we shall require to consider later.

[1] *Philosophy of the Unconscious*, vol. II, p. 59.
[2] Op. cit., vol. II, p. 55.
[3] Op. cit., vol. II, p. 56.
[4] While this is passing through the press, a new work on Instinct has appeared, in which a theory very like that of v. Hartmann is developed, the interesting book, *What is Instinct?*, by C. Bingham Newland.

The development of natural science, from about the middle of the eighteenth century onwards, brought upon the scene other views of Instinct, involving a discussion and interpretation of the phenomena from an entirely different point of view—from two different points of view, in fact, as we shall see presently. We must remember, however, that, apart from the purely biological aspect of Instinct, the views we have already considered have also influenced the views of the physiologist and the biologist, Schopenhauer's and von Hartmann's more or less directly, the psychology of the Scottish School through Cabanis and the phrenologists. The influence has really been mutual, an influence of physiological and biological study on psychological and philosophical conceptions, an influence of psychology and philosophy on physiological and biological conceptions of Instinct.

Physiological psychology had made a strong bid for recognition as the only scientific psychology by the middle of the eighteenth century. Hartley's[1] *Observations on Man* and Bonnet's[2] *Contemplation de la Nature* were published almost contemporaneously just before the middle of the century, while Bonnet's more important work, the *Essai analytique sur les facultés de l'âme*, appeared in 1760. Von Haller's[3] *Elementa physiologiae humani corporis* saw the light about the same time. Swammerdam[4], the Dutch naturalist, had done important biological work, as, for example, in the study of insects, a century earlier.

There were two directions in which the work done in physiology and biology contributed to a clearer and fuller knowledge of Instinct. On the one hand, there was a contribution, mainly physiological, developing as a pure physiology of the brain and nervous system, and influencing psychology through phrenology, and later through the physiological psychology of the present day. On the other hand, there was a more important contribution, mainly biological, developing, more especially during the nineteenth century, through the various theories of evolution into a comparative study of the physiology and psychology of living organisms, and represented

[1] 1705–1757.   [2] 1720–1793.   [3] 1708–1777.   [4] 1637–1680.

in the psychology of to-day by Comparative and Social Psychology[1].

The physiological psychology of the earlier physiologists, Hartley and the rest, was in the main a somewhat crude attempt to express the psychology of Locke in physiological terms. Equally crude was the attempt made by Erasmus Darwin[2] towards the end of the same century. The first really scientific physiological psychology made its appearance in the *Traité du physique et du moral de l'homme* of Cabanis[3], published for the first time as a separate work in 1802.

Cabanis starts from the conception of 'sensibility' as a general and characteristic property of all living organisms. He tries to show how all the higher intellectual processes are evolved from 'sensibility,' how they all depend upon organic conditions, and also to determine the organic conditions. His explanation was, therefore, intended to be an explanation throughout in physiological rather than psychological terms, science not 'metaphysics.' His aim was to show how ideas, instincts, passions, depend upon, are modified by, and involve only physiological conditions.

Lewes quotes[4] a very interesting example of the method of Cabanis, as applied to Instinct, what he calls Cabanis' experimental proof of the fact that an instinct is developed by certain organic conditions. An artificial maternal love is, according to this account, produced in a capon by plucking off the feathers from his abdomen, rubbing the abdomen with nettles and vinegar, and then placing the capon on eggs for hatching. This artificial instinct, it is said, not only endures till the chickens are hatched, but until they no longer need care and protection.

The attempt of Cabanis, in spite of the defects of both his physiology and his psychology[5], must receive due recognition, as a genuine attempt, prompted by the true scientific spirit,

---

[1] 'Social Psychology' is here used in the widest sense.
[2] 1731–1802. *Zoonomia*, published 1794–6.
[3] 1757–1808.
[4] *Biographical History of Philosophy*, p. 627.
[5] Cabanis defines Instinct as "Le produit des excitations dont les stimulus s'appliquent à l'intérieur." See Bostock, *Elementary System of Physiology*, vol. III, p. 228.

to interpret the facts of experience in terms of physiological processes, and to develop a scientific psychology on the basis of physiology. The kind of recognition we ought to give to another and somewhat analogous attempt, viz. phrenology, is more doubtful. Nevertheless phrenology and the work of the phrenologists may justly be regarded as really more important than the work of Cabanis. C. S. Sherrington[1] speaks rather slightingly of the work of Gall[2] and implicatively of the whole phrenology movement. We cannot entirely share his views. Gall was certainly more than half charlatan, as were many of his followers, and Cranioscopy can claim no respect from the scientist. But Spurzheim[3] and Combe[4] were not charlatans, and phrenology as such was not only very significant historically, but it exercised an important influence on the development of psychology, of educational theory, and to an even greater extent of physiology.

In order duly to appreciate the historical position of the phrenologists, we must carefully avoid the error, into which most psychologists, apparently following James[5], seem to have fallen. The *modus operandi* of the phrenologist's reasoning cannot fairly be described as merely classifying the various psychical phenomena, hypostatizing the class names as powers, and then assigning these powers distinct organs in different parts of the brain. It is true that this line of argument holds against phrenology to the extent to which the phrenologists adopt the 'faculty psychology.' But it quite ignores the real historical position and significance of phrenology.

No doubt the psychology of Gall was of the nondescript order, containing elements of Aristotelian and mediaeval psychology, of the psychology of Locke and Hartley, as well as of the psychology of Reid, Stewart, and the Scottish School. Under these circumstances, if we are disposed to criticise destructively, it is, as one would expect, a very easy matter to criticise the psychology of the early phrenologists. But we ought to discriminate. In order to come to a clear

[1] Article "Brain" in *Encyclopaedia Britannica*, 11th ed.
[2] 1758–1828.   [3] 1778–1832.   [4] 1788–1858.
[5] *Principles of Psychology*, vol. I, p. 28.

and definite decision regarding the merits and demerits of this
early nineteenth century development of thought, in order to
reach a just evaluation of the work done, we must seek to
understand what the phrenologists were really trying to do.
What was their problem? How did they set about its solution?
These are the questions that must be asked and answered.

Like Cabanis the phrenologists were attempting to develop
a physiological psychology. But their method of approach
was different. It was also different from the method of
approach to psychology adopted by physiological biologists
like Bonnet and Erasmus Darwin. The notion of 'natural
law,' very prominent in Combe[1], and underlying the thought
development as a whole in its typical manifestations, implies
the conception of nature as a mechanism through and through,
a mechanism contrived for the purposes of the Author of
Nature. The 'laws of nature' are the laws which regulate
action and reaction among things in the inorganic world, and
similarly action and reaction among living things, every thing
and every organism acting in accordance with the constitution
bestowed upon it. In virtue of its constitution each thing
has certain powers of acting with regard to other things. All
objects, therefore, are regarded as manifesting distinct forces,
each acting according to the laws of its nature[2]. The laws of
nature apply in the intellectual and moral life of man, as in
animal life, and as in the inorganic world.

Turning now to the human being, we find that he has a
definite constitution expressing itself in definite activities, the
activities being the actions of the various powers, forces, or
faculties of man. The same holds of animals, only man has
certain powers or faculties which animals have not got. As
regards the life processes, each power is represented in the
activity of a definite organ. The same ought to hold of the
mental and moral faculties of man, the animal propensities of
man and the lower animals. Hence the problem arises of
determining the organs, corresponding to the mental and moral
faculties of man.

[1] See *Constitution of Man*, Introduction.
[2] Loc. cit.

The preliminary problem of determining the various mental and moral powers or faculties does not seem to have presented itself as a problem at all. Herein, we might say, consists the first error of phrenology. But it must be remembered that there were certain forces, recognized by the psychologists of the time as real forces, impelling man to act in definite ways, expressions of the constitution bestowed upon him by the Divine Author of his being. These forces were the instinctive tendencies, the 'animal propensities,' common to man and the lower animals[1]. To these were added, more or less arbitrarily, powers or faculties, in virtue of which man was able to know, compare, and reflect upon objects, together with powers or faculties, representing sentiments, or qualities of character or will. All were equally regarded as due to the functioning of certain organs, and the problem was to find the respective organs.

The chief human instincts, recognized by the phrenologists, were sexual love (amativeness), parental love (philo-progenitiveness), the gregarious instinct (adhesiveness), pugnacity (combativeness), destructiveness, appetite for food, acquisitiveness, constructiveness, self-esteem, love of approbation, wonder, and imitation. This list is strongly suggestive of the development of introspective psychology we have already studied, and is additional evidence of the extent to which this psychology had become the current psychology of the early nineteenth century.

It is evident from this account of the underlying ideas of phrenology that the criticisms, levelled and valid against the 'faculty psychology,' are not necessarily valid against phrenology, as such. Animal propensities, instinctive tendencies, may quite legitimately be conceived as forces, without any hypostatization of general terms, and the search for a corresponding organ seems a quite legitimate scientific problem. It is true that the search was conducted very unscientifically, and that, while pretending to have succeeded, it really failed. But the failure to solve the problem, they set out to solve, must not be attributed to the phrenologists, as a crime against reason and common sense.

[1] *Constitution of Man*, chap. II, section III.

It is interesting to see how phrenology was related to the orthodox physiology of the day. Take first Magendie[1]. Magendie's psychology was essentially that of Cabanis. The phenomena of human intelligence he regarded as simply functions of the brain[2], and, as such, capable of being studied only by "observation and experience." The phenomena of the intellect were merely modifications of the 'faculty of perception,' and he recognized four chief modifications: sensibility, memory, judgment, and desire or will. Magendie himself made an important contribution to our knowledge of the physical basis of sensibility in his determination of the difference in function between the anterior and posterior nerve roots. As a result of his own work, and that of other physiologists like Rolando and Flourens, he finds no difficulty in localizing the principal seats of the special senses in the cerebrum and lower centres. With these results of physiological investigation the phrenologists seem to have been very imperfectly acquainted. As regards memory, Magendie makes no attempt to localize it, but refers in a curious, facing-two-ways footnote to the attempts of the "pseudo-science" phrenology, attempts "laudable in themselves, but hitherto unable to bear examination[3]."

Instincts are defined by Magendie as "propensities, inclinations, wants, by which animals are constantly excited and forced to fulfil the intentions of nature[4]." An instinctive feeling, which has become "extreme and exclusive," is a passion. Again in this connection, in a footnote, there is allusion to the problem, at least, of phrenology, when he says: "This should be the proper place to treat of the different parts of the brain in regard to the understanding and instincts....I have been engaged at intervals on experiments directed to this point, and will make the results known, as soon as they appear worthy of public notice[5]."

---

[1] 1783–1855.

[2] Magendie, *Elementary Compendium of Physiology*. Translation by E. Milligan, p. 109. Fourth edition, Edinburgh, 1831.

[3] Op. cit., p. 113.

[4] Op. cit., p. 116. Magendie's own words are:—"des penchants, des inclinations, des besoins, au moyen desquels ils sont continuellement excités et même forcés à remplir les intentions de la nature." (*El. Phys.* t. I, p. 207.)   [5] Op. cit., p. 118.

Take another physiologist, Bostock, who approaches the matter from a different point of view. He devotes a whole chapter to a serious examination of the claims of phrenology[1], and, though he comes to the conclusion that the claims are not substantiated, there is no ridicule. Bostock's own psychology was eclectic, derived mainly from Hartley, Reid, and Dugald Stewart, but he does not hesitate to speak of powers and faculties, and he also attempts to localize them. His definition of Instinct is in terms of capacity—"a capacity for performing, by means of the voluntary organs, certain actions, which conduce to some useful purpose, but of which purpose the animal is itself ignorant[2]." This later becomes sometimes a motive, sometimes a faculty, and is localized, in a tentative way, in the lower brain centres[3]. Bostock too has evidently a problem which is not essentially different from that of the phrenologists.

The fact is, that, with the generally prevailing view of Instinct, and the stage of development reached by the physiological study of the brain and nervous system, the physiologist could not help having some such problem as the phrenologist had. The rapidity with which evidence against the conclusions of phrenology accumulated is itself a remarkable proof of the extent to which phrenology influenced the direction of physiological investigation. As real knowledge of the cerebral cortex extended, the motley array of faculties, with which the phrenologists wrought, fell more and more into the background. Nevertheless Carpenter, in his *Mental Physiology*, still in 1874 localized the instincts in the 'sensory ganglia[4],' just as he had done thirty years earlier in his *Human Physiology*[5].

At the present day the physiologist is generally inclined to be more cautious, and merely to view Instinct in a somewhat vague way as an innate nervous arrangement, mechanism, or disposition. But, after all, the notion of such an organ, as subserving instinctive activity, is not essentially different from the notion of a definite part of the brain, as the organ performing

[1] *An Elementary System of Physiology*, vol. III, chap. XIX.
[2] Op. cit., vol. III, p. 228.   [3] Op. cit., vol. III, p. 232.
[4] Carpenter, *Mental Physiology*, p. 81.
[5] *Human Physiology* (4th ed., 1846), p. 375.

the same function. Nor is there any need to assume that this notion, in itself, and physiologically regarded, is an erroneous one. Error will only arise, when, and if, we attempt to explain Instinct psychologically as the functioning of this or any such organ.

The importance of the development of biology for the psychology of Instinct has a double source. In the first place, this development led to an enormous increase in the facts of animal life bearing upon Instinct, which were made available for psychological interpretation. The development of comparative psychology is by no means bound up with the evolution theory, Lamarckian or Darwinian, except perhaps in so far as it depends upon the recognition of essential continuity between animal and human mind. Important work had been done before the beginning of the nineteenth century, that is, before there was any evolution theory in our modern meaning of evolution[1], by Bonnet, Reimarus[2], Buffon[3], Cuvier[4], and others. The same kind of work, leading to an accumulation of facts belonging to animal psychology, went on with increased zeal under the stimulus of the evolution theory, and such work, represented at its best by Lubbock (Lord Avebury), Darwin, Fabre, the Peckhams, has a value for psychology, independent of any value it may have for a biological theory.

In the second place, the psychological interpretation of Instinct was supplemented by the biological. This was more especially the work of the evolutionists, but this too had its beginning in pre-evolution biology. The common, though erroneous, view, that the biological account of Instinct can take the place of the psychological, has been discussed above[5]. It is true that some of the biological theories of Instinct leave no place for the psychological account, but such theories are not now the theories generally accepted.

This erroneous view seems to have originated from the fact that many biologists, both of the pre-evolution and of the evolution period, have actively sought to combat a view of

---

[1] See article 'Evolution' in *Encyc. Brit.*, 11th ed.
[2] 1694–1768.   [3] 1707–1788.   [4] 1769–1832.
[5] See chap. I Introduction.

Instinct, which has apparently been mistaken for the psychological, but which ought rather to be called the religious-metaphysical, or, as Karl Groos calls it, the "transcendental-teleological[1]." The success of these biologists in their controversy is somewhat problematical, but at any rate, they have very successfully suggested that their view of Instinct was a new view to be substituted for this antiquated one, so successfully that, at the present day, the suggestion is generally accepted without any careful examination of the rights and wrongs of the controversy.

What then is this religious-metaphysical view of Instinct? There is more than a suspicion of it in many of the views of Instinct we have discussed, more particularly perhaps in those of Hume, von Hartmann, the phrenologists, but the clearest, and at the same time the popular, form of this view is admirably expressed in Addison's definition of Instinct, quoted by Romanes[2]:—"I look upon instinct as upon the principle of gravitation in bodies, which is not to be explained by any known qualities inherent in the bodies themselves, nor from any laws of mechanism, but as an immediate impression from the first mover and divine energy acting in the creatures[3]." In so far as such a view shuts the door against any scientific study of Instinct, it is of course quite inadmissible, and the psychologist, equally with the biologist, must protest. But, in so far as such a view represents a philosophical or ultimate view of Instinct, it does not appear that biology can touch it at all. If there is such a thing as Instinct, the ultimate philosophical account of it is, as we have tried to show, in an entirely different category from the scientific biological account.

The most direct attack upon this religious-metaphysical view of Instinct consisted in the denial or rejection of such a conception altogether. Among older biologists Erasmus Darwin, and among more modern Brehm[4], Büchner[5], Bain[6], if we may

---

[1] *The Play of Animals*, Engl. Trans., p. 26.   [2] *Animal Intelligence*, p. 11.
[3] See also Kirby, *History, Habits, and Instincts of Animals* (1835), and Newland, *What is Instinct?* (Lond. 1916), for views which tend in a similar direction.
[4] *Thierleben*, vol. I, p. 20.
[5] *Aus dem Geistesleben der Thiere*, Engl. Trans., by Annie Besant.
[6] *The Senses and the Intellect*, 3rd ed. p. 409. But see also *The Emotions and the Will*, pp. 53 and 613.

count him, and at one time Alfred Russel Wallace[1], have taken
this line of attack in one form or another.   In some cases the
attack has been directed mainly against the notion of an innate
and unerring knowledge, and Büchner more especially emphasizes in this connection the mistakes of Instinct, in others
against the notion of a divine origin.   Alfred Russel Wallace
for a time took the view that so-called instinctive actions could
be explained as a result of imitation and experience.   After
the publication of Darwin's *Origin of Species* most biologists
abandoned this line of thought, though some of the more
extreme opponents of the religious-metaphysical view continued to urge the desirability of ceasing to employ the term
'instinct,' and most of them saw in Darwin's 'natural
selection' a complete explanation of Instinct, which of course
it is not.

What of the biological account itself?   The history of its
development is the history of the modern evolution theory.
The evolution theories of the eighteenth century, though they
prepared the way, were entirely superseded by the evolution
theory of Lamarck, which first saw the light in the early years
of the nineteenth century[2].   The fundamental principle of
this theory is the inheritance of characteristics acquired
through functional adjustment to an environment.   Between
the publication of the *Philosophie zoologique* and 1858, when
Darwin and Wallace published their *Theory of Natural Selection*,
the notion of evolution, though frowned upon by the orthodox
and 'respectable' zoologists, kept appearing every now and
again in one form or another, and, with the year 1859, when
the *Origin of Species* came, the modern theory of evolution
may be regarded as definitely established in biology.   According to this theory changes in the organic world, like changes in
the inorganic, take place in accordance with law; these changes
include the gradual development and differentiation of the

---

[1] *Contributions to the Theory of Natural Selection.*
[2] Lamarck first indicated his theory of evolution in 1801, and in his *Philosophie zoologique*, published in 1809, he formulated the theory in detail.   Trevi-
ranus apparently arrived at a theory of evolution independently and almost
simultaneously, his *Biologie* (at least the first volume) which contained the
theory appearing in 1802.   See art. "Evolution" in *Encyc. Brit.*, 11th ed.

various species of animal life; among the animal characters, and not the least important, which have been so developed and differentiated, is Instinct.

The evolution theories of Lamarck and Darwin really represent two different accounts of Instinct. According to the former Instinct is originally a character, consciously acquired, and established as a habit, in successful adaptation to an environment, and then transmitted to descendants, the inherited character being subsequently modified by new successful adaptations, which are in turn transmitted. A complex instinct is thus due to a number of successful adaptations, made at different times in the history of the race, and transmitted as gradually changing 'race habit.' In other words Instinct is largely "lapsed intelligence[1]." According to the Darwinian view, on the other hand, Instinct is due mainly to the operation of natural selection upon accidental or spontaneous variations.

The 'lapsed intelligence' view of Instinct, in some form or another, is adopted by Ribot, by Preyer[2], by Wundt[3], by Schneider[4], by Herbert Spencer and others. Darwin admits it as a possible view of the origin of some instincts but lays chief stress upon natural selection. Romanes follows Darwin, and distinguishes the two kinds of instinct as 'primary' and 'secondary[5].'

More recently the whole notion of the inheritance of acquired characteristics has been assailed, notably by Weismann[6], and on grounds so strong, that biologists of the present day are inclined to give up the theory of 'lapsed intelligence' altogether, and to explain Instinct, as regards its origin, through the operation of natural selection alone. There are, however, still some difficulties, which seem to point to some kind of inheritance of acquired characteristics after all. To meet these difficulties, H. F. Osborn, Lloyd Morgan, and J. M. Baldwin have, still

---

[1] Lewes, *Problems of Life and Mind.* Ribot, *L'Hérédité psychologique.*
[2] *Die Seele des Kindes.*
[3] *Vorlesungen über die Menschen- und Tierseele.*
[4] *Der thierische Wille*, p. 146. *Der menschliche Wille*, p. 68.
[5] *Mental Evolution in Animals*, p. 178.
[6] *Die Continuität des Keimplasmas. Das Keimplasma.*

more recently, elaborated a theory of 'organic selection[1],' which reintroduces the factor of individual adjustment, and is otherwise very important in throwing a light upon the operation of natural selection in the case of societies rather than individuals. This theory is based upon the notion of possible coincidence in tendency between congenital variations and adaptive modifications, developed during an individual's lifetime. Such adaptive modifications are those which are produced in the individual because of their suitableness to a particular environment, by his conscious adjustment to that environment. Even though the adaptive modifications may not be transmitted, the coincident congenital variations are, and the operation of natural selection in the ordinary sense may therefore tend to be greatly modified in the long run, through the cumulative influence of particular elements, in the social *milieu*, for example, with which the individual, in the course of his life, may require to keep in adjustment. To some extent the same kind of modifications would be produced in this way, as if acquired modifications were transmitted. It is partly through this 'organic selection' that 'social heredity,' as Baldwin has called it, operates.

Such may be considered to be the general outcome of the biological account of the development of instincts, and the fundamental importance of Darwin's work must be recognized. But Darwin did not attempt a biological account of Instinct itself, in fact, deliberately avoids the issue[2], that is, he did not define the view which the biologist, as such, must take of the nature of Instinct. Consequently, though all biologists are now practically agreed as to the general mode in which instincts originate and develop, there is by no means agreement with regard to the view which the biologist ought to take of Instinct. Two views are still in the field. On the one hand is the view of those who, while not denying that intelligence may cooperate with Instinct in certain cases, hold that "the idea of consciousness must be rigidly excluded from any definition of instinct

[1] See *Science*, 1896, April 23rd, 1897; *Nature*, April 15th, 1897; Groos, *Play of Animals* (trans.), p. 329; *Mental Development in the Child and the Race*; *Social and Ethical Interpretations*.
[2] *Origin of Species* (5th ed., 1869), p. 255.

that is to be of practical utility[1]." On the other hand is the view of Romanes and those who think with him, that Instinct cannot be distinguished from reflex action, unless the idea of consciousness or experience is introduced. The dispute seems to arise partly from the old difficulty of the knowledge apparently involved in Instinct, and partly from the fact that the psychologists have taken a share in the discussion, and are, many of them, now as eager to exclude the term 'instinct' from psychology, as the biologists, not very long since, were eager to exclude it from biology.

Leaving some of these points for discussion later, in so far as they are psychological points, we may, in the meantime, simply sum up the result of both the physiological and the biological developments of the nineteenth century in a definition of Instinct, which will represent both physiology and biology, and which, as far as it goes, would probably be accepted by both physiologist and biologist. Such a definition may be worded thus:—As a factor determining the behaviour of living organisms, Instinct, physiologically regarded, is a congenital predisposition of the nervous system, consisting in a definite, but within limits modifiable, arrangement and coordination of nervous connections, so that a particular stimulus, with or without the presence of certain cooperating stimuli, will call forth a particular action or series of actions; this predisposition, biologically regarded, is apparently due to the operation of natural selection, and determines a mode of behaviour, which secures a biologically useful end, without foresight of that end or experience in attaining it. Such a definition appears to represent in a fairly satisfactory way the outcome of the physiological and biological study of Instinct, and leaves the psychological questions as open as possible.

[1] Karl Groos, *The Play of Animals* (Engl. trans.), p. 62.

CHAPTER IV

THE PSYCHOLOGICAL NATURE OF INSTINCT—
THE 'KNOWLEDGE' OF INSTINCT

Modern Philosophy, so far as it has been psychological, has largely confined itself to the study of cognition, and twice in the course of its history has led to its own *reductio ad absurdum*. The "ideal system" of Descartes, as Reid called it, led to the scepticism of Hume; the new beginning in cognition of an essentially similar philosophy, in the Critical Philosophy of Kant, led to the Absolutism of Hegel, which must equally be regarded as its refutation. Reid sought to escape Hume's scepticism by a new starting-point in what he rather unfortunately called "Common Sense," just as Schopenhauer sought to escape Hegelianism by a new start in the notion of reality as "Will," rather than as "Idea." It will be noticed that, in all cases, psychological notions seem to have afforded the basis for an ultimate metaphysic. So accustomed have we become to this way of looking at philosophy, that it comes as a genuine shock of surprise to find Bergson founding his philosophy upon biological, rather than psychological, conceptions. Bergson's philosophy may nevertheless be a genuine advance in the direction in which Modern Philosophy was moving.

A few years ago it seemed as if the Critical Philosophy represented the culmination of the philosophical thought of the modern world. To-day it is becoming ever clearer that the Critical Philosophy, if it was not a false step, was at any rate a side issue in post-Renaissance thought, and that the real achievement of Modern Philosophy is still to come. Moreover, there is increasing likelihood that, when this achievement does come, it will be apparent that Reid's "Common Sense," Schopenhauer's "Will" and Bergson's "Life Impulse" have been as significant advances as Kant's transcendental principles.

However that may be, there can be no doubt that the return of psychology to the study of the whole of experience, instead of one aspect of it, and that an aspect which has no meaning apart from the rest, is full of promise for psychology, if not for philosophy. The *reductio ad absurdum* of philosophy was no less a *reductio ad absurdum* of psychology, if psychology is the science of experience as such, and of experience as determining behaviour. The psychology, which set out from thought in isolation, returned to thought in isolation, but did not seem ever to reach experience in its life setting.

We must regard Fichte's and Schopenhauer's as valuable attempts to get to living experience, but the psychology itself was not wrought out as a psychology. At the present time we seem to have a still more fundamental starting-point offered us in the "life impulse" of Bergson, a starting-point that is behind the Ego, and behind Will. It is necessary, before accepting such a starting-point, to determine whether psychology can adopt as its starting-point something which is perhaps itself outside experience, and, if so, whether this is the starting-point it can with most advantage adopt.

We have already[1] taken up the position, in connection with psychology, that the psychologist is entitled to frame hypotheses which go beyond the facts of experience themselves, if such hypotheses are necessary to account for the facts psychologically. That is a right claimed by all sciences. The ultimate meaning of such a hypothesis is of course the concern of philosophy. Hence the legitimacy of some such starting-point as Bergson's "life impulse" cannot be questioned, always provided that these conditions are satisfied. The difficulty is as regards the way in which such a hypothesis should be formulated, in order to be of use psychologically. It would be an easy matter, without hypothesis at all, to substitute for the Cartesian "cogito, ergo sum," some such principle as "I am living, therefore life exists." But it is not easy to see how such a principle could carry us very far in philosophy, and its use in psychology is not very obvious. Psychology has as its task the explanation of experience and of behaviour in terms of experience. One essential

---

[1] See above, p. 12.

characteristic of any starting-point, unless it is one forced on
the psychologist, is that it should further the psychological
explanation of experience and of behaviour.

That we have an experience of living seems to be a fact.
The simplest hypothesis, based upon this fact, is that experience
depends upon life. Such a hypothesis, expressed in this form,
is not very obviously either a helpful one or a necessary one.
But it can be modified so as to become helpful, and, we believe,
necessary. In a great part of our experience, possibly in all,
we experience ourselves as active. Our whole notion of activity
arises from this experience. Not only when we experience
impulse, or desire, or endeavour, have we this experience of
being active, but also when we perceive, when we imagine,
when we judge, when we reason. A very strong case—which
we do not mean to argue at present—can be made for the view,
that our whole experience is determined by an activity which
is also experienced, but which does not arise from experience.
For the origin of this activity we must look, as it were, behind
experience. Assuming meanwhile that this view is sound—
its justification will appear as we proceed—we seem to find
that some kind of hypothesis becomes necessary at this point,
and our hypothesis is that this activity, which we experience,
but which also determines experience, is the 'life impulse'
become conscious in us.

Another condition which the hypothesis, furnishing the
starting-point of any science, must satisfy is that it should,
at any rate, be a possible way of regarding actual phenomena,
that is, that it should not contradict other known facts, laws,
or principles, but rather should be capable of being harmonized
with them, or even of throwing further light upon them, that,
in short, it should represent a possible, if provisional, way of
regarding the world of reality, when looked at from the standpoint of philosophy. It is of course clear that the most extra-
vagant hypotheses could be framed by the human imagination,
and organized structures of thought built upon such hypotheses,
which would represent science for those imaginary worlds to
which the hypotheses could apply, but only for such worlds.
Hence the necessity for this further condition or criterion,

by which the legitimacy of the hypotheses of any real science must be judged.

Now the hypothesis of a 'life impulse' becoming conscious in experienced activity, and determining experience itself, also satisfies this condition. The existence of such a life impulse is taken for granted in biology, may even be said to be the main topic discussed by biology, and physiology no less assumes it, while seeking to explain it. Philosophy also recognizes this as a way of looking at a part, at least, of the universe. On all grounds such a hypothesis can be more easily justified than the hypothesis of psycho-physical parallelism, which has long been adopted, almost without question, as a psychological hypothesis. Besides such a hypothesis saves us from requiring to talk of 'soul,' which it may ultimately be necessary for the psychologist to postulate, but which we do not apparently require to postulate in order to explain our facts, if we are allowed this simpler hypothesis of a 'life impulse.'

Let us consider this hypothesis as provisionally admitted, and try to apply it in order to get a definite idea of what Instinct really is, as far as the universe of discourse of psychology is concerned, that is to say, what the meaning of the term 'instinct' is to be for psychology. As we have already seen, most of the older psychologists recognized that there are certain determinate conscious impulses, which are experienced as impulses, but of the origin of which, as impulses, experience can afford us no explanation. Take, for example, as Hutcheson does, the anger impulse. Why should the pain, say of a blow, determine us to retaliate, rather than to relieve the pain?- Experience cannot answer. Or again, why should the sight of a certain object determine A, who has had no previous experience of such objects, to approach it, with a view to getting to know more about it, while B, who has had previous experience of similar objects, withdraws as hastily as possible? At the same time A has the emotional experience we call curiosity, B that which we call fear. We might possibly say that B's impulse and emotional experience were due to previous experience, but surely not A's. Really B's impulse is as little explicable from previous experience as A's. C, who has also had previous experience of such objects, and a similar experience to A, may attack and destroy it, experiencing at the same time the emotional experience we call anger or hate.   Moreover, if A, B, and C are animals belonging to different species, we may have each showing the characteristic behaviour of a different one of the three impulses, on the perception of an object, never met before by any one of them.   In this case we should have no hesitation in calling the impulses instinctive in all three cases.

But what should we mean psychologically by calling them instinctive?   One answer is, that, by calling them instinctive, we mean that they are determined by heredity.   That is to say 'instinctive' = 'determined by heredity.'   This is not satisfactory.   It is tantamount to saying that we are speaking biologically, and not psychologically, when we call such impulses instinctive, for 'heredity' is a biological conception, and to use it in this connection and context appears to imply the failure, at this point, of our psychological explanation of experience.   There is a further objection.   To speak of an 'instinctive impulse,' meaning this by 'instinctive,' is apparently to speak of a phenomenon which is neither biological nor psychological. The term 'impulse' indicates here a psychological phenomenon. Instinctive behaviour may be discussed by biology, but 'instinctive impulse' must be defined by psychology, if it is capable of definition at all.

Instead of avoiding the issue in this way by an appeal to biology, it is evidently the duty of the psychologist to attempt a description of 'instinctive impulse' in terms of experience. The first step towards this is the psychological analysis of the experience as a whole, of which the instinctive impulse is a constituent.   A first analysis yields us three factors, perception or cognition of an object, which we can denote by x, conscious impulse in relation to that object, which we may denote by y, and a feeling element correlated with both x and y, which we shall call z.   The whole psychosis may then be denoted by xyz, the factors all determining one another, and being also determined on the one side by the nature of an object, on the other side by the life activity of the experiencer.

An example from ordinary life will perhaps make clear the

way in which the three factors must be related to one another.
I am going a walk.   Passing the hall-stand, I perceive my
walking-stick and grasp it.   At the time of perceiving the
walking-stick, I had the impulse to grasp it in order to take it
with me.   The psychosis was, let us say $a'b'c'$, where a' is an
apprehended walking-stick, b' an impulse to grasp it, c' a faint
accompanying interest in walking-sticks, a' being determined
partly by the actual object before me, b' and c' partly by my
intention at the moment, the intention of going for a walk.   But
it is not difficult to show that the intention at the moment
also partly determines a', and that the nature of the object
partly determines b' and c'.   On a lonely part of the road I am
attacked by a tramp.   I now apprehend the walking-stick as
a suitable weapon of defence, and use it accordingly.   The
psychosis at the moment when I apprehend, as a weapon, the
object, which I originally apprehended as a walking-stick, may
be denoted by $a''b''c''$, where a'' is an apprehended weapon,
and is determined partly by the nature of the object but partly,
like b'' and c'', by the 'intention' at the moment, and where
b'' is an impulse to use a weapon of defence, and c'' an interest
in weapons, both determined partly by the 'intention' at the
moment, but partly also by the nature of the object apprehended
as a''.   In crossing a bridge, my cap blows off into a stream.
I now apprehend the object, which was previously apprehended
as a' and a'', as a hook, which will enable me to draw the
cap out, impulse and interest being concomitantly changed,
and the new psychosis being $a'''b'''c'''$.   One and the same
object has thus been apprehended as a walking-stick, a club,
and a hook.   In ordinary life I call the object a walking-stick,
but only because that is its ordinary function.   In the dynamic
of living experience, the apprehended object changes with the
impulse and the interest, but no less the impulse and the
interest change with the nature of the apprehended object.
The main point we wish to make at present is that the total
psychosis, the experience at any moment, is determined
partly by the nature of the object, but partly also by the
need of the individual at that moment, manifesting itself
in experience as impulse, with a correlated feeling or interest,

and further that all the elements in the psychosis are determined both by the nature of the object and the need of the moment.

Experience is essentially bipolar, with a bipolarity analogous to the subject-object bipolarity of cognition, but a bipolarity which can only be conceived in dynamic terms. The psychosis mediates between an object and a living being. Its determining factors are the nature of the object and the activity of the living being—what we are calling the 'life impulse.' May we not, for psychological purposes, regard experience in some such way as this? A conscious being, as conscious, is capable of being affected in a characteristic way by the nature of objects. This affection by the nature of an object, considered by itself, we may term 'sensation.' A conscious being, as conscious, is also capable of experiencing the 'life impulse,' when it becomes a particular conscious impulse. But undefined conscious impulse is an abstraction, as is also pure sensation. In the living experience, which the psychologist must describe and explain, the sensation, depending upon the nature of the object, is determined by the conscious impulse as perception or cognition of an object—or perhaps it is better to say situation—and at the same time the conscious impulse becomes a particular conscious impulse with regard to that perceived object or situation.

Now we are proposing to call the conscious impulse 'Instinct[1],' when and so far as it is not itself determined by previous experience, but only determined in experience, while itself determining experience, in conjunction with the nature of objects or situations determining experience as sensation. This is what Instinct seems to be psychologically. Instinct is the 'life impulse,' becoming conscious as determinate conscious impulse. But this, in itself, is only one side of the psychological fact, and an abstraction. The other side—also an abstraction—is sensation. The psychological fact itself is experience in its lowest terms.

This involves an important conclusion at the very outset.

[1] Cf. McDougall, "Instinct and Intelligence," in *British Journal of Psychology*, vol. III, p. 258.

The ground of experience is intelligence or mind. Popularly actions are called instinctive, when what we may call the potency of experience is low, intelligent, when it is high. But psychologically Instinct and Intelligence cannot be placed in opposition. The potency of experience will vary with the degree of intelligence. But the degree of intelligence is simply the degree of 'psychical integration[1].' The primary 'psychical integration' is the integration of instinct and sensation in the rudimentary and fundamental experience of a determinate conscious impulse, defined by a perceived situation or object, and correlated with a feeling, which we may for the present describe as 'worthwhileness.'

With this view of Instinct, let us next attempt to give a more detailed account of the various elements involved in the 'instinct-experience,' and to solve some of the difficulties, which recent discussions of Instinct have revealed and made prominent. We may appropriately begin with the cognitive element. The nature of the cognitive element will be best brought out by a consideration, first of all, of the view of Instinct put forward by Bergson[2], which however does not differ very materially from the view of Instinct we have already described as von Hartmann's.

Bergson seems to have set out from some such notion of Instinct as ours, but, apparently under the influence of the long-standing and popular opposition between Instinct and Intelligence, he finally reaches the position that Instinct and Intelligence represent entirely different developments of conscious life, the most characteristic difference between them being the different kinds of 'knowledge' which they represent, or which constitute their content. This difference in kind of knowledge is analogous to, if not identical with, the difference between intuitive and conceptual knowledge.

In order to understand this position psychologically, it seems necessary to get a clear idea of what is to be understood by 'intuitive knowledge.' The claim is that Instinct and

---

[1] This term is used in a sense analogous to that in which Sherrington uses 'nervous" and "cerebral integration." See *Integrative Action of the Nervous System*, especially Lect. IX.

[2] *Creative Evolution*, chap. II.

Intelligence mediate different orders of knowledge.   Apparently
then we must seek to determine the psychological nature of
intuitive knowledge, that is of intuition, for only here is there
a psychological problem at all.   That the one knowledge is
reached as a result of experience, and the activity of Intelligence
working on experience, and the other knowledge is a knowledge,
which is not based upon experience at all, though it determines
experience, is a contention which can only be met by the
psychologist, after he has examined, in the first place, the
process called 'intuition,' and, in the second place, the so-
called 'intuitive knowledge' of Instinct.

What is intuition from the psychological point of view?
Is it a way of knowing reality, different from other ways, and
sui generis?   That is apparently our first question.   Introspection ought to be able to settle the matter once for all, so
far as 'intuition' describes a certain mode of experiencing.
Intuition, we all agree, is direct apprehension of some reality,
of some real situation.   Perception is also direct apprehension
of a real object or situation.   Is there any difference between
the two?   As ordinarily used and understood, intuition
certainly involves more than perception, as bare cognition.
Intuition is always perception of that thing in particular,
which at the particular moment is the one thing needed, and
hence the peculiar 'satisfyingness,' which is so characteristic
of it.

Let us take some examples of intuition.   A sudden situation
presents itself in perceptual experience; we apprehend 'intui-
tively' the very object, which meets the needs of the case, and
we act upon or with that object 'instinctively.'   Again, we
have mislaid something we require, and are groping in our
memories for some suggestion or clue; the clue flashes upon
us suddenly in a remembered past event, which determines at
once the place of the required something.   Again, we are
striving to find some conceptual law or principle, which will
unite and organize a number of particular facts in some domain
of science; in a moment, as it were, we apprehend the key
relation, and the mass of discrete particulars is organized.   All
these are cases of what we call intuition.

We might go on giving instances of what is usually called intuition from art, from philosophy, from the practical life of commerce or industry. In every case we should find the same elements present, an object, situation, or relation apprehended or perceived, and apprehended as the very object, situation, or relation we require at the particular moment. Intuition is then perception, but something more; it is Reid's 'belief,' but something more. That 'something more' is, however, nothing mystical or occult. It is merely a pronounced feeling element, 'satisfyingness,' determined by the merging of the impulse of the moment in its required object, a pronounced feeling element that will only arise, when there has been previously a glow of 'worthwhileness,' accompanied by an experienced 'tension.'

What of intuitive knowledge? Intuition, if this analysis is correct, cannot yield a new and unique kind of knowledge. Intuitive knowledge is perceptual knowledge, qualified, if you like, by a feeling of its value and significance at the moment, but not thereby altered in its cognitive aspect. We can distinguish, on the cognitive side of mind, three grades or levels of intelligence, the perceptual level, the level of ideal representation, and the level of conceptual thought. Intuition may appear at all levels. So also may perception. One level is not superseded by the development of a higher level. Moreover the difference in levels is merely a difference in the degree of 'psychical integration'[1] that is possible, and a corresponding difference in the possible range of perception or of intuition. At the perceptual level perception and intuition are limited to sense perception, and the immediate apprehension of a presented situation, in the 'psychical integration' of impulse or interest and determining or satisfying sensation. At the second level the range of both is extended, owing to a 'psychical integration,' which includes the representation of past situations and of objects not immediately presented. There seems no object in confining perception, any more than intuition, to

---

[1] Sturt comes very near the idea of 'psychical integration' in this context by his 'noesis' or 'noetic synthesis.' See *Principles of Understanding*, especially chaps. III, VIII, IX, X.

sense perception, for the immediate apprehension of a single
and simple real is perception, whether the real be presented
or ideally represented. The same principle holds of the third
level. Conceptual thought involves analysis as well as synthesis, and therefore it involves the immediate apprehension
of objects presented or represented, as well as of relations
between objects. Here, too, apprehension of a single and
simple real, whether object or relation, is perception. In all
cases, the perception which glows with 'worthwhileness' and
'satisfyingness' is also intuition.

Bergson cites the knowledge displayed by the solitary wasp,
Ammophila, in its action on its caterpillar prey, as an illustration of the nature and perfection of the 'intuitive knowledge'
of Instinct[1]. According to Fabre's observations, which Bergson
accepts, the Ammophila stings its prey *exactly* and *unerringly*
in *each* of the nervous centres. The result is that the caterpillar is paralysed, but not immediately killed, the advantage
of this being, that the larva cannot be injured by any movements of the caterpillar, upon which the egg is deposited, and
is provided with fresh meat when the time comes.

Now Dr and Mrs Peckham[2] have shown, that the sting of
the wasp *is not unerring*, as Fabre alleges, that the number of
stings *is not constant*, that sometimes the caterpillar *is not
paralysed*, and sometimes it *is killed outright*, and that *the
different circumstances do not apparently make any difference
to the larva*, which is not injured by slight movements of the
caterpillar, nor by consuming as food decomposed rather than
fresh caterpillar.

Lloyd Morgan[3] is inclined to hold with Bergson, that it does
not much matter for Bergson's thesis, whether the wasp "acts
like a learned entomologist and a skilled surgeon rolled into
one," or not. But it does matter. If the facts are not as
stated by Fabre, and by Bergson following Fabre, then calling
the instinct a "paralysing instinct" seems to be largely a
begging of the question, and very little is left in the illustration,

[1] *Creative Evolution*, p. 182.
[2] *Wasps, Social and Solitary*, chap. II.
[3] *Instinct and Experience*, p. 223. But see for the opposite view the same
writer in *British Journal of Psychology*, vol. III, p. 226.

that is relevant to the hypothesis, in support of which it is cited.

We can call the instinct an example of 'sympathetic insight,' if we like, but there is really no proof that knowledge in any sense, sympathetic or other, is implied at all, any more than knowledge of the nature of chlorine is implied in the ammonia that selects it out of the air and combines with it to form ammonium chloride. Perhaps it may be argued that this is too extreme a statement, and that, in the case of Ammophila and her caterpillar, vital processes at least are involved. Even conceding this, we are still far from anything that can be called knowledge, for a reflex action, like that of the heart or of the stomach, is also a vital process, but hardly any one would maintain that it involves sympathetic knowledge. The rootlets of a plant select and absorb the elements of the soil, necessary to the growth of the plant. Do they exhibit sympathetic or intuitive knowledge in doing so?

For all we know to the contrary, the stinging of the caterpillar by the wasp may be due simply to reflexes, stimulated by the contact of the caterpillar, and the places in which the stings are given determined partly by accident, and partly by the shapes of the two bodies—that is, for all we know to the contrary, in the established facts among the total mass of presumed facts cited by Bergson. If we take the whole hunting of the caterpillar by the wasp, from the first view to the final sting, the case is not in the least altered, unless we can show definitely that consciousness or experience must have been present, to account for facts actually observed. In the mere process of stinging, as carefully described by the Peckhams, no such fact appears to be involved.

If 'knowledge' represents a psychological phenomenon at all, if it is to be possible to attach a psychological meaning to the knowledge of Instinct, the hunting instinct of Ammophila and similar instincts, must be described and interpreted in quite different terms. Further, if the knowledge of Instinct is of the nature of intuitive knowledge, and if intuition, as we have shown or at least tried to show, is essentially perception, as far as its cognitive aspect is concerned, then the knowledge

of Instinct must be interpreted psychologically as of the nature
of perceptual knowledge, and the working out of an instinct
is accompanied by what is essentially nothing more than
perceptual experience, perceptual experience at the first level,
with the lowest degree of 'psychical integration.'

How far can we interpret the facts from this point of view?
Every act of Ammophila, in the working out of its hunting
instinct, to take this as an example of the whole type of instinct
to which it belongs, is either accompanied by perceptual experience, or is of the reflex order, that is, without the intervention of experience. Let us assume that all the acts, in place
of only a few of them, as may be really the case, are accompanied
by perceptual experience. If they were all of the reflex order,
then we should have merely a compound reflex, and no instinct
at all. It must be noted, however, that such compound reflex
would fit into Bergson's theory of Instinct as well as anything
else. The instinctive impulse, which we may denote by Y,
starting the whole movement, so to speak, enters consciousness
as l, on perception a of, let us say, certain organic sensations,
indicating certain coming changes, in the body of Ammophila,
associated with the depositing of the egg. Act $X1$ follows,
the result of which, that is the situation which supervenes
upon the act, apprehended as b, determines a new particular
impulse m, and action $X2$ follows, the result of which in turn,
apprehended as c, determines a third particular impulse n,
and action $X3$ follows, and so on. We have therefore the
underlying impulse Y, which may be regarded as really the
instinct from the philosophical, or even from the biological
point of view, appearing successively as l, m, n, o, ..., according
as it is determined by percepts—or intuitions, if that word is
preferred—a, b, c, d, ..., and a chain of actions, constituting
the instinctive behaviour $X1$, $X2$, $X3$, $X4$, ... In the meantime we are leaving the feeling element out of account, because
it does not appear to be significant for our present purpose.

We might have such a series as $X1$, $X2$, $X3$, $X4$, ..., as a
chain of reflexes, the end of one action stimulating the beginning of the next. As we have just said, such a chain of reflexes
will suit Bergson's view quite as well, for we might speak of it

figuratively, as representing, on the part of nature or of life, a perfect insight or intuitive knowledge. But how do we know that the hunting instinct of Ammophila, or any such instinct, is not of this description? How do we know that the other series are present? We know that $X1, X2, X3, X4, ...$, is not a series of reflexes, because we get evidence in the behaviour itself of the intervention of experience at certain points—we are assuming at all points for the sake of simplicity of exposition—and we get evidence, or may get evidence, of the presence of both the other series. Close observation of the wasp discloses that it is not the action $X1$ that stimulates to $X2$, but the presentation of a certain situation, giving rise to perception b. For example, the action may be completed without the normal situation appearing as a result. Or we may interfere in such ways as to produce repetition of certain actions over and over again, by altering the situation so as to give perception b over and over again[1]. In fact it is not at all difficult to convince ourselves by experience that there is a series $a, b, c, d, ...$ But we can also, though it is slightly more difficult, occasionally modify the series $l, m, n, o, ...$, by interfering at any point with the underlying impulse Y, working itself out. For example we may produce a new underlying impulse Z, for which the situations presented as $a, b, c, d, ...$, either have no meaning, or have a different meaning, say a', b', c', d'. Even though we could not actually produce this change, it could still be shown that the series $l, m, n, o, ...$, is psychologically necessary to explain the facts psychologically, that is on the basis of our own experience.

A close parallel for the kind of behaviour, which characterizes the hunting instinct of Ammophila, as we are interpreting it, as well as all similar instincts, including even such instincts as the nest-building of birds, is to be found, in the case of human beings, in a series of acts like those involved in riding a bicycle through a crowded thoroughfare. This series has of course been learned, but, when learned, it involves, as far as experience is concerned, a fundamental impulse, generally not itself experienced, a mental setting, determined from time

---

[1] Examples will be found in the cases of instinctive behaviour cited later.

to time by the perceptual apprehension of situations, as a
series of particular conscious impulses, and determining a succession of corresponding acts. The consciousness, or experience,
or mind, involved, is merely a series of sparks or flashes, lighting up a particular cross-road, so to speak, at the moment
when the choice between roads must be made.

It now becomes possible for us to see more clearly what
the development of intelligence, in connection with the working
out of an instinctive impulse, involves, and what is meant by
degree of 'psychical integration.' A chain of acts, $X1$, $X2$, ...
Xn, constituting a course of behaviour, may be simply a chain
of reflexes, in which case the process, once started, works itself
out inevitably from $X1$ to Xn, and, apart from any possible
results of organic adaptability, is practically unmodifiable. In
such a case there could be no unequivocal evidence that any
consciousness or experience was present. If, however, the
course of behaviour is instinctive, and not reflex, then, at some
point or points, between $X1$ and $X2$, $X2$ and $X3$, or $X3$ and $X4$,
there is a spark or flash of perceptual experience, a psychical
relating or integrating of particular impulse and particular sensation determined by the situation at the moment. At that point,
or those points, the behaviour will no longer be unmodifiable,
since there it is not mechanically but psychically determined.

Such is the lowest stage in the development of mind or
intelligence, the lowest degree of 'psychical integration.' The
first traces of mind are in the nature of sparks or flashes of
perceptual consciousness, psychically relating particular impulse
and particular situation. Wherever this spark of perceptual
consciousness appears, the action of the animal is modifiable,
but only after the activity up to that point has run its course.
The whole subsequent course of behaviour may obviously be
modified as a result. The first development of intelligence
may take place at the same level, by a mere multiplication of
the sparks or flashes of perceptual consciousness, so that ultimately every act in the chain may become modifiable, but
only after the previous act has been performed. This is the
stage at which we assumed the hunting instinct of Ammophila
had arrived.

At the next level of intelligence the spark has become a glow. In place of the psychical relating of a to x, there is a relating of a to b and c, and therefore to y and z, which is not a conceptual or noetic relating, but which is nevertheless psychical, and which manifests itself in experience by anticipation of, or preparation for, what is coming, rather than by purposive determination of what is to come. Or we may say a becomes a sign of c, z begins to be acted at x. Perceptual consciousness is no longer confined to presentative, but contains also representative elements. Any evidence as basis for inference from observed behaviour to experience may be more or less equivocal at the first level; at the second level the inference is practically certain. If an animal's behaviour is determined, not by a as such, but by a as the sign of some result, already experienced in similar situations, as the sign of something coming, not by the 'primary' meaning alone of a, but by 'secondary,' as well as 'primary' meaning, the only possible inference seems to be that the animal is capable of a 'psychical integration,' including more than the immediate experience, referring back to what has been experienced, and forward to what is coming. Again there are grades of intelligence at this level, according to the range of the 'psychical integration,' according to the extent, so to speak, consciousness is capable of lighting up[1].

At the third level of intelligence there is 'noetic' relating and synthesis of the perceptual elements, to one another and in a conceptual whole, whereby the underlying impulse itself, rather than the separate particular impulses, may become clearly conscious, in its relation to the final term of the series, which has become conscious end. The range of 'psychical integration' may thus become practically unlimited, since the relation and the synthesis are general, and not particular. The highest degree of 'psychical integration' we find in the human being, but again there are differences in degree in different individuals, and these differences are also differences of intelligence. In all cases man is capable, though in degrees, of looking before and after. He foresees the end from the

---

[1] Cf. Hobhouse, *Mind in Evolution*, chap. VI.

beginning, and—we are speaking of the ideal, rather than the real human being—in all its relations. Consequently he is independent of the intervening presentations, except in so far as these are necessarily involved, and he sees that they are necessarily involved, in the attainment of the end.

Another way in which the degree of 'psychical integration' may be regarded is its relation to time order or succession in presentations. The higher the degree, the greater the independence of time order of the behaviour. This seems to indicate, in the limiting case, the entire independence of time of the behaviour guided by perfect 'psychical integration.' Schopenhauer's assertion of the timelessness of instinctive knowledge[1] is thus paralleled by a similar statement with regard to the behaviour controlled by perfect conceptual knowledge. Do beginning and end coincide?

The statement, that the cognitive element in instinct-experience is perceptual and nothing more, does not quite meet the needs of the case. It must be conceded that no sufficient evidence has yet been adduced, to show that this is the only kind of instinct-knowledge the psychologist can recognize. Writers of the most diverse views, from Lord Herbert of Cherbury to von Hartmann and Bergson, have stated that Instinct itself involves a knowledge, and they all mean more than the perceptual cognition accompanying instinctive behaviour. Moreover there are three aspects of Bergson's treatment of Instinct, a philosophical aspect, which does not concern us in the meantime, a psychological aspect, and a biological aspect. Though the alleged 'knowledge' of Instinct still demands further consideration, it would naturally leave the reader with an uneasy sense, that the discussion so far was incomplete, unsatisfactory, and misleading, were we entirely to ignore the biological aspect, and we may besides find in this biological aspect something which will help us to a just view of the further psychological question.

Biology studies the behaviour of living organisms from the objective point of view. According to Bergson's view, the behaviour of an "unintelligent animal" is the using of "an

---

[1] See above, p. 65.

instrument that forms part of its body" by "an instinct that knows how to use it[1]." Let us see what the biologist himself says. Romanes defines instinctive behaviour as "conscious and adaptive action, antecedent to individual experience, without necessary knowledge of relation between means employed and ends attained, but similarly performed, under similar and frequently recurring circumstances, by all the individuals of the same species[2]."

Apparent knowledge without experience, skill without learning, actions adapted to an end without prevision of the end, these are the characteristics of instinctive behaviour. Spalding's and Lloyd Morgan's observations and experiments with chicks, Fabre's observations on insects, afford numerous instances of these characteristics[3]. Spalding hooded chicks, immediately after he had removed them from the egg, and kept them hooded for periods varying from one to three days, his object being to eliminate any possibility of learning by experience, imitation, or instruction. On unhooding them, he found, that "often at the end of two minutes they followed with their eyes the movements of crawling insects, turning their heads with all the precision of an old fowl. In from two to fifteen minutes they pecked at some speck or insect, showing not merely an instinctive perception of distance, but an original ability to judge, to measure distance, with something like infallible accuracy. They did not attempt to seize things beyond their reach, as babies are said to grasp at the moon; and they may be said to have invariably hit the objects at which they struck—they never missed by more than a hair's breadth, and that too, when the specks at which they aimed were no bigger, and less visible, than the smallest dot of an *i*. To seize between the points of the mandibles at the very instant of striking seemed a more difficult operation. I have seen a chicken seize and swallow an insect at the first attempt; most frequently, however, they struck five or six times, lifting once or twice before they succeeded in swallowing their first food...."

---

[1] *Creative Evolution*, p. 146.
[2] *Animal Intelligence*, p. 17.
[3] Article in *Macmillan's Magazine*, Feb. 1873. Quoted by Romanes, *Mental Evolution in Animals*, pp. 161-2.

A chicken that had been made the subject of experiments on hearing was unhooded when nearly three days old....For twenty minutes it sat on the spot, where its eyes had been unveiled, without attempting to walk a step. It was then placed on rough ground within sight and call of a hen with a brood of its own age. After standing chirping for about a minute, it started off towards the hen, displaying as keen a perception of the qualities of the outer world as it was ever likely to possess in after life. It never required to knock its head against a stone to discover that there was 'no road that way.' It leaped over the smaller obstacles that lay in its path and ran round the larger, reaching the mother in as nearly a straight line as the nature of the ground would permit. This, let it be remembered, was the first time it had ever walked by sight."

Waiving for a moment the question of the apparent knowledge, involved in behaviour of the kind here described, let us examine the behaviour itself. The first question that presents itself is, whether there is anything in such behaviour, apart, that is, from any modification or learning due to experience, to differentiate it from behaviour or activities, with which, as such, the psychologist has no concern, like reflex action, or unconscious functional organic processes. "Reflex action," says Romanes, "is non-mental, neuro-muscular adaptation to appropriate stimuli[1]." It is possible, he continues, only theoretically to draw the line between instinctive and reflex action. The difficulty of drawing a distinction arises from the fact, that "on the objective side there is no distinction to be drawn[2]." If we accept this statement, and there is every reason that we should, seeing that it is a statement upon which most biologists would be agreed, it seems to imply, that the necessary bodily structure (using 'structure' widely), for the carrying out of such actions, can be developed by heredity, through the operation of natural selection. This view is confirmed by Herbert Spencer's definition of Instinct as compound reflex action.

Objectively considered, then, instinctive behaviour, as described by Spalding, and generally characterized by Bergson,

[1] *Animal Intelligence*, p. 11.   [2] Op. cit., p. 12.

may be regarded as merely the functioning of a complex organic structure. Essentially, therefore, it does not seem to be different from the functioning of the lungs in breathing, or the digestive apparatus in digesting. It is the modifiability of the behaviour, a modifiability, according to Romanes, depending upon consciousness or experience, that differentiates it from these other forms of functional activity. Since this modifiability depends upon experience, a psychological phenomenon, it is, *qua* experience, that instinctive behaviour claims the attention of the psychologist. This is indeed a decision to which we had previously come, but at this point it clears the way for our final psychological problem in connection with Bergson's view.

What then of the apparent instinctive or innate knowledge displayed? There are many ways in which we might approach the problem involved here. We might refer once more to reflex action, or to the digestive functioning of the digestive apparatus, and point out that these also display the same kind of evidence of knowledge or insight into the true inwardness of things and relations. But, assuming that von Hartmann's 'clairvoyance' and Bergson's 'intuitive knowledge' can be regarded as psychological phenomena, we may meet the contention in another way. We may hold, with Hobhouse, that imputing 'innate conception' to an animal "is to infer, on the ground of actions similar to those of man, an intellectual method opposed to that of man[1]." Bergson's answer is that instinctive knowledge is not of the same order as conceptual knowledge. This seems to leave only one satisfactory way open, and that is the examining of the manifestations of instinct, to see how far these support the position that Instinct involves anything that the psychologist can call knowledge.

There are three considerations which seem specially relevant in this connection. Consider first of all the part which the sense of smell can be shown to play in so many typical and well-developed instincts. As Mitchell has pointed out, in this very connection[2], no sense is less fitted than smell to give us knowledge of a complex object. It would seem to follow that no

---

[1] *Mind in Evolution*, p. 50.   [2] *Structure and Growth of the Mind*, p. 127.

sense is less fitted than smell to mediate innate or intuitive knowledge of a complex object.

When Spalding, who had just been working with puppies, put his hand into a basket containing kittens only three days old, and still blind, they at once began "puffing and spitting in a most comical fashion[1]." Romanes made a similar observation as regards young rabbits and the smell of a ferret[2]. The flesh-fly, which normally deposits its eggs on putrid meat, will deposit them on the flowers of the carrion plant[3]. The strong smelling secretion of the udder attracts the lamb; otherwise it would not know what to suck. "It will take into its mouth whatever comes near, in most cases a tuft of wool on its dam's neck, and at this it will continue sucking for an indefinite time[4]."

More striking still is the apparent instinctive recognition by ants, of ants belonging to the same nest or community, while a stranger ant, put into the nest, is also at once recognized and killed[5]. Sir John Lubbock (Lord Avebury) repeated and confirmed the observations of Huber in this respect, and observed further that an ant, separated from the nest for over a year, was still recognized, that, even when ants were taken from the nest in the condition of pupae, and restored as perfect insects, they were still recognized, and finally that ants hatched from the eggs of different queens taken from the same nest received one another as friends. Sir John Lubbock concludes, that the recognition is not due to any 'password' or 'gesture sign,' nor to any peculiar smell. Here, if anywhere, we appear to have a case of innate knowledge or 'clairvoyance.' But a subsequent investigator has discovered that the recognition is due to smell[6], that it is not the sight of a stranger ant, or the recognition of him as an intruder, that excites the ants in a nest to fury, and, on the other hand, it is not the sight of a kindred ant, or the recognition of him as of their kin, that

---

[1] *Mental Evolution in Animals*, p. 164.
[2] Op. cit., p. 165.   [3] Op. cit., p. 167.
[4] Hobhouse, *Mind in Evolution*, p. 48, quoted from Lloyd Morgan, *Habit and Instinct*.
[5] Romanes, *Animal Intelligence*, p. 14 f.
[6] Bethe, in *Pflüger's Archiv*, LXX, pp. 33–37, quoted by Mitchell, *Structure and Growth of the Mind*, p. 126.

causes them to receive him as a friend, but in each case a peculiar smell, or at least something analogous to that. For this investigator succeeded in turning "friend into enemy among them, and with more difficulty enemy into friend, and both in degrees," by rubbing a particular enemy ant in the dead bodies of friends, or a particular kindred ant in the dead bodies of enemies.

What are we to say then? What is our psychological interpretation of such behaviour to be? Surely not that there is a mysterious kind of innate knowledge, which becomes functionally active, and determines behaviour, on the presentation of a certain smell. Rather that the smell itself has a certain interest, and, on being presented, inaugurates a certain course of action of the kind we call instinctive. Have we no examples in our own experience of unaccountable liking or aversion, which is entirely independent of knowledge, and entirely perceptual? The animal or insect knows nothing except that it apprehends an object or situation, the smell of which is agreeably or disagreeably interesting, as the case may be, and which *must* be reacted towards in a certain way. We might term the whole experience, including the behaviour-experience, a 'this—of course' experience, only, by so doing, we are making it more definite, and more approximating our own kind of experience, than it in all probability really is[1].

The second consideration is the extent to which, and the way in which, a slight modification in a situation is sufficient to throw the whole instinctive series out of gear. "The brute cannot deviate from the rule prescribed to it," says Rousseau[2]. Of course this is not invariably true, but the really surprising thing is that it is so near the truth.

Illustrations of this characteristic of instinctive behaviour are fairly numerous, especially among insects. Here are three, all due to Fabre's observations.

The young of Bembex are shut up in a cell, covered over with sand. From time to time the mother brings food, finding

---

[1] Cf. Mitchell, *Structure and Growth of the Mind*, pp. 125–8, for a discussion of this point.

[2] *Discourse on the Origin of Inequality*, part I.

her way unerringly every time, though to the ordinary human
eye, there is nothing to distinguish the spot.   Fabre removed
the sand, on one occasion, exposing the cell and the larva.   As a
result the Bembex was quite bewildered, and evidently did not
recognize her own offspring, which she had all the time been
feeding.   "It seems as if she knew the doors, the nursery, and
the passage, but not the child[1]."

The larva of Chalicodoma is enclosed in a cell of earth,
through which it must eat its way when the time comes for
its exit.   Fabre first pasted a piece of paper round the cell,
and found that the insect ate its way through this without
difficulty, in the same way as it ate its way through the earthen
wall of the cell.   He next placed round the cell a paper case,
with a small distance between the wall of the cell and the paper.
This time the paper formed "an effectual prison."   The Chalicodoma was determined by Instinct to bite through one wall,
but not through two[2].

One of the solitary wasps, *Sphex flavipennis*, hunts grass-
hoppers.   When returning to its nest with the grasshopper,
it invariably leaves the grasshopper outside, "so that the
antennae reach precisely to the opening," goes in, as if to see
that all is right inside, then puts out its head and drags in the
grasshopper.   On one occasion, while the Sphex was in its
nest on its visit of inspection, Fabre removed the grasshopper
to a small distance from the entrance.   Out came the wasp,
missed the grasshopper, searched round for it, dragged it to
the entrance as before, laid it down, and proceeded again to
inspect the nest.   Once more Fabre removed the prey, and
the wasp repeated the whole process, and again, again, and
again, in all forty times.   Fabre then removed the grasshopper
altogether.   The Sphex did not search for another grasshopper,
but closed up its nest in the usual way, as if everything was all
right inside, though in reality it was closing the nest up, without
any food for the larva[3].

This last case of Instinct has been cited many times.   It

---

[1] Romanes, *Mental Evolution in Animals*, p. 166, quoting Sir John Lubbock.
[2] Op. cit., p. 166.
[3] Hobhouse, *Mind in Evolution*, p. 55; Romanes, op. cit., p. 179.

must be noted, however, that on another occasion Fabre failed
to get the same unvarying process repeated so often, and that
Dr and Mrs Peckham, in their study of American species of
Sphex, describe the process somewhat differently[1]. It seems
as if the urgency of the next succeeding impulse gradually
becomes accentuated, until finally the grasshopper may be
dragged into the nest, without the preliminary visit of inspection
taking place, or the nest may be closed up without a grasshopper.

Now what is the nature of the knowledge involved in these
three cases? Obviously perceptual knowledge. That is the
only answer the psychologist can give. If we suppose a mind
confined to perceptual experience, that will account for everything in the phenomena, so far as they are psychological, and
nothing else will.

The third consideration is the kind of error which characterizes Instinct. This is a point that has been much emphasized
by those writers who have sought to combat the notion of
Instinct altogether. Büchner is a notable instance[2]. We may
distinguish simple errors made by Instinct, from what we
should rather call aberrations of Instinct. Let us begin with
a few typical errors.

The larva of the Sitaris beetle attaches itself to a bee, and
is carried to the hive, where it is hatched and maintained on
the honey[3]. The knowledge that would really matter to the
Sitaris larva is knowledge that would inevitably enable it to
distinguish a bee from other passing insects. This knowledge
it evidently does not possess. "Although they are close to
the abodes of the bees, they do not enter them, but seek to
attach themselves to any hairy object that may come near
them, and thus a certain number of them get on to the bodies
of the Anthophora, and are carried to its nest. They attach
themselves with equal readiness to any other hairy insect,
and it is probable that very large numbers perish in consequence
of attaching themselves to the wrong insects[4]."

---

[1] *Wasps, Social and Solitary*, pp. 69–71, 304–5.
[2] See *Aus dem Geistesleben der Thiere*, English translation by Annie Besant,
under the title *Mind in Animals*, Introduction.
[3] Darwin, *Origin of Species*, chap. xiii.
[4] *Cambridge Natural History*, vol. vi, p. 272, quoted by Hobhouse, *Mind
in Evolution*, p. 49.

Romanes records, on the authority of two independent observers, that wasps and bees occasionally visit representations of flowers on the wallpapers of rooms, and quotes a case, where a parrot, which ordinarily feeds on the flowers of the Eucalyptus, attempted to dine off the flowers represented on a print dress, and another case of a hawk-moth mistaking the artificial flowers in a lady's bonnet for real ones[1]. Brehm relates that the pine-moth, the caterpillars of which live on pine leaves, may by mistake lay its eggs on oak-trees, growing in the neighbourhood of pines[2]. The same point is illustrated by some of our previous cases of Instinct, for example those of the flesh-fly and the lamb. Errors in connection with the migratory instincts of birds and animals[3] might be added, but, owing to the unsatisfactory state of our knowledge regarding the phenomena of migration, we could hardly with safety draw conclusions from them.

One example will suffice of what we may call aberration of Instinct. The larva of the Lomechusa beetle eats the young of the ants, in whose nest it is reared. Nevertheless the ants tend the Lomechusa larvae with the same care they bestow on their own young. Not only so, but they apparently discover that the methods of feeding, which suit their own larvae, would prove fatal to the guests, and accordingly they change their whole "system of nursing." Hobhouse, who quotes this illustration from Wasmann, comments: "After all is an ant, nourishing parasites that destroy its young, guilty of a greater absurdity than, say, a mother promoting her daughter's happiness by selling her to a rich husband, or an inquisitor burning a heretic in the name of Christian charity, or an Emperor forbidding his troops to give quarter in the name of civilization[4]?"

Though the comparison is no doubt a just one, yet from the psychological point of view it is rather misleading. The

---

[1] *Mental Evolution in Animals*, p. 167.
[2] Quoted by Büchner, op. cit., p. 15 (translation).
[3] See Darwin, *Descent of Man*, 2nd ed., pp. 105, 107. Also "Posthumous Essay on Instinct" in Romanes, *Mental Evolution in Animals*, and also pp. 281–297 of latter.
[4] *Mind in Evolution*, p. 75.

mother, the inquisitor, and the Emperor have all certain conceived ends, and judge that the means taken are such as to realize those ends. The behaviour of the ant is what it is, precisely because there is no conceived end, nor judgment regarding the means for realizing it, but merely perceptual consciousness, determining the acting out of an instinctive impulse from moment to moment.

These examples—and they are all more or less typical—seem to make it abundantly clear that we have no right to speak of knowledge, in any psychological sense of knowledge, as characterizing the operations of Instinct, beyond the knowledge involved in perceptual consciousness. That the instinct structure is a marvellous adaptation to the conditions in which it must function, and that this adaptation is the result of evolution, working in the main through natural selection, no one would attempt to deny. But similar adaptations of structure to conditions of functioning may be found in processes of animal life, which do not, in the psychologist's opinion, involve consciousness at all. Of course we may speak figuratively of knowledge as determining action in these cases also, but to do so is to use the term in a meaning that is scientifically quite unjustifiable. Or we may regard the knowledge, as residing in a Mind, which has created both the structure and the conditions to which it is adapted. Psychologically the only possible interpretation of instinctive behaviour seems to be in terms of specific impulse determining specific act, on presentation in perceptual consciousness of a specific situation.

So far as Bergson's description and analysis of Instinct is psychological, this view of the nature of the instinctive consciousness will apply to it, and will even help in the interpretation of its often highly figurative language. Take this for example: "Instinct is therefore necessarily specialized, being nothing but the utilization of a specific instrument for a specific object. The instrument constructed intelligently, on the contrary, is an imperfect instrument. It costs an effort. It is generally troublesome to handle. But, as it is made of unorganized matter, it can take any form whatsoever, serve any purpose, free the living being from every new difficulty that arises, and bestow on it an unlimited number of powers. Whilst it is inferior to the natural instrument for the satisfaction of immediate wants, its advantage over it is the greater, the less urgent the need[1]." Understand "perceptual experience" for the "specific instrument of instinct," and "conceptual thought" for the "instrument constructed intelligently," and everything becomes clear and acceptable to any psychologist.

Let us return to our example of the cyclist riding through a crowded thoroughfare. He has to rely upon perceptual experience, and he must perceive, and act immediately on the perception of, the precise element in each newly presented situation, which is essentially concerning him. Cyclists die young, who try to ride through crowded thoroughfares, and who perceive and act towards the wrong things, or who require to think about relations, before they can decide to act at all. The situation in which the cyclist often finds himself is precisely such a situation, that the only possible guide to right action is perceptual experience. Neither purely mechanical adjustment, nor knowledge of the velocities and masses of various loaded and unloaded vehicles, and the relation of such velocities and masses to the velocity and mass of himself and the machine he is riding, will serve his purpose. Purely mechanical adjustment will not, because the situations do not present themselves in any form, which can be grasped under a general law or principle, capable of being embodied in any mechanism. Conceptual knowledge will not, because it involves a delay of action, when immediate action is imperative, when even the representation of the act in idea is "held in check by the performance of the act itself[2]."

A final point, which may be made against Bergson's view of Instinct, is that his contrast between Instinct and Intelligence, as ways of knowing reality, depends, not only on a psychologically illegitimate use of the word 'knowledge,' in connection with Instinct, but also on an interpretation of Intelligence, which, as confining that term to its highest manifestations, is also misleading. Intelligence, he holds,

---

[1] *Creative Evolution*, p. 148 (translation).
[2] Op. cit., p. 151.

implies an "innate knowledge" of relations, rather than things. Once more the use of 'knowledge' is scarcely legitimate, for, by this statement, he means simply to assert that Intelligence makes use of intellectual categories, and comprehends reality under these forms, the use of a form implying 'innate knowledge' of the form, which seems to be precisely the same argument as that used with regard to instinctive 'knowledge.'

According to a disciple, Bergson means to define Intelligence as the "power of using categories," since it is "knowledge of the relations of things[1]." But, to quote again the same writer, "beside the intellect, and implied in our knowledge of its limitations, is a power of intuition, that is, of apprehending reality not limited by the intellectual categories[2]." Exactly so. This intuition, as we have seen, is what we call perceptual experience, and, as we have also seen, this *is* characteristic of instinctive behaviour. It is true that perceptual experience does not make use of the intellectual categories, because, *qua* perception, it does not think relations, but apprehends single and simple reals, though, in the human being, as 'conceptual' perception, it may employ or, at all events, be modified by, the results of such use of the intellectual categories. But, in any case, the contrast between Instinct and Intelligence has thus become nothing more than the distinction between perceptual consciousness and conceptual thought. If we choose to limit 'Intelligence' to the latter, then the separation between Instinct and Intelligence, as regards the form under which each knows reality, is inevitable.

We are really using Bergson as a type of those theories of Instinct, which attribute to it a kind of 'innate' or 'clairvoyant' knowledge. He is, of course, really opposing Instinct and Intelligence on an apperceptive background of philosophy, not of psychology, and of a peculiar philosophy, which requires him to use terms, which are used in psychology, but with a different and specialized or 'polarized' meaning. It is Life, which is the ultimate reality, a Life, which 'acts' and 'knows,' but with a transcendent 'action' and 'knowledge,' not the

---

[1] H. Wildon Carr in *British Journal of Psychology*, vol. III, p. 232.
[2] Op. cit., p. 236.

action and knowledge of the individual, with which psychology deals.

Desiring to express this transcendent 'action' and 'knowledge,' so as to make it clear to himself and to others, Bergson seizes upon the difference between Instinct and Intelligence, as presenting in some way an analogy to the difference between ordinary action and knowledge and this perfect action and knowledge. At this point Bergson seems to be thinking of Instinct partly in the way in which the biologist thinks of it, but still more—and this is where the importance of the view for psychology comes in—in a more or less popular way, and in a way which had shown itself in several of the older writers on Instinct, from Lord Herbert of Cherbury to E. von Hartmann.

When Bergson comes to an analysis of the characteristics which distinguish Instinct from Intelligence, he is compelled by his whole line of argument to oppose the two. Psychologically the opposition is really that between perceptual experience and conceptual thought, biologically that between a 'connate' and an acquired disposition, structure, or organization of nervous elements. Apart from philosophical implications, these are really the oppositions he makes. But, in order to support his thesis, immediate apprehension of reality must be emphasized on the one hand, as over against indirect, relational, and hypothetical knowledge on the other. Hence the implied conclusion, that, only in so far as we lay aside the forms of the intellect, and trust to intuition, can we know reality as Life. In order to get the best view of the stars through a telescope, we ought to shut our own eyes, as some one—was it not Locke—once expressed a somewhat similar situation.

CHAPTER V

THE PSYCHOLOGICAL NATURE OF INSTINCT—
INSTINCT AND INTELLIGENCE

The discussion of Bergson's opposition between Instinct and Intelligence naturally leads us on to attempt to determine, more closely than we have yet done, the exact relation between the two. This has lately become a highly controversial question, but we shall try to show that there is really no reason why it should have. The whole controversy—or, at least, the main controversy—seems to have arisen from different writers using the respective terms in different senses, and our old friend, the biological meaning of Instinct, has played no mean part, and has been perhaps the most fruitful source of confusion.

The *British Journal of Psychology* of October, 1910, contained a statement of the views, regarding the relation of Instinct to Intelligence, of several of our leading British psychologists, Myers, Stout, McDougall, Lloyd Morgan, and Wildon Carr. Lloyd Morgan has since given us a more fully elaborated statement of his views in his *Instinct and Experience*. The main lines of the discussion may, therefore, be regarded as laid down for us. Five more or less different views regarding the relation of Instinct to Intelligence are before us. Of these, one is Bergson's and need not further concern us for the present. Lloyd Morgan's view appears to be the generally prevailing view among comparative psychologists. It will, therefore, be best to take our start from that. Myers puts forward what may be called the opposing view, with McDougall in close agreement, while Stout's view mediates between Lloyd Morgan's and Myers', with leanings towards the latter, as regards essential elements.

It may be well to state here, that our purpose in utilizing this whole discussion is not merely to clear up the relation of

Instinct to Intelligence, but also to arrive at a fuller analysis
of the instinct-experience itself. Hitherto we have been concerned mainly with the instinct-experience, in so far as it is
determined by the nature of an object or situation, and with
the assumption of an innate knowledge of some kind or other,
determining the course of action. We have still to consider
the instinct-experience, in so far as it is determined by the
relation of situation to impulse, by what we shall call later
the 'meaning' of the situation, and our attempt to get a psychological account of this factor will be very greatly assisted by
following the discussion, in the way in which we intend to
follow it.

It is a little unfortunate that Lloyd Morgan's conception
of Instinct should be the biological, a conception which we have
already rejected as practically useless for psychological purposes, and as likely to lead sooner or later to insoluble difficulties.
Nevertheless his paper yields some very interesting psychological
points, when he seeks to attach to his biological conception
of Instinct the notion of experience, and attempts to give
a genetic account of what he terms the 'primary tissue of
experience[1].'

A start is made with instinctive behaviour, defined as
dependent "entirely on how the nervous system has been
built up through heredity, under the mode of racial preparation
which we call evolution[2]." As opposed to instinctive behaviour,
intelligent behaviour depends on the way in which the nervous
system has been built up through heredity, but "depends also
on how the nervous system has been modified and moulded
in the course of that individual preparation, which we call the
acquisition of experience[3]."

Both definitions are psychologically unsatisfactory, the
latter the more obviously so. It would include under intelligent
behaviour the most unintelligent and unconsciously formed
individual habits, like habits of speech and gesture. On the

---

[1] Lloyd Morgan has since, in *Instinct and Experience*, explicitly abandoned
this phrase.   We are inclined to continue its use, but rather in the form 'primary
tissue of meaning,' as below.
[2] *British Journal of Psychology*, vol. III, p. 220.
[3] Op. cit., p. 221.

other hand it is very doubtful how far we can regard what is essentially intelligent in intelligent behaviour as due to the acquisition of experience. As to the former it is necessary, in order to differentiate instinctive behaviour, so defined, from mere organic process and reflex activity, to add that the behaviour, conditioned by inherited dispositions of the nervous system, which we call instinctive, is also accompanied by experience. It is only at this point that the psychology of instinctive behaviour begins. The questions which interest the psychologist are: What is the nature of this experience? How does it arise? What is its function? All these questions Lloyd Morgan attempts to answer in his genetic account of the 'primary tissue of experience.'

The whole argument as to the origin of experience and the relation of Instinct to Intelligence centres round the development of the experience of a moorhen, which Lloyd Morgan has observed. He begins with the moorhen about two months old, which he has observed on the occasion of its first dive, and, working backwards in the moorhen's experience, he finally reaches the 'primary tissue of experience,' where the 'factors of reinstatement' are practically non-existent. We may profitably reverse the order, and begin with the 'primary tissue.'

If we consider the moorhen chick, "at the time when the little bird was struggling out of the cramping egg-shell," then we have the time when the first experience arose, "when there came what we may regard as the initial presentation, generating the initial responsive behaviour, in the earliest instinctive acts, accompanied we may presume by the initial emotional tone, coalescent to form what I have ventured to call the primary tissue of experience[1]." This is the birth of experience. It is the stage "at which the experiencer, as such, has its primary genesis." Is this also the beginning of mind, as far as the chick is concerned? This is a question which we might ask, but which we do not intend to press in the meantime, since the answer seems to be involved in what follows.

"All those primary and inherited modes of behaviour,

---

[1] *British Journal of Psychology*, vol. III, p. 224.

including reflex acts," which contribute to the 'primary tissue of experience,' are, "for psychological purposes," to be regarded as included under Instinct. This earliest experience—instinct-experience—described as the coalescence of the first presentation, the first emotional tone, and the first instinctive act, renders possible, according to Lloyd Morgan's view, an intelligent factor in subsequent behaviour. The first act, however, is not at all intelligent, but purely 'instinctive.'

Two other instances of the moorhen chick's behaviour, are cited, and it will be well to have these also before us, when considering this account of the nature of instinct-experience. The genesis of the moorhen as experiencer has been described. When this experiencer had had a few days of such experience, it was one day placed gently in a tepid bath. "Even then he was an experiencer, though his store of factors of revival was exceedingly limited. Of swimming experience he had none. Racial preparation had, however, fitted the tissues, contained within his black fluffy skin to respond in a quite definite manner. And, in the first act of swimming, there was afforded to his experience a specific presentation, a specific response, a specific emotional tone, all coalescent into one felt situation[1]."

Two months later, this moorhen dived for the first time, when it was scared by the appearance of a dog. "There was the moorhen, swimming in the stream. Sensory presentations through eye, ear, and skin, from the organs concerned in behaviour, from the internal viscera, from the whole organic 'make-up'—these, together with a supplement of 'factors of reinstatement,' gained during two months of active, vigorous life, constituted what I conceived to be the actually existent experience of the moment. Here was a body of experience, then and there present, functioning as experiencer and ready to assimilate the newly introduced instinctive factors. Then comes along that blundering puppy; and the moorhen dives[2]."

Lloyd Morgan's thesis is, that, though in a moorhen two months old Instinct and Intelligence cannot be separated, yet they are theoretically and psychologically distinguishable. In the "scare-begotten dive" the behaviour is predominantly

[1] *British Journal of Psychology*, vol. III, p. 222.   [2] Op. cit., p. 221.

instinctive, because it is dependent mainly on the way in which the "nervous mechanism has been built up through heredity," and to a very slight extent determined by the previous experience of the moorhen. From his own point of view, he is of course right, and popularly also, as we have seen, we call actions instinctive when the 'potency of experience' is low. But that is not where the real difficulty arises, nor where the real interest of the psychologist lies. The real difficulty arises in the account given of experience.

What Lloyd Morgan's exact idea was, when he used the word 'coalescent,' it is not easy to determine, but, on his own statement of the various cases, there is no coalescence. There is only a succession of two experiences. There is the presentation-experience a, and there is the behaviour-experience b, and b succeeds a, is not synthesized with a, by any means of which he makes mention in the descriptions. It is impossible to see how 'factors of reinstatement,' unless they contain more than the original experiences, as so described, can ever make any difference in the instinctive behaviour of the moorhen. The "scare-begotten dive" is determined, not merely to a very slight extent, by experience, but, on any such account of experience, not at all. It is as purely instinctive as the first instinctive response of the newly hatched chick.

The most valuable part of Stout's paper is probably his conclusive refutation of Lloyd Morgan's views, as regards the nature of the experience, which accompanies the first or any subsequent instinctive response. Lloyd Morgan has expanded, and somewhat modified his views, in a more recent work[1], to meet the objections of Stout and others. It is therefore necessary that we should consider here his fuller and more detailed statement, before leaving this point.

The first important addition made is that experience, as such, is synthetic. "Any given experience at any moment is a synthetic product, or, from a different point of view, a phase in a continuous synthetic process[2]." Now this is undoubtedly

---

[1] *Instinct and Experience.* London, 1912.

[2] Op. cit., p. 8. Lloyd Morgan in a private letter has pointed out that he recognizes 'synthesis' as a fact and a fundamental fact of *vital* process. Hence to some extent the two of us are speaking of different things when we use the word, and as a result some of what follows may be unjust to his real views.

true, and it apparently gets over the 'coalescence' difficulty, but what does it really mean for Lloyd Morgan? What is the exact nature and manner of this synthesis? He says it is essentially the synthesis involved in what Stout has called 'primary meaning[1].' In an experienced series—if there is conative unity and continuity, according to Stout—each element except the first is qualified by the fact that certain others have preceded, as well as by the *quale* of these others, and is therefore presented with a *meaning*, which is something over and above the bare presentation itself. In other words, our experience of the object is determined, not by the nature of the object exclusively, but also by our immediately preceding experience of objects. Though we cannot accept Stout's account of 'primary meaning,' it must be conceded that this position presents no difficulties for him, since, with him, experience is shot through and through with conation, and conation always synthesizes. For Lloyd Morgan the explanation of the synthesis is an entirely different, and much more difficult matter.

Lloyd Morgan admits that "all experience involves a consciousness of process as transitional[2]." There are really two points which arise. The first is the kind of explanation we can give of synthesis or coalescence—they cannot be considered synonymous—on the basis of transition in experience and experience of the transition. That enquiry we are for the present postponing. The second is the way in which this transition in experience and experience of transition affects 'primary' meaning, in Stout's sense. That is the point we are discussing.

A 'puppy presentation' *a* is followed by a 'behaviour-experience' *b*. Theoretically at least, we may suppose other presentations interposed between *a* and *b*. Practically that is probably impossible in this case, owing to the fact that *b* follows almost immediately upon *a*, but theoretically there is no impossibility. In the small fraction of a second, intervening between *a* and *b*, let us suppose other presentations, *x*, *y*, *z*, etc., as of a stone thrown into the water, a trout leaping, and the like. How will this affect the primary meaning of *b*? Is *b* now qualified by *x*, *y*, and *z*, as well as by *a*, and presumably

[1] *Manual*, book I, chap. II.　　[2] *British Journal of Psychology*, vol. III, p. 223.

to a greater extent by z than by a? Obviously the answer is that b is not qualified to any appreciable extent by x, y, and z, and certainly not to a greater extent by z than by a, *because b is the response to a.* This is the chief factor giving meaning to b, not the mere transition in experience from a.

The two experiences belong together, and are experienced as belonging together. But experienced transition and 'primary' meaning, as understood by Lloyd Morgan, will not explain this experience of belonging together. For a also represents a transition from some other presentation or behaviour-experience, say swimming, and acquires 'primary' meaning from such antecedent experience, which we may denote by A; but the connection between A and a, and the qualification of a due to A, are worlds away from the connection between a and b, and the qualification of b due to a.

Take for illustrative purposes an analogous, or nearly analogous, case from human experience. I am cycling in a leisurely way along a country road, listening to the song of a lark, when a motor whizzes suddenly round a bend in the road, some twenty yards away, and I hurriedly take the side of the road. Here we have 'song of lark' as presentation A, 'approaching motor' as presentation a, and 'getting hurriedly out of its way' as behaviour-experience b. It is clear that the relation of b to a is quite different from the relation of a to A, and that the difference is due to the fact that more is involved than the mere experience of transition.

But there is another side of the psychological series of phenomena. So far we have considered only the meaning of b with relation to a. What of the meaning of a with relation to b? In our opinion the answer to this question presents a difficulty, which Lloyd Morgan is no more successful in surmounting on the second statement of his case, than on the first. He can only give an account of this meaning in terms of 'secondary' meaning, that is to say, as the result of past experience, the 'factors of reinstatement.' According to this account, on its first presentation a has no meaning, but it acquires meaning from the behaviour-experience which follows. This seems a very strange transposition of Stout's 'primary' meaning. So far as Stout's 'primary' meaning is concerned, *a* is qualified not by *b*, which succeeds, but by *A* which precedes it.

Waiving this difficulty, we come upon another. On a subsequent presentation similar to *a*, owing to 'secondary' meaning, there is preperception of what is coming. This is what we call learning by experience. If it were not that Stout interprets Lloyd Morgan's position, in the same way, we should be afraid that we were misinterpreting him. But Stout, very pertinently, as it seems to us, asks whether this learning must be considered as taking place on the first occasion or on the second. If it did not take place on the first occasion, he sees no way of accounting for its taking place at all. This Lloyd Morgan cannot help admitting[1].

The most interesting point is the preperception itself, or the "prospective reference," of which preperception "is the first genetic stage[2]." The position would seem to be, that, so far as the purely instinctive element is concerned, there is no "prospective reference" in the first "puppy presentation," that the moorhen experiences, but, because of the results which follow in experience, the second such presentation would have "prospective reference," and the behaviour, which followed, even within the limits in which it was previously purely instinctive, would be suffused with intelligence. The "prospective reference" of *a* on the second occasion, therefore, can only arise from the association of behaviour-experience *b* with *a* on the first occasion. Every other explanation is excluded, and how association supplies a characteristic of looking forward, which was not present in *a* on the first occasion, which determines the association, appears to us, as to Stout, an entire and incomprehensible mystery.

It must be admitted that Lloyd Morgan is quite aware of the associationist implications of his position. He seeks to avoid them by pointing out that he is describing the 'experienced,' not the 'experiencing[3].' If this means that he is concerned with the objective, and not at all with the subjective

---

[1] *Instinct and Experience*, p. 36.
[2] Op. cit., p. 45.   [3] Op. cit., p. 51.

aspect of experience, it would seem, in the circumstances, a somewhat extraordinary admission. It is surely scarcely legitimate, in a genetic account of experience, to begin by theoretically distinguishing object and subject in experience, and then to describe the development of the objective, in isolation from the subjective, when, in actual experience, no such development is possible or conceivable. It may, of course, imply the view, that there is in 'experiencing' something which is not 'experienced,' and that with this something a psychological account of instinct has nothing to do. Such a view can only be accepted, if, and so far as, psychology can be shown necessarily to fail in giving an account of this factor.

Before attempting a solution of the problem of meaning which all this really involves, it will be advisable to dispose of the problem of the relation of Instinct to Intelligence, by following out the discussion. We pass, therefore, in the next place, to Stout's attempted solution.

Stout's views are not so definite as Lloyd Morgan's. On the one hand, he maintains that all instinctive behaviour is, as such, intelligently determined, but, on the other hand, asserts or implies that there may be intelligent behaviour, which is not instinctively determined. On the one hand, he maintains that all instinctive action is accompanied by experience, which is conative on the perceptual level from the very beginning; on the other hand, he urges that we require the term Instinct "to distinguish congenitally definite modes of behaviour[1]." One explanation of the apparent inconsistencies would be that he is vacillating between the two possible ways of regarding Instinct, the psychological and the biological.

His argument starts with a very valuable and acute criticism of Lloyd Morgan's views, which, in most respects, is pretty much on the same lines of thought, which we have indicated. What mainly interests him is Lloyd Morgan's account of the process of learning by experience. "How can the actual

---

[1] *British Journal of Psychology*, vol. III, p. 245.

Most of what follows was written before Stout's most recent pronouncement on 'Instinct' in the third edition of the *Manual* (1913), but, although we find ourselves in agreement with many of these later views, we have not seen reason to alter anything here.

process of learning by experience," he says, "which is supposed to generate intelligence, be itself entirely unintelligent? How can a series of experiences in the way of blind sensation and feeling result, on a subsequent occasion, in the open-eyed pursuit of an end? So far as I can discover, this is supposed to take place merely through the revival of past experiences by association. But the bare revival of an experience cannot be or contain more than the original experience itself. If this consist of blind sensation and feeling, so will its reproduction. No intelligent alteration of behaviour such as animals actually display could be accounted for in this way. The intelligence is shown in a more or less systematic modification of the whole conduct of the animal when a new situation arises resembling the old one[1]."

He quotes an illustration from Lloyd Morgan's *Habit and Instinct*. A chick had been taught to pick out pieces of yolk, from among pieces of white of egg. Bits of orange peel, cut so as to resemble the yolk, were then mixed with the white. One of these was seized, but almost immediately dropped. A second time a bit of orange peel was seized, held in the bill for a moment, and then dropped. Afterwards nothing would induce the chick to touch the peel. The orange peel was then removed, and pieces of yolk of egg substituted once more. For a time these were left untouched. Then the chick looked doubtfully, pecked tentatively, merely touching, finally pecked and swallowed.

"How can such adaptive variation," he concludes, "in the whole method of procedure be explained by the mere repro-duction of meaningless sensations and feelings? On this view, when present sensations are combined with revivals of past sensations, both the present and the revived experiences will give occasion to their appropriate reactions. This, of itself, will only account for resultant movements, in which the different reactions will be combined in so far as they are compatible, and will neutralise each other so far as they are incompatible.... What actually happened in the case of the pieces of orange peel was that the chick, after learning its lesson, definitely

[1] *British Journal of Psychology*, vol. III, pp. 242–3.

refused from the outset to have anything to do with them. And when he is again presented with the piece of yolk his whole conduct is modified in a still more systematic way. He looks hesitatingly at the yolk; he then makes a tentative peck, only touching it, not seizing it. When this preliminary trial proves satisfactory, he pecks again, seizes and swallows. The original process in which the animal learned to behave in this manner, cannot, I think, have been wholly unintelligent[1]."

But Stout, in his description of the intelligent activity, which accompanies all instinctive activity, and differentiates it from reflex action, goes farther than we think the psychologist, in the meantime, should find it necessary to go. He apparently takes up the position that the operation of the "congenital prearrangements of the neuro-muscular mechanism for special modes of behaviour," as he regards Instinct, must be "sustained, controlled, and guided by intelligent interest in the pursuit of ends[2]." "Instead of a sequence of psychologically isolated reactions, we find the unity of a single activity, developing itself progressively, through its partial phases towards its end[3]."

The "psychologically isolated reactions" are reflex actions. The word 'psychologically' is presumably used to emphasize the fact, that, though such actions possess a continuity in the underlying vital process, it is not a psychological continuity. But are the reactions themselves psychological? If they are not, why use the expression 'psychologically isolated' at all? On the other hand, is there any need to assume that a course of instinctive behaviour possesses psychological—that is conative—unity and continuity from beginning to end? Is it not more reasonable, from all we know at present, to suppose that Instinct itself appears as a single link, as it were, in a reflex chain, and that the conative unity and continuity—or 'psychical integration'—at first refers to that link alone, the continuity of the vital process accounting for the continuity as a whole?

We do not seem to find anything in instinctive behaviour, or the learning from experience which characterizes it, to render

---

[1] *British Journal of Psychology*, vol. III, pp. 242–3
[2] Op. cit., p. 244.   [3] Loc. cit.

it necessary for us to assume such conative unity and continuity, as Stout assumes, except in the case of the higher animals and man, and only in the latter is conative unity and continuity complete, with clear foresight of end, and relation of means to end. To hold the contrary is to find a great gap between reflex and instinctive activity. Moreover, if we take the analogy of habit in the human being--and in many ways this is a very helpful, though sometimes dangerous, analogy—we find habitual acts representing practically every grade from the unconscious reflex, as when we respond to a certain visual stimulus with the sound of a word in reading aloud, to the series of consciously controlled acts involved in playing a game like cricket, or in working at any skilled occupation or profession.

Stout regards the instinctive endowment of man as insignificant, as displaying a "minimum of complexity and specialization, so that careful scrutiny is required to detect its presence at all[1]." It is not surprising therefore that he finds it easy to conclude that there may be intelligent behaviour which is not at all instinctively determined. As regards this part of the argument, three observations require to be made.

In the first place, he finds it possible to look on 'instinct' as, strictly speaking, a purely biological term, employed to mark off "biological adaptations comparable to the prearrangements of structure and function, which, in human beings, subserve the digestion of food[2]." In view of his own previous discussion, such a restriction of the meaning of the term is quite inadmissible. If this biological adaptation conditions in any way conation, interest, and perceptual meaning in experience, 'instinct' must obviously be a psychological term, as well as a biological, and the biological meaning will not serve in the psychological universe of discourse, as we have already tried to show.

In the second place, intelligent behaviour in pursuit of ends may, in the process, show no trace of the instinctive. Yet it is incumbent upon Stout to show also that there are *ends*, which are not at all instinctively conditioned, before he can hold that there may be intelligent behaviour without a trace

---

[1] *British Journal of Psychology*, vol. III, p. 245.   [2] *Op. cit.*, p. 243.

of Instinct. This he nowhere succeeds in doing, nor indeed attempts.

In the third place, were it any psychologist but Stout, we should say that he tends to confuse capacity with tendency. That is at all events the effect of part of the argument. The "capacity for acquiring skill and knowledge[1]" he claims as not instinctive. In our sense of instinctive, it is not. But the tendency to acquire, the motive for acquiring, skill and knowledge may, nevertheless, be instinctively conditioned. Ultimately, we believe, it is always so conditioned, so that the working out of the capacity in intelligent behaviour will involve an instinctive element. Mozart's gift for music[2] was not instinctive, though his interest in music was probably instinctively conditioned. The congenital aptitude for music we do not call instinctive, but the congenital tendency we do. Hence there is no reason why we should not say that Mozart had an instinct for music, in precisely the same sense that we say Ammophila has an instinct to hunt caterpillars, in the sense, that is to say, of a certain experience being interesting, we know not how or why, and a certain action seeming the one and only proper thing to do in a certain situation.

With the essential aspects of McDougall's view of Instinct we intend to deal later. We are therefore left with Myers, with whom, indeed, McDougall professes general agreement. According to Myers, Instinct and Intelligence are in reality inseparable. But this statement seems to have for him two meanings, sometimes the one meaning, and sometimes the other dominating his thought. With the statement, in one of its meanings, we are in agreement.

On the one hand, we have the view, that "the separation of Instinct and Intelligence is a purely artificial act of abstraction[3]," because the relation of the one to the other is essentially similar to that of object to subject[4]. The separation between the two arises simply from our regarding behaviour from two points of view, from the inside, or from the outside, subjectively or objectively. So far as we regard behaviour from the inside,

---

[1] *British Journal of Psychology*, vol. III, p. 247. [2] Op. cit., p. 248.
[3] Op. cit., p. 209. [4] Loc. cit.

it is characterized by finalism, and is therefore intelligent. So far as we regard it from the outside, it is characterized by mechanism, and is therefore instinctive. Instinctive behaviour can be regarded in the former way "from the standpoint of the individual experience of the organism[1]." Intelligent behaviour can equally be regarded in the latter way "from the standpoint of observing the conduct of other organisms[2]." This view seems to be based upon the biological conception of Instinct as a nervous mechanism or neural prearrangement. Wherever experience can be shown to be present, we must assume that there is Intelligence. Consequently, since Instinct is differentiated from reflex action by the fact that experience is present, Instinct must necessarily involve Intelligence in every case. This is rather too simple an argument to represent Myers' real views.

On the other hand, there is running through the whole treatment, though more or less obscurely, the recognition of behaviour as determined by *ends* which are 'innate,' and the meaning of Instinct, implied in the notion of instinctive impulse, as impulse determined by this 'innate' end. "When a mother sacrifices her life to save her child," he says, "does she recognize that she is acting instinctively[3]?" From our point of view, this second meaning of Instinct is the important one, in fact the only meaning, which can necessitate the discussion of Instinct by the psychologist, as such.

Psychology, as aiming primarily at a description and explanation of experience, is primarily concerned only with the elements of experience, and the factors which directly condition experience, and so far as they directly condition it. A biological mechanism, as such, does not concern the psychologist. If this is necessarily the only view that can be taken of Instinct, then the psychologist must perforce agree with Stout, that the word and its meaning belong to the universe of discourse of biology, and not of psychology. But, in so far as this biological mechanism directly conditions experience, in so far as there are emotions and impulses, interests and ends, which we can describe as instinctive, just so far is the psychologist concerned with Instinct, but then also, for the psychologist, Instinct denotes

[1] *British Journal of Psychology*, vol. III, loc. cit.   [2] Loc. cit.   [3] Op. cit., p. 215.

primarily those very emotions and impulses, interests and ends, and only secondarily the neural mechanism, or 'disposition,' with which they are correlated.

It appears to us that Myers has failed to make good his contention, largely because, while conscious all the time of this possible way of regarding Instinct, he keeps it in the background, and puts the biological view in the foreground. He maintains that Instinct and Intelligence are inseparable, that there is but one psychological function, 'instinct-intelligence,' because, in the most rudimentary instinctive behaviour, there are evidences of learning from experience, and therefore of Intelligence. But this is not sufficient. This is only one half of the story. This does not meet Stout's argument that there is no instinctive factor, necessarily determining the behaviour of the highest intelligence. Nor is it enough to say that, considered objectively, intelligent behaviour may present the characteristics of being instinctive or 'mechanistic,' that, if we knew all the conditions determining our behaviour, we should "extend the mechanistic interpretation to ourselves[1]." From the psychological point of view, at least, the latter statement seems far from self-evident. It is certain that, if we called our behaviour 'mechanistic,' we should contradict the evidence of our own experience. In fine, it must be confessed, that Myers has not proved his thesis. He has only proved that Intelligence is involved in all instinctive behaviour, and that is the basis of his definition of Instinct.

Nevertheless, from his other point of view, Myers indicates the lines, along which his thesis may be satisfactorily established. He insists strongly on the fact, that instinctive behaviour is conative, that Instinct determines ends. Now Intelligence, as such, does not determine ends. It only devises means for their attainment, that is, if we are to understand Intelligence in any sense, in which it can be opposed to Instinct. Had this line of thought been pursued, the whole thesis could have been established forthwith. Unfortunately, it seems to us, this point of view is overlaid by the suggestive effect of two more or less misleading conceptions. The first of these is

---

[1] *British Journal of Psychology*, vol. III, p. 217.

the conception of Intelligence as practically coextensive with experience or consciousness, in place of being merely the cognitive aspect of experience or consciousness, the suggestion from which thrusts Instinct aside from its proper place. The second is the thought underlying the subject-object analogy. Hardly anything could be so unhappy as the comparison of the relation between Instinct and Intelligence to the relation between object and subject in experience, for it is presumably the subject-object relation in experience, to which the reference is made. The suggestion of the analogy leads us to look for Instinct on the wrong side of experience, so to speak, as far as human behaviour is concerned. The conation of Instinct, the instinctive impulse, the instinct-feeling, fall on the subject, not the object side, and it is precisely these, which are the instinctive factors in developed intelligent behaviour.

Had this line of argument been taken and developed by Myers from the start, it is questionable whether any difference of opinion, or, at least any essential difference of opinion, would have appeared on the part of any one of the five psychologists. It is of course the central feature of the teaching of McDougall in his *Social Psychology*. It is also in line with a great deal of Stout's teaching. Both Lloyd Morgan and Wildon Carr express themselves, as prepared in the main to agree to it. The latter, however, holds that this view "breaks down entirely, if called upon to explain or account for those highly specialized and complicated actions, that we meet with only in what we call the lower forms of life[1]." The former qualifies his acquiescence by stating that the connotation of the term 'instinct,' which he has accepted, is accepted from his standpoint "as biologist and comparative psychologist[2]."

If we have not already been successful in showing that Lloyd Morgan's point of view is sound for the biologist, but mistaken for the comparative psychologist, it is not likely that we shall be any more successful by prolonging the argument. In any case, we have nothing to add. Our answer to Wildon Carr is essentially on the same lines. If he asks that the psychological explanation should "explain and account for"

[1] *British Journal of Psychology*, vol. III, p. 231.   [2] Op. cit., p. 229.

the whole fact, in the philosophical sense of explanation, then it must be conceded that this it cannot do. For the psychological explanation is only intended to cover a part of the whole fact—the psychological part—just as the biological explanation is meant to cover the biological part. Together, a d supplemented by the physiological, chemical, and physical explanations, they may be said to cover the whole fact from the point of view of empirical science, but not even then from the point of view of philosophy, which requires that we show what the fact means in relation to other facts in an ordered universe, and in relation to the scheme of things as a whole.

Upon the use of the terms 'finalistic' and 'mechanistic' by Myers, in describing the two aspects from which behaviour may be regarded, Lloyd Morgan, in his *Instinct and Experience*, bases a long, important, and, from his point of view, sound argument on the principles that ought to be applied in a scientific explanation of the facts of life and experience. Most of the argument is entirely beyond the scope of the present discussion. The part of the argument, which might be available and applicable, is, in our opinion, largely invalidated by an identification, or apparent identification, of conation, or conscious impulse, with preperception of end[1]. This identification also marks his paper on 'Instinct and Intelligence,' and the paper of Dr Myers appears to share in it. It seems to arise from what we cannot help regarding as a misconception of the nature of conation. It certainly carries a suggestion that tends towards misconception.

Avoiding the wider issues raised, and confining ourselves to the psychological interpretation, we might enquire once more, with a view to a possible distinction between Instinct and Intelligence on this basis, how far intelligent behaviour can ever be regarded as characterized by mechanism. The psychologist may safely grant, that, if we knew all the conditions, we could prophesy the outcome in intelligent behaviour. He could, of course, take refuge in the plea that such knowledge is impossible, because each individual is unique, and, further, all the conditions are only known, when the act has taken

---

[1] *Instinct and Experience*, pp. 287, 288, etc.

place, even to the individual acting. But there is no need. The psychologist merely requires to point out that, among the conditions determining the act, there are some, of which no mechanistic, and at the same time psychological, account is possible, and no other than a psychological account can be called an account in any real sense. Take, for example, purpose. What mechanistic interpretation of purpose can be given, which will include all the facts, and what explanation, other than a psychological one, can be attempted?

If a mechanistic explanation of instinctive behaviour, as such, can be given, and a mechanistic explanation of intelligent behaviour, as such, cannot be given, then theoretically, at least, it is possible, and indeed desirable, that we should separate and distinguish the two kinds of behaviour. But if instinctive behaviour comes within the purview of the psychologist, then a mechanistic explanation is impossible, since it involves experience, and it can be shown to involve conation, if only through the learning from experience which takes place. Hence, as far as psychology is concerned, the attempt to distinguish between Instinct and Intelligence on the basis of mechanism and finalism entirely breaks down.

We find it possible, therefore, while differing from Myers on many points in the course of his argument, to agree with his main conclusions: (1) that there is no instinctive behaviour without an intelligent factor, and (2) that there is no intelligent behaviour without an instinctive factor. But we should prefer to express his final conclusions in somewhat different terms. "Throughout the psychical world there is but one physiological mechanism, there is but one psychological function[1]," which we should call experience, and not 'instinct-intelligence.' Experience is determined by the nature of the experiencer and the nature of the experienced object or situation, and, in the elementary case, this reduces itself, as we have seen, to 'instinct' and 'sensation.' But " pure instincts deprived of meaning are like pure sensations deprived of meaning; they are psychological figments[2]." And this, because experience, as carrying meaning, involves both in relation to one another.

[1] *Instinct and Experience*, p. 270.   [2] Op. cit., p. 269.

With the development of 'psychical integration' both sides develop, and their relation, that is experience, therefore expands into a meaning inclusive of more and more, till, in the human being, it may be inclusive of all things actual and possible, the universe in space, and history in time from the remotest past, and, in imagination, to the most distant future. But analyse the most elaborate and complex processes of thought, or the deepest and widest operations of the human reason, and we come inevitably upon our two poles of all experience, determining for the individual the primary meaning of all.

CHAPTER VI

THE PSYCHOLOGICAL NATURE OF INSTINCT—
INSTINCT-INTEREST AND 'MEANING'

We are now in a position to take up the discussion of
'meaning.' The general position we shall try to defend is that
the 'meaning' in instinct-experience is affective, not cognitive,
on its first appearance[1]. This part of the discussion will also
involve, therefore, the discussion of 'instinct-interest,' as
fundamental in the 'primary tissue' of meaning. This aspect
of Instinct we have up to now passed over somewhat lightly,
but any psychological account of instinct-experience must
necessarily be incomplete, which does not describe what Lloyd
Morgan calls the emotional tone, but we prefer to regard as the
interest of the situation, as well as the cognition of the situation
in perceptual experience.

Returning once more to the instinct-experience of Lloyd
Morgan's moorhen, let us try to determine where meaning
emerges, and to give some account of the synthesis or 'coalescence' which takes place. As we have seen, Lloyd Morgan's
own account of the genesis of meaning professes to be a rendering of Stout's explanation of the 'acquirement of meaning[2].'
According to this view the 'acquirement of meaning' is dependent upon 'primary retention.' As we have also seen, the
view presents difficulties for Lloyd Morgan, which are not felt
by Stout, but even against Stout's statement of the theory we
should hold that meaning emerges prior to the process called
'acquirement of meaning,' and this on grounds similar to those on
which Stout himself bases his criticism of Lloyd Morgan's views.

The psychological problem is the emergence of meaning in
its most rudimentary form. Confusion will inevitably arise,

[1] See Appendix I.   [2] See *Manual*, p. 91 f.

unless, at the outset, we distinguish clearly between meaning, strictly so called, meaning in its root notion, and the more developed and more complex secondary meaning, which ought rather to be called 'significance.' Significance is a pointing forward of the present experience to some other coming and related experience or experiences. Hence it is always the outcome of experience, and we may legitimately speak of the 'acquirement of significance,' or the acquirement of 'secondary meaning.' Significance also implies a certain synthesis, which may or may not be 'noetic,' but which, as far as behaviour is concerned, has the effect of 'noetic' synthesis, a synthesis involving 'psychical integration' which is inclusive of more than the immediate present. Primary meaning is something more fundamental, upon which significance depends. Essentially the 'primary tissue of experience' ought to be regarded as composed of meanings rather than of presentations or impressions. At all events the earliest conscious behaviour must be regarded as reaction to a meaning, without which reaction to a presented situation appears inexplicable.

By a very interesting coincidence, Condillac and Bonnet[1] both chanced to strike upon the same illustration, in order to explain how knowledge is built up. And this illustration is an excellent one for our present purpose. They imagined a statue, which was endowed with the five senses in succession, beginning with smell. The meaning they attached to 'sensation' was somewhat different from the meaning we attach to the term. But let us try to work out such a case with our meaning of sensation.

All experience being of the nature of sensation, all knowledge will be composed of sensations, combined through association, while meaning will be either of the nature of significance, that is secondary meaning, or of the nature of simple recognition of another of the same kind as one previously experienced, if we can speak of either significance or recognition, where everything due, either directly or indirectly, to the activity of the subject is eliminated. The sensations themselves must be

---

[1] Condillac, *Traité des Sensations.* Bonnet, *Essai Analytique sur les Facultés de l'Âme.* See Erdmann, *History of Philosophy*, vol. II, pp. 138 and 143.

regarded as in some way determining 'psychical integration' and recognition.

Under such conditions we could not have even perceptual experience, which involves the apprehension of a single and simple real, and implies also, as an essential element, primary meaning. The sensation is but one aspect of perceptual experience, and no number of sensations, as such, will give us the other aspect.

Unfortunately we cannot get an illustration quite like the statue illustration, to enable us to realize the other aspect of perceptual experience. If we were to try to imagine pure mind active in an empty world, we should have the other side in a certain sense, but it is quite impossible to make such a thought definite. All we can say is that in this case we have form without content, as in the other we have content without form. And, after all, this does not bring us to the point at which we wish to arrive. For form without content is obviously nothing, while it is not quite clear that the content of the 'statue's' experience is entirely without form, since it appears to have some sort of pattern, determined by the nature of the world from which it proceeds.

We may perhaps get a nearer approximation to what we want by imagining, instead of a statue with senses, a being with, say, three instinctive impulses, and the power of move-ment, but without senses. Endow this being with the single capacity of feeling satisfaction or the reverse. Place it in an environment, which is of such a kind, that movement in one direction will tend to satisfy, or lead to the satisfaction of, one impulse, movement in another direction to satisfy a second, and movement in a third direction the third. In this case the experience would consist of three different satisfactions succeed-ing each other in a quite random manner, since, on the hypo-thesis, there is no consciousness of the respective movements. Endow now this being with memory and a single sense—that of sight is easiest to work with—and observe the difference. Since an instinctive impulse, as such, is capable of being deter-mined by a specific object, the three instinctive impulses being assumed of equal strength, whichever is first determined by the apprehension of an object seen, will tend towards satisfaction. Neglecting the behaviour of such a being, we see that its experience is an experience of a situation or object, seen and also felt. On analysis, the experience will necessarily be found to contain (*a*) a felt impulse, (*b*) a visually apprehended object or situation, and (*c*) a feeling of interest or 'worthwhileness,' passing into 'satisfyingness.' This interest it is not quite correct to call an interest in the visually apprehended object, nor an interest qualifying the impulse. It is essentially a feeling dependent upon the whole relation of impulse to object.

We conclude, therefore, that, while perceptual experience cannot be imagined without two factors, it really involves three, for with its constitution there emerges the interest of the situation, which is its meaning, and which is for elementary experience the most important element of the three. The emotional factor Lloyd Morgan recognizes, but he makes no use of it in his subsequent analysis of meaning. If, however, it is the meaning, and involves the apprehension of an object as a simple real, on the one side, and experience of the impulse, thereby determined and become conscious, on the other, it is of the very first importance. It is the very core of the experience itself. We define then primary meaning as the feeling of relation between an object or a situation and an impulse towards that object or situation, that feeling being best described as interest or 'worthwhileness.'

The same conclusion is arrived at in another way. It seems clear, that, in order that an object should have any meaning for us, there must be a reference to something that is not in the object, but in us. "Suppose that, by a miracle, a developed intelligence suddenly fell passionless, was moved by no desire, felt no pleasure or pain, hoped nothing, feared nothing, loved nothing, hated nothing. Would it not straightway tend towards extinction, and dwindle like a flame deprived of air? It would surely go out, and with it its world[1]." One might even go farther and say, it could never cognize a single object, it could never perceive, and it is doubtful how far it could even experience. On the other hand, as the writer quoted also

[1] Sturt, *Principles of Understanding*, p. 201.

points out, "the best observers now agree that the behaviour of the lowest active creatures cannot be explained by automatism, and that the movements of an amoeba, pursuing a smaller amoeba, imply cognition of an object[1]." Instinct-experience is cognition of an object or situation, never before cognized, because of the instinctive interest of the situation, that is, because of the felt relation of the object to an impulse which it determines as conscious impulse, and which seeks and finds its end with reference to it.

This psychological analysis of primary meaning enables us to interpret the instinctive behaviour and experience of Lloyd Morgan's moorhen from another point of view. Though practically there is what may be called 'coalescence,' there is, strictly speaking, no 'coalescence' of 'puppy presentation' and behaviour experience. There is merely conative unity and continuity, the normal working out of the interest of a situation, and 'psychical integration.' 'Puppy presentation' does not seem adequately to describe the first part of the experience. There was cognition of an object, "puppy," determining and determined by an instinctive impulse, the origin of which must be sought in the race history of the moorhe , with felt interest or primary meaning, arising from this relation; then there was the behaviour of the moorhen, determined by the situation and its meaning or interest, constituting the working out or satisfaction of the impulse and the interest, contributing secondary meaning to the original perceptual experience, and possessing primary meaning of its own, at all its experienced stages. Any emotional disturbance there may have been, over and above the interest of the situation, must be left over for later consideration, but, except for the part played in it by experiences from the internal organs, it was of a piece with the interest. The important point is, that there was meaning, as well as instinctive impulse, involved in the perceptual experience from the start; meaning was not given to the original presentation by some incomprehensible back-stroke from the resulting behaviour experience.

[1] *Principles of Understanding*, loc. cit. Cf. Jennings, *Behaviour of Lower Organisms.*

Instinct-Interest and 'Meaning'

Though we can analytically distinguish in perceptual experience impulse, interest, and sensation, it is only by abstraction that we do so. All three are necessary constituents of the perceptual experience, but all exist only as its constituents. One of the most futile of all attempts at psychological simplification appears to be the attempt to reduce all experience to sensation. Owing to the nature of mental process, we can make the sensational element in perceptual experience the object of cognition, but we can make neither the impulse nor the interest the direct object of cognition. The one always, from its very nature, falls on the subject side, the other, as a *felt* relation, on the subject side also, though, as a relation, it can fall on neither side. Hence, as James, was it not, pointed out, to try to cognize impulse or interest as object is like trying to turn round rapidly so as to see our own eyes looking. If we analyse the object side of experience, we must inevitably find nothing but sensation; nevertheless we experience both impulse and interest, and to deny their existence as ultimate constituents of experience is to deny experience in a twofold sense, to deny its evidence and to deny its existence.

At the same time it must be recognized that impulse, interest, and sensation are not on quite the same footing as constituents of perceptual experience. Impulse becomes determinate conscious impulse only in relation to the nature of the object, and in perceptual experience of the object; sensation, dependent upon the nature of the object, can only be said to exist, as such, in the other term of the relationship in perceptual experience; interest is the relationship felt as primary meaning. There is no succession or sequence in time, but impulse may be said to be logically prior to the cognitive aspect of the perceptual experience, and both impulse and sensation to its affective aspect or interest. Nevertheless we must regard interest as the central and relatively stable factor in behaviour experience, preserving, as it were, the character of the initial and underlying impulse, while subordinate impulses and determining sensations proceed in the working of it out.

The calling of interest the ' primary tissue of meaning' seems to require some further explanation. The chief difficulty for this conception arises from the fact, that, when we use the term 'meaning,' we generally use it in a logical, rather than a psychological reference. Hence, when we think of meaning at all, we are apt to think of logical meaning, and to talk of this as interest seems rather absurd. But meaning is also a phenomenon of experience, and, as such, demands a psychological explanation. This is not the place to develop a psychological theory of meaning. Still the main points of such a theory seem to be necessary in order to justify our position.

That position is briefly the following. Primary meaning must be distinguished from secondary. Secondary meaning is acquired through experience, but primary meaning is involved in the first instinct-experience. In secondary meaning two elements can be distinguished, a cognitive and an affective, and to the cognitive element in secondary meaning the term 'significance' in its strict sense may be applied. Primary meaning, or the primary tissue of meaning, is affective only, is interest.

The psychology of meaning has always presented difficulties, and more especially to the psychologist of sensationalistic bias. Such a psychologist will probably reject our interpretation of primary meaning at once. In his analysis of experience he finds meaning represented by image and by nothing else. But, if a psychologist in analysing experience looks only for a particular kind of psychical element, the chances are that he will find only what he looks for. The sensationalist will of course deny the insinuated accusation. But, if he refuses to recognize as a psychical element, anything which cannot be attended to in introspective analysis of consciousness, it seems obvious that he is only looking for a certain kind, or certain kinds of psychical elements, those which can be attended to.

We may take Titchener as a type of the mode of thought we are calling sensationalistic. It goes without saying that a psychologist of Titchener's calibre will not consciously err in this way. Nevertheless the bias keeps showing itself, and always characteristically. Thus he replies to Bühler's "It is impossible to ideate a meaning; one can only know it," with "Impossible? But I have been ideating meanings all my life. And not only meanings but meaning also. Meaning in general is represented in my consciousness by another of these impressionist pictures. I see meaning as the blue-grey tip of a kind of scoop, which has a bit of yellow above it (probably a part of the handle), and which is just digging into a dark mass of what appears to be plastic material....It is conceivable that this picture is an echo of the oft-repeated admonition to 'dig out the meaning' of some passage of Greek or Latin[1]." The inference seems to be, at this point at any rate—for we would not willingly misrepresent Titchener—that meaning is analyzable into imagery.

Sometimes he finds that there are kinaesthetic, as well as visual images. "Not only do I see gravity, and modesty, and pride, and courtesy, and stateliness, but I feel or act them in the mind's muscles[2]." And, later on in the same work, he comes to the conclusion that "meaning is originally kinaesthetic; the organism faces the situation by some bodily attitude, and the characteristic sensations, which the attitude involves, give meaning to the process that stands at the conscious focus, are psychologically the meaning of that process[3]." This last is practically Lloyd Morgan's 'behaviour experience.'

We have no quarrel with Titchener's inference from such facts to the non-existence of imageless thought, if by the existence of imageless thought we mean, that there is a third order of substantive cognitional element, say the concept[4], in addition to percept and image. Also it must be said that there are few more subtle psychological analysts than Titchener, so that any conclusions to which he has come, as a result of psychological analysis, must be treated with respect. Still there is always the sensationalist bias to be discounted, and assuredly it appears to have influenced the analysis here.

To say that meaning is psychologically a kind of 'scoop' is not the same as saying that it is represented in consciousness, when he tries to think of it, by such an image. Quite apart from this criticism, which is after all somewhat superficial, there are two fundamental criticisms of this view of meaning. The

[1] Titchener, *Experimental Psychology of the Thought Processes*, pp. 18, 19.
[2] Op. cit., p. 21.
[3] Op. cit., p. 176.
[4] See Aveling, *Consciousness of the Universal.*

first is that which we, following Stout, urged against Lloyd
Morgan's theory of the process of learning by experience in
instinctive behaviour. The experiences of bodily attitude in
facing a situation—the very fact that the earliest meaning is
found in these is itself very significant to us—may qualify the
meaning of that situation for subsequent experience, and the
kinaesthetic imagery may come to represent the meaning of
that situation in subsequent thought of it, but the primary
meaning, without which there could be no such secondary
meaning, must be in the first experience of the situation, and
prior to the behaviour experience. The second is, that the
kind of experience, upon the analysis of which he relies for his
discovery of the psychological nature of meaning, is precisely
that in which psychological, as distinct from logical, meaning
is most difficult to find.

The latter statement is obvious if our analysis of meaning
is correct. Introspection, under the conditions even of the
Association Experiment, may fail to reveal anything in consciousness, except visual, auditory, or kinaesthetic imagery,
as far as the cognitive aspect is concerned, and yet we may
still be able to maintain that imagery is not meaning.

As a matter of fact, the results of association experiments,
devised and carried on by Marbe, Ach, Messer, Watt, Woodworth,
and others, for the express purpose of throwing light upon the
thought processes, have not been negative, but positive, as
regards our present contention or its implications, and against
the contentions of sensationalists, in spite of Titchener's efforts
to explain these results away, and telling in favour of views
expressed long ago by psychologists, otherwise differing so
widely from one another, as Wundt, James, and Stout. Thus
Watt found that "what distinguishes a judgment from a mere
sequence of experiences is the problem[1]," that "the repro-
ductive tendencies represent the mechanical factor in thinking,
while the problem is what makes it possible that ideas shall be
significantly related[2]," and Marbe that "all experiences may
become judgments, if it lies in the purpose of the experiencing

[1] *Experimental Psychology of the Thought Processes*, p. 120.
[2] Op. cit., p. 175

subject, that they shall accord, either directly or in meaning, with other objects[1]." These results are probably as much as we can expect this kind of experiment to yield[2].

But, after all, the laboratory results merely confirm the results of introspection under everyday conditions of everyday experience, and so far have added little, if anything, to these results. Meaning, in its most obvious and easily recognizable shape, is an attribute of what we might call the wholes of experience, and it is meaning that largely determines that they should be the wholes of experience. I am 'at a loose end,' and taking up a magazine, turn over the pages idly, until I am arrested by the title of an article, "Eskimo Traditions and the Discovery of America by the Norsemen," let us say, though whether there ever was such an article in any magazine, we do not know. This title has meaning for me both primary and secondary, or both meaning and significance. It has meaning because I am deeply interested in Old Norse history; it has significance because it refers to events of history, with which I am already familiar, though from a new standpoint. Hence, before I have read a word of it, the article has meaning for me, meaning both affective and cognitive, and it has a meaning whole. As the reading progresses, this meaning whole is continuously modified, on the affective side by the satisfaction of interest here, the development of new interest there, on the cognitive side by becoming continuously more definite and particularized. But the meaning of every word is with reference to the sentence that contains it, of every sentence to the paragraph, of every paragraph to the meaning whole.

To say that this or that part of the meaning is not in my consciousness at any particular moment is, it appears to us, to speak unpsychologically, just as much as to say that part of the meaning at any moment is in the form of a physiological state determining consciousness. The facts for psychology are, that the experience at any moment cannot be divided without remainder into the particular percepts and images of that moment, and that the remainder is explicable only in terms of the

---

[1] *Experimental Psychology of the Thought Processes*, p. 128.
[2] See McDougall, *Body and Mind*, chap. XXII.

meaning whole and its progressive determination up to that point.

Or, take an example from perceptual experience, that will perhaps be more relevant to our purpose, which is the analysis, not of thought processes in general, but of instinct-experience. I am engaged in a game of cricket, and have just gone in to bat, to open the innings, let us say. The bowler delivers the first ball, apparently straight for my legs. Under ordinary circumstances, if any one threw a fairly large, round, hard object like a cricket ball at my legs, I should get hastily out of the way. But in cricket the meaning of the situation is different, and prompts to behaviour of a different kind, mainly because of the particular determination of the cricket interest which is dominant at the time—to keep up the wicket and make runs. I might even have seen something in the delivery of the bowler, which was significant of a break on the ball, and prepare for the event, so that the kind of meaning we are calling significance might also be involved, in this form, if not in any other.

What should we find on introspective analysis of consciousness in such a case? We may analyse the presented situation into a sensation-complex. But what of the meaning of that situation which determines behaviour towards it? There is not much time for imagery, if we consider that the simple reaction to the visual stimulus will take about a fifth of a second, and, by that time, the ball is almost on the batsman. But let us grant some kinaesthetic imagery of the movements about to be made. Is this the meaning? Surely not.

It seems clear that the meaning of the perceptual situation is primarily in its relation to my aim, purpose, or 'need' at the moment, which relation defines itself in consciousness as the interest of the situation. To prevent the possibility of misunderstanding this expression 'defines itself,' it is necessary to point out that the interest is not a fixed state of consciousness, but is a qualification of the dynamic of the living activity dealing with the situation, and therefore changes with the changing phases of that activity.

Summing up once more our whole view with regard to interest and meaning, we may say that meaning is a relation, either of the situation to the self, or of the situation, as a part, to the whole of which it is a part, or of the situation, as part of a whole, to the other parts of the whole. Primary meaning is affective, secondary meaning both affective and cognitive, and inclusive of significance, as we have seen. Secondary meaning therefore covers the relational elements, constituting meaning on the objective side, and is essentially based upon primary meaning, both as regards its affective, and as regards its cognitive aspect, for a whole is a whole, and a part a part, in cognitive meaning, only through the fundamental relation to the self, that is, through primary meaning or interest.

We ought now to be able to get a clearer notion of the interest factor involved in instinct-experience. One writer has described instinctive behaviour as our "instinctive prosecution of the interest of a situation[1]." All conscious behaviour may be described in the same way, as the conscious prosecution of the interest of a situation, the situation being perceptual, ideally represented, or conceptual. Interest is the universal characteristic of behaviour-experience. It is also the primary meaning of a situation, in that it is the immediate consciousness of a relation between self and presented situation, a relation that is primarily *felt*. The only aspect in which instinct-interest differs from interest in general, is that it is not determined by or derived from previous experience of the situation, or due to needs which have arisen as a result of experience, but is due to original needs, of the determination and modification of which the biologist professes to give an account in his evolution theory.

Beyond these statements, can we give any further account of instinct interest or of interest in general? At first sight it does not appear that we can. The main difficulties in the way seem to be two, the first arising from the nature of language, which is fitted to express either cognition or action, but not to express the felt relation that mediates between them, the second arising from the fact that interest seems to be the very factor in experience, which introspection finds the greatest difficulty in reaching, just because it is the central factor.

[1] Mitchell, *Structure and Growth of the Mind*, p. 125.

Nevertheless interest is a factor in experience, and, in spite of these difficulties, its description ought not to be impossible. At all events the attempt further to describe it must be made, and the attempt should at least indicate by questions where the main problems lie.

On several occasions previously we have described interest as a feeling of 'worthwhileness.' The first question is as regards the reference of the 'worthwhileness.' What is it that is felt as 'worth while'? Is it the perceived situation or object? Or is it a certain action towards that situation or upon that object? Or is it the situation arising from the action? The answer seems to be that it is all three in a certain sense, but the sense will depend upon the degree of 'psychical integration.'

Interest is dynamic, not static, that is, it is always transition in living experience. In purely perceptual experience, situation and action towards situation practically 'coalesce,' and there is transition in feeling from 'worthwhileness' to 'satisfyingness' or 'dissatisfyingness.' The whole experience is in the present, but it is a changing present. Where the degree of 'psychical integration' is high, the 'worthwhileness' attaches primarily to the result as end, spreads to present situation, and action towards present situation, as means, but, as before, the prosecution of the interest involves the transition to 'satisfyingness' with progress towards the attainment of the end, or 'dissatisfyingness' with failure to make progress. In the event of the transition being from 'worthwhileness' to 'dissatisfyingness,' the interest in either case, that is with the lowest as with the highest degree of 'psychical integration,' will take on the form of emotion, which we shall discuss more fully later.

The second question is as regards the 'qualities' of interest which are distinguishable in experience. So far we have mentioned the three possible phases of interest as 'worthwhileness,' 'satisfyingness,' and 'dissatisfyingness,' each evidently involving a definite *quale* of experience. It must be recognized that this is the exceedingly difficult psychological problem of the qualities of affective experience. Consequently the solution we offer must not be taken as laid down in any dogmatic spirit, but rather as a tentative suggestion. We should be inclined to take these qualities as the fundamental and ultimate qualities of affective experience, and these three alone. This appears to involve the denial of ultimate qualitative differences between emotions on the affective side. But it really involves the explanation of these qualitative differences on a basis other than the interest as such.

Without anticipating our discussion of the emotions, and their relation to Instinct, we should suggest that the undeniable qualitative differences between different emotions may be explained thus. So far as the prosecution of the instinct-interest takes its normal course, and 'worthwhileness' passes normally into 'satisfyingness,' through the definite behaviour provided for by the neural prearrangement we call Instinct, when we are speaking biologically, so far there is no emotion. But if in any way this normal prosecution of the instinct-interest is checked, 'tension' will arise, a tension in feeling which is emotion. The difference between this 'tension' and the simple instinct-interest or 'worthwhileness' is a difference in the affective consciousness in some respects analogous to the difference between conception and perception in the cognitive. That is to say, feeling 'tension' represents a further, though secondary, development of affection. None the less is it for experience purely affective.

The qualitative differences between the different emotions cannot be explained in terms of the organic resonance, though this will undoubtedly accentuate the differences, nor can they, we believe, be explained in terms of the experienced impulse, the conation, but only in terms of qualitative differences in affection. The feeling 'tension,' therefore, which is emotion, must show these qualitative differences. But that there should be affective differences in the felt 'tension' or emotion, which are not in the original affective element, from which the 'tension' arises, can apparently only be explained, though itself not impulse but affection, as the effect of the urgency of a particular impulse, temporarily denied the appropriate issue in action.

An illustration of emotion, fairly low down the scale of organic life, which seems entirely unambiguous, and is therefore valuable, is given by the Peckhams in describing the behaviour of an Ammophila: "Her stops were so frequent and so lengthy that nearly an hour was occupied in going about twenty-five feet. When, at last, the nest was reached, the plug was removed from the entrance and the caterpillar dragged in, but almost immediately the wasp came out backwards with the point of an egg projecting from the extremity of her abdomen. She ran round and round the nest in a distracted way four or five times and then went back, dragged the caterpillar out, and carried it away. The egg came out further and further, and finally dropped on the ground and was lost[1]."

This illustration from insect life emphasizes one characteristic of the emotion, which is perhaps too often forgotten, and that is its ineffectiveness in securing its end, when roused in an excessive degree. We should not like to assert that this is characteristic of all emotions, but it is certainly characteristic of most. The illustration also shows us one kind of circumstance, under which the 'tension' of feeling, which is emotion, will be produced, that is, when the urgency of the impulse is such that action cannot keep pace with it.

Another kind of circumstance, under which 'tension' will arise, is when there is no inherited provision for the precise reaction which is appropriate to a particular situation. Looking at the matter from a biological standpoint, we see that the survival value of precise reactions for particular situations is distinctly limited to a stable and not too complex environment. In a changing and complex environment plasticity of reaction, that is to say, the lack of a fixed provision for particular reactions to particular situations, may involve a biological advantage, in spite of the fact that the plasticity involves some delay of reaction, and therefore some feeling 'tension.' Hence in the higher animals and man we should expect to find, as we do find, plasticity of reaction, and going along with this, and *pari passu* with it, signs of emotional development.

In addition to this felt 'tension,' as an affective experience, which is due to the temporary suspending of the normal transition from 'worthwhileness' to 'satisfyingness,' we must also recognize another affective quality, in the vague 'restlessness'

[1] *Wasps Social and Solitary*, p. 47.

or 'uneasiness,' which is present when a 'need' is neither definite nor determinate, but is merely a 'need' of something else than the present experience affords. This affective state, while evidently in the main a variety of 'dissatisfyingness,' seems to be emotional and complex.

The usual view that 'pleasure' and 'pain' are the fundamental qualities of our affective consciousness is not quite so easily reconciled with our view regarding the fundamental characteristics of affection, nor indeed with our whole position as regards the nature of instinct-experience. To some extent the view is a popular, rather than psychological, view, since both terms connote a considerable variety of affective experience. There is no real difficulty about pleasure, which, where it has not an emotional character, may be regarded as on the whole synonymous with our 'satisfyingness.' What we call pain, on the other hand, may or may not be 'dissatisfyingness.' Generally it is more. In fact pain, so far as it is affective, is usually emotional, or at least may be explained as emotional. The relation of pleasure and pain to action, is, however, so important that we must consider the question in its wider bearings, and, in the course of the discussion, the real nature of pain, in the usual sense as an affective experience, will become clearer.

We have all along taken for granted, that, in describing instinct-experience, we were describing the original form of all experience, and we have maintained that it is impossible to understand instinct-experience in any other way than as perceptual experience. In other words, we have maintained that our description holds of the most elementary experience, such experience as an amoeba, for example, if it has experience at all, must have. The chief difficulty for such a view will arise in connection with the pleasure-pain factor in experience.

In many quarters the opinion is strongly held that, though instinctive behaviour may be determined in some such way as described, that is independently of previous agreeable or disagreeable experience, yet it cannot be denied that behaviour is also determined as a result of agreeable or disagreeable experiences, and, in such cases, the meaning or interest being taken as the agreeableness or disagreeableness, we cannot hold that the impulse is prior to it, either logically or temporally, while perceptual experience does not seem the starting-point of the behaviour, and may not indeed form part of the behaviour-experience at all.

The difficulty is undeniable, but possibly not insoluble. If we accept such a view with regard to behaviour originating in agreeable or disagreeable feelings, it appears to involve either giving up the view that in Instinct we have the sole original driving forces in human nature, or defining Instinct in such a way as to include such cases of behaviour determined originally by agreeable or disagreeable experience, and therefore giving up the view that instinct-experience is, as such, perceptual experience.

Are we compelled to choose one of these alternatives? There seems to be one way of avoiding the difficulty and escaping the alternatives, and that is by a view, which again it would be absurd to present in a dogmatic way, which can only be put forward as a hypothesis, but which seems to explain the facts, without involving the abandonment of our position with regard to instinct-experience and instinctive behaviour.

The hypothesis depends upon the sensational character of pain. Practically all sensations are either agreeable or disagreeable, but pain, as a sensation, is nearly always disagreeable. Hence the painful has become identified with the disagreeable, or rather the highly disagreeable, in all sensations, and has been opposed to the pleasant, whereas painful, or something corresponding to it, was originally a sensational quality with no opposite.

That pain really is an independent sensation can hardly be doubted, with the accumulating evidence we now have. The exploration of pain spots, the experiments of Dr Head and his assistants[1], abnormal conditions, artificial or morbid, all point that way unmistakably. The extraordinary case of natural analgesia, quoted by Ribot[2], of an intelligent and successful professional man, who had as little sensation of pain as a

---

[1] *Brain*, xxviii (1905), p. 99.
[2] *Psychology of the Emotions*, p. 33, footnote,

marble statue, who bit off his own wounded finger, and under-
went various surgical operations without anaesthetic, has
·always seemed to us impossible of interpretation, except on
the analogy of the blind or the deaf.

There is still, however, the difficulty with regard to the
extent to which pain sensation will determine cognition of an
object or situation in perceptual experience. Pain, it has been
asserted, as a sensation does not externalize itself[1], that is,
does not determine the perception of an object. Now this
may be the case with the human being, but it does not seem
to settle the matter. The question really is whether pain as
sensation could, under any conceivable conditions, determine
the cognition of an object or situation, as, for example, sight
does in the case of the human being, whether it has cognitive
value in this sense. And we must discriminate. It may be
that for us the cognitive value of pain as sensation is not zero,
but infinitesimally small. But for us cognition is determined
by sight, hearing, touch, taste, smell, and so on. Imagine an
organism with all the other senses wanting, and with only the
pain sense, or what corresponds to it under these conditions.
Such may be the lowest organisms, in which there is some
slight trace of experience; such in all likelihood they are.

Our perceptual world is largely a world of visible and audible
things. Helen Keller's world is a world of things tactual. She
longed to "touch the mighty sea and feel its roar." On the
other hand, taste and smell have for us a very much lower
cognitive value with less pronounced objective reference. In
fact the agreeableness or disagreeableness of a smell—especially
the latter—is much more prominent in our experience than its
quality or its objective reference. For a dog, on the contrary,
smell must have a much higher cognitive value, that is, relative
to his other senses, and apparently still more for lower forms
of life.

In the organism, which is confined to pain sensation or its
analogue, there seems no reason to deny that pain may function
in determining cognition of an object or situation. The experienced world of such an organism must be narrow, and

[1] See Ribot, *Psychology of the Emotions*, p. 38.

apparently monotonous, though that is by no means certain. But that it has an experienced world of some kind may reasonably be maintained. If the possibility of an experienced world of objects or perceptual situations, mediated by pain sensation, or what corresponds to it, is admitted, our main theoretical difficulty has disappeared. It is not easy for us to imagine the nature of such experience, or to express it even if we could imagine it. For we do not seem to be able to revive the sensational element of pain as image, and our language is the conceptual analysis and synthesis of our own experience. Nevertheless we might attempt to characterize such experience in a general way, and, in so doing, we must inevitably fall back upon the form of our previous description of instinct-experience.

There is impulse, becoming conscious and determinate in relation to pain sensation, which is conditioned by the nature of the object or situation, the result being perceptual experience of a situation, perceptual experience of a kind we cannot imagine, yet not unintelligible to us. Further there is meaning or interest, which, in the 'tension' form is quite intelligible to us, if we consider it as the disagreeableness or pain affection. The interest, as such, is not logically or temporally prior to impulse and sensation, but temporally simultaneous with, and logically posterior to both.

There is nothing inherently absurd in regarding sense pain, on its affective side, as of an emotional nature, in our sense of emotional, in a primordial consciousness. The emotional experience of an organism, the whole of whose presented world of situations is mediated by pain sensation, would almost inevitably be as undifferentiated as its sense experience. With the usurping of the cognitive function of this primordial sensation by the more highly differentiated special senses, there has gone the development of an equally differentiated affective life. Pain now corresponds simply to disorganization, not only disorganization of the physical organism, but also disorganization of this primordial experience through the submerging of the cognitive function of the original sense, and the consequent impossibility of the development of a normal impulse or interest. If among experiences of the pleasant there is any element which cannot be explained, as already suggested, in terms of 'satisfyingness,' it would be interpreted in the same way. In this case, however, the lack of any special sensations of the same nature as pain sensations would constitute a rather formidable difficulty.

From the general point of view, therefore, of the nature of instinct-experience, pain does not present an insoluble difficulty. It must, however, be granted that, in the human being, pain in its affective phase, as it were, originates the impulse to avoid it or escape from it, and that prior to cognition of object or situation. It must also be granted that, in the human being, in addition to the instinctive springs of action, or motive forces which determine behaviour prior to individual experience, pleasure and pain are also motive forces depending upon individual experience.

Our solution of the difficulty is mainly of theoretical interest, but we shall later include the so-called appetites among human instincts, and these seem to differ from the instincts proper in an analogous way. The suggested psychological view is, therefore, that sense pain, and the uneasiness which determines the appetites (specific), represent the emotional or 'tension' form of the interest of the most primitive consciousness, the cognition of which was in terms of a sensation or sensations of which pain sensation is the survival, and that the interests of the human being are on a higher stage of affective development, correlated on the cognitive side with the development and differentiation of the cognitive element dependent on the nature of objects or situations, through the development and differentiation of the other avenues of sense experience.

CHAPTER VII

CLASSIFICATION OF INSTINCTIVE TENDENCIES OF MAN—
INSTINCT AND EMOTION

The basis of the developed mind and character of man must be sought in the original and inborn tendencies of his nature. From these all development and education must start, and with these all human control, for the purposes of education and development, as for the purposes of social and community life, must operate. These are more or less truisms, but they are truisms which have been ignored in much of the educational practice of the past, and in many of the best-intentioned efforts at social reorganization and reform. The original human nature, with which the psychologist is concerned, consists, first of all, of capacities, such as the capacity to have sensations, to perceive, to reason, to learn, and the like, and, secondly, of conscious impulses, the driving forces to those activities without which the capacities would be meaningless. To the latter we are applying the term 'Instinct.' We have tried to describe what is psychologically involved in Instinct; we must now enter upon a study of the manifestations of Instinct in Man.

It seems hardly necessary to emphasize once again the fact, that the psychologist's problems are different from the biologist's, in precisely the same way in which the meaning of Instinct for the psychologist differs from its meaning for the biologist. The biologist, as we have seen, is concerned with animal behaviour in reference to its biological origins and biological results. He argues from the behaviour, and the conditions which determine it, to the existence of a more or less modifiable nervous structure, of which the behaviour is the functioning, and which he attempts to explain biologically, and the physiologist physiologically. The psychologist is concerned with the experience, which underlies, we may say, instinctive behaviour, determines that it is perceptual experience, and that it involves a characteristic impulse and interest. Both the biologist and the psychologist will naturally attempt to describe the whole fact as it appears to them, and, in doing so, the biologist may refer to experience, and the psychologist to nervous structure; but they will only be fully intelligible to one another, so long as they realize that they are concerned essentially with different aspects, and that experience cannot be described in terms of the one science, any more than nervous structure can be described in terms of the other.

This constant emphasis upon the contrast between the psychological and the biological point of view would not be necessary, were it not for the fact that the prevailing view of Instinct, during the last generation or so, has been the biological, the result being that we have become accustomed to oppose animal behaviour to human behaviour, regarding the one as typically instinctive, the other as typically intelligent, and also to maintain that the instincts and instinctive tendencies of human nature are insignificant. Had the psychologist been clear as regards the psychological nature of Instinct, this position could not have developed. For, though perceptual experience is more and more overlaid by the higher mental processes, it always underlies them, and, though control of primitive impulse becomes more and more complex, it is always a control by that which draws its controlling force, ultimately and fundamentally, from primitive impulses, never a control *ab extra*.

The psychology of the present day is much indebted to McDougall for his constant emphasis upon this latter principle, though, as we have already seen, Hutcheson, Hume, Schopenhauer were no less emphatic. It must be confessed, however, that there are at least two rather formidable difficulties with regard to the recognition and enumeration of the instinctive tendencies of man. The one is that indicated by James[1], the

[1] *Principles of Psychology*, vol. II, p. 390.

fact that there is foresight of the end on every occasion, save the first, of acting out an instinctive impulse, and the human being cannot therefore be said to act instinctively save on the first occasion. The other, which is more serious, is that in man an instinctive impulse is comparatively seldom definite and determinate, with regard either to the objects or situations, in connection with which it becomes conscious, or to the actions or modes of behaviour to which it leads. This latter difficulty is probably the main explanation of the opinion so very generally held, and expressed, as we have seen, by a psychologist of the standing of Stout, that in the human being the instincts are relatively few and unimportant.

The tendency to belittle the influence of Instinct on the behaviour of man was accentuated by the constant discussion, on the part of the biologist, of that very type of instinctive behaviour, which is most remote from human instinct, the instinctive behaviour of insects, like the ant, the bee, the wasp, 'pure' instinct, as the biologist termed it. 'Pure' instinct of this type, it must be admitted, though not wholly absent from human nature, especially in the early stages of child development, is relatively unimportant in the developed life and experience of the adult human being. But such instinct is 'pure,' precisely because, and in so far as, the accompanying experience is 'pure' perception, because, and in so far as, the consciousness is a 'present moment' consciousness, the mental life a series of sparks or flashes.

The discussion of 'pure' instinct by the biologist is easily understood. In this type of instinct, he feels that he can describe the whole fact more adequately in biological terms, because there is apparently but a slight departure from reflex action, the departure being, it is true, due to the only factor, which he cannot describe in biological terms, but that factor seemingly playing an insignificant part in the whole, so insignificant that he could neglect it, and without great error regard instinctive action as merely compound reflex action, as Spencer did.

Further, it is behaviour that concerns the biologist, and, in the case of 'pure' instinct, the functioning of an original nervous structure comes very near being a full explanation of all the observed facts of the behaviour. In the adult human being, on the contrary, the functioning of an original nervous structure can explain but a small part of the whole fact. If then the psychologist adopts the standpoint of the biologist, as several psychologists have done, and looks only for 'pure' instinct in man, he easily finds it possible to hold that this is to all intents and purposes absent, that it can be ignored in psychology, and that the human being differs from the animal in respect that his behaviour is controlled by ideas and purposes, while the animal's behaviour is controlled by feelings and instincts.

We have seen that many of the older psychologists did not take this view, recognizing that the original springs of human action are either instinctive or of the instinctive order, and that human reason is in the main applied in the seeking out of means for the attainment of ends, determined ultimately by these original instinctive forces. McDougall has recently revived the view of these older psychologists, and it is the view which we also intend to adopt. In what follows, therefore, we shall deal mainly with those impulses in the human being, which have been generally acknowledged to be instinctive or innate, concentrating attention, like McDougall, upon those which seem to be of primary importance for education and for community life, rather than upon those which may be regarded as manifestations of 'pure' instinct, unless these are important on other grounds.

We cannot, however, adopt the general point of view of McDougall without at least mentioning the fact that there is another way of dealing with the human instincts, in support of which a strong line of argument may be developed. No one can fail to be struck in reading James's account of human instincts[1] with the very heterogeneous nature of the group of native tendencies discussed. From highly specific types of behaviour, like sucking, or carrying an object grasped to the mouth, he passes to such general modes of behaviour as those shown under the influence of the play tendency and curiosity, of emulation and imitation, without indicating that there is

[1] *Principles of Psychology*, vol. II, chap. XXIV.

any marked difference between actions determined by instinctive tendencies at the one extreme, and actions determined by those at the other.

At the very beginning of his treatment of instincts, James deprecates the method of classifying "definite tendencies by naming abstractly the purpose they subserve, such as self-preservation, defence," and the like[1], and insists further that the strict psychological way of regarding instincts is to regard them as actions, which "all conform to the general reflex type[2]," that is the type of a definite response to a definite situation.

It seems as objectionable to speak of an instinct of imitation, or play, or curiosity, as it is to speak of an instinct of self-preservation, if we apply to human instincts the criteria, which James wishes to apply. As it turns out, he himself finds it convenient to ignore his own criteria, as soon as he comes to discuss the more important human instincts and instinctive tendencies, and for a reason, which we shall presently find to be psychologically very significant.

A more recent writer has revived James's criteria, and also the point of view from which James starts, and has, with some success, maintained this point of view throughout his discussion of human instincts[3]. Thorndike, looking upon instinctive tendencies as tendencies to respond with a definite response to certain definite situations, makes an elaborate attempt to displace "the vague facts that man has instincts of 'pugnacity,' 'gregariousness,' 'cruelty,' 'curiosity,' 'constructiveness,' 'play,' and the like[4]," by a description of the definite responses to definite situations, which are, in his opinion, what we really find in human nature, and what we classify in this way merely for convenience, but not without sacrificing to some extent, or at least imperilling, a sound psychology.

We might admit—though as a matter of fact we do not—that Thorndike's position is theoretically sound, and yet prefer to adopt McDougall's point of view, for two reasons, either of which seems sufficient. In the first place, we believe that

[1] *Principles of Psychology*, vol. II, p. 383.   [2] Op. cit., vol. II, p. 384.
[3] Thorndike, *Educational Psychology*, vol. I. *The Original Nature of Man*, or *Educational Psychology*, Briefer Course.
[4] Briefer Course, p. 11.

Thorndike's 'definiteness' is more or less illusory, when we come to the practical business of enumerating and classifying the human instincts, and, not only is it illusory, but it is misleading, since it gives the impression or the suggestion that specific responses, as in the case of the behaviour determined by fear, with respect to specific objects, characterize the actions of the human child, in the same way as they characterize the behaviour of the young of lower animals. We shall attempt to show later that this is not the case, at least to any significant extent. In the second place, for the understanding of human interests and motives, more especially with a view to the development of a psychology of education, the 'class names' are exceedingly valuable, since their very 'vagueness' indicates that indeterminateness, which is, for the educator, so significant a feature of the instinctive equipment of the human being.

That Thorndike's position cannot be maintained even theoretically, that his formula is inapplicable, not only to many human instincts, but also to some of the instincts of lower animals, even of animals fairly low down the scale, will appear, when we have considered one important aspect of McDougall's position, viz., the relation assumed between instinct and emotion. Whether McDougall is right or wrong in his contentions in this regard, he clearly indicates one characteristic of human instincts, which would apparently be quite inexplicable on Thorndike's view of the essential nature of all instincts. Whether right or wrong, we say, because the facts are undeniable, and it is only with regard to his interpretation of the facts, that McDougall can be wrong, while the facts themselves seem to be of such a kind that Thorndike cannot be right. But let us consider McDougall's position.

By defining Instinct as he does[1], McDougall raises a very important question regarding the fundamental nature, not only of Instinct, but also of Emotion. Is Emotion primarily and fundamentally the affective element in Instinct? Or, to put the question in another form, which will probably be more convenient for us at present, is the interest involved in the instinct-experience always of such a character psychologically,

[1] See above, p. 15, or *Social Psychology*, p. 29. See also Appendix III.

that we ought to, or can, call it an emotion?   The question is not whether, under certain conditions, the interest may develop into an emotion, but whether it is necessarily an emotion from the outset.   Our answer has to some extent been anticipated in our discussion of instinct-interest.   But it is now necessary to consider the question in fuller detail and with special reference to the instincts of Man.

McDougall himself grants, that, in the case of some of the simpler instincts of Man, the affective element would not be called an emotion in the popular sense of the word.   In such cases "the affective element is not at all prominent; and, though no doubt the quality of it is peculiar in each case, yet we cannot readily distinguish these qualities, and have no special names for them[1]."   But we have names for the affective elements of our experience "in the case of the principal powerful instincts," the names in fact which we generally use in speaking of the instincts themselves, and the experiences are of the kind to which the generic term 'emotion' is applied.   But McDougall maintains that, psychologically speaking, the term 'emotion' ought not to be restricted to such experiences, while he later shows that there are cases where it is applied quite illegitimately in ordinary speech.   Hence the inference from McDougall's whole argument is, that, even as regards the simpler instincts where the affective element is not prominent, this affective element is psychologically emotion, while, in other cases, affective experiences—as, for example, surprise— ordinarily regarded as emotions, are not emotions psychologically.

Several questions are involved, but the first question seems to be whether, in our adoption, for psychological purposes, of the popular term 'emotion,' giving it thereby a definite and scientific meaning, we are justified, on the one hand, in extending it to cover the affective elements in every instinct-experience, and, on the other hand, limiting its meaning in such a way as to exclude several experiences popularly included.   In the first instance, it is worthy of note, that, by so extending the meaning of 'emotion,' we may cause it to usurp the place of another

[1] *Social Psychology*, p. 46.

equally good word, and at the same time leave without any definite descriptive term a mode of experience, for which the term 'emotion' seems peculiarly suitable. Is not 'interest' the better word to apply to the affective element in instinct-experience, as such, and is not 'emotion' something more than this, something in a sense secondary? That is the view we have taken in the previous chapter. In the second place, by excluding such experiences as surprise and the like, we appear to be narrowing the application of the word 'emotion' on the other side, so to speak, in such a way as to necessitate the employment of still another descriptive term to cover modes of affective experience of this kind.

An alternative view to McDougall's has already been sketched on general lines, but we may recapitulate, in order to place the two views side by side. A decision between them must depend on the results of introspective study of the various kinds of experience involved.

The alternative hypothesis to McDougall's is that the affective element in instinct-experience becomes emotion, only when action in satisfaction of the interest is suspended or checked, when, as we expressed it before, interest passes into 'tension.' If impulse immediately realizes itself in the appropriate action towards the situation, then there is no emotion in any strict sense of emotion. At a first glance this hypothesis seems to account best for the facts, when we consider especially those instinctive activities which are accompanied by no pronounced emotion. On the other hand, there are undoubtedly certain facts, which favour McDougall's hypothesis. For example, in the 'fear' instinct, or in the 'fighting' instinct, the emotion is the predominant characteristic of the whole experience. This suggests at any rate that in the human being, we have at least two types of instinct to deal with, and that, if Thorndike's formula is applicable to the one type, it can scarcely be expected to apply to the other.

In the meantime, however, let us attempt to settle this question of the relation of Instinct to Emotion, and return to the bearing of the facts on Thorndike's view.

Some definition of emotion would seem to be necessary,

before we proceed to decide between these alternative hypotheses regarding this relation. Unfortunately a generally accepted psychological definition of emotion is not easy to find. Psychologists, who have defined emotion, have generally defined it in such a way as to lead on to, or support, a particular theory of the emotions. Thus Külpe regards emotion as a "fusion of feeling and organic sensation," Höffding as "pleasure-pain in association with the idea of its cause," Sully as "a mass of sensuous and representative material with a predominant affective tone," Ward as a "complete psychosis involving cognition, pleasure-pain and conation[1]." The best course therefore is apparently to enumerate those features which characterize all emotional experiences, and to start from such an enumeration as a provisional psychological definition of emotion.

The definitions cited indicate most of the prominent characteristics of emotion as an experience.

(a)   In the first place, emotion always involves an affective relation to an object, either perceptual or ideal.

(b)   In the second place, the pleasure-pain colouring is nearly always pronounced. One might in fact maintain that 'emotion,' as popularly understood, always involves this accentuated pleasure-pain factor, so much so, that a considerable number of psychologists have taken this as the essential characteristic of the experience.

(c)   In the third place, 'organic resonance,' as it has been called, is in general well-marked. Again certain psychologists, the most notable being James, have taken this as the essential characteristic, but it has been recognized as a prominent characteristic from Descartes and Malebranche onwards.

(d)   In the fourth place, emotion involves a feeling-attitude of such a kind, that "actions of a special sort, and these alone, appeal to us[2]." Our consciousness is, as it were, narrowed, and also specialized, the emotion affecting cognition and action both by way of inhibition, and by way of reinforcement. This again has been taken as the fundamental fact by some psychologists.

---

[1] For the various definitions see Irons, *Psychology of Ethics*, p. 1 f.
[2] Irons, *Psychology of Ethics*, p. 3.

(e) In the fifth place, emotion involves an impulsive force, a source of driving power, so to speak, which, in the more marked cases, tends to suspend the higher mental processes, and to overwhelm purposes, resolutions, and principles, by its irresistible urgency towards immediate action.

If we consider that all emotions, to a greater or less extent, show these characteristics, we must apparently decide against McDougall's view, which would include only the first and fourth as essential to emotion, the others appearing only when the emotional state becomes accentuated. But these are the characteristics merely of that interest, which we have all along recognized as a necessary accompaniment of instinctive activity.

A recent writer on this subject, Alexander F. Shand[1], comes to practically the same conclusion, but on somewhat different grounds. He points out, that, "when the activity of the instinct is most sudden and unopposed, the emotion, if it be brought into activity at all, will be of less intensity and definiteness." This seems incontrovertible, and in the limiting case the emotion may be considered entirely to disappear. When Shand passes on to argue that "many instincts of great individual importance and distinctness have no corresponding distinctive emotion[2]," and cites, as an instance, the nest-building instinct in birds, he is on much more doubtful ground. The obvious rejoinder is, that we are in no position to say whether there is a distinctive emotion involved in the nest-building instinct or not. Shand's analysis of Instinct into impulse and sensation is also open to grave objection. If there is not an affective element involved in all instinctive activity, it is difficult to see how the characteristic instinct-emotions could develop under any circumstances, and that there are such Shand acknowledges.

We seem then compelled to take the view that the instinct-emotion is not an invariable accompaniment of instinctive activity, but that the instinct-interest is, that the instinct-emotion is due to what we previously called 'tension,' that is, in the ordinary case, to arrest of the impulse, to the denying of immediate satisfaction to the interest.

[1] *The Foundations of Character*, London, 1914.   [2] Op. cit., p. 371.

This arrest of the impulse may arise from a variety of circumstances, but, as we have seen, in the case of the human being one set of circumstances is specially important. With many instinctive impulses, and, among these, some of very great significance, there is no provision in the organism, by means of any neural prearrangement, for that particular course of action, which will meet the particular individual case. Thorndike disagrees, but we shall consider his views immediately. It follows, that there must be at least momentary arrest of the impulse, while the particular course of action is being intelligently determined—intelligently, if only on the perceptual level.

If this is a valid explanation of the instinct-emotion, then we ought to find in a comparative study of the instincts of animals, representing different stages or levels of intelligence, that, in the case of certain instincts, the development of the emotional element in instinctive behaviour proceeds *pari passu,* on the whole, with the dropping out of inherited special adjustments for particular reactions to particular situations. And that is what we apparently do find. Romanes has discussed the emotional manifestations of organisms at different levels[1], and though, as he points out, the inference to the emotional life of animals "necessarily becomes of less and less validity, as we pass through the animal kingdom to organisms less and less like our own[2]," we cannot fail to be struck by the fact, that the manifestations of emotion become rarer and rarer, and more and more ambiguous, as we descend the scale, and as instinctive activities become more and more fixed and definite. First the self-feelings disappear, then the emotions connected with the distinctively social instincts, then curiosity, and finally we are left with fear and anger, even these disappearing in the lowest.

What appears to be the biological function and significance of emotion would lead us to expect precisely this phenomenon. Biologically the function of emotion is apparently to reinforce

[1] *Animal Intelligence,* pp. 45, 155, 204, 242, 270, 329, 334.   *Mental Evolution in Animals,* chap. xx.
[2] *Mental Evolution,* p. 341.

impulse and interest. This reinforcement will be necessary
in two cases, either where an obstacle must be surmounted, or
where a more or less prolonged course of trying to find the
appropriate reaction is necessary, owing to the fact that no
neural prearrangement provides for the precise action in a
particular case. In the first set of circumstances, in addition
to the appropriate emotion, whatever that may be, anger
generally develops, as a further reinforcement. In the second,
anger will not meet the needs of the situation, since only actions
of a certain kind will satisfy the impulse and interest involved,
and only the appropriate emotion can secure such actions.

Though we cannot accept McDougall's view, that the
primary emotion, as such, is merely the affective element in
instinct-experience, we are in entire agreement with him on
what appear to be the main points. There are certain instincts,
of vast importance in both human and animal life, of which
an emotion is, under normal conditions, one of the most prominent characteristics. At the same time there are, it is true,
in addition, minor instincts, characterizing the behaviour of the
young child, where the interest is not usually of the emotional
type. But the important point is that the great instincts of
human nature have all their accompanying and typical emotion.

We must, therefore, in the case of man and the higher
animals, distinguish between instincts, which approximate the
'pure' type, and the great instincts which are characteristically
emotional. We may now turn to Thorndike's view, for which
this fact would seem to be an insurmountable difficulty.
Thorndike would recognize but one type of instinct, and the
great instincts, like fear, anger, curiosity, and the like, he would
regard, not as single instincts, but rather as groups of instinctive tendencies, all of the normal 'pure' type. Hence, in his
opinion, the psychologist cannot rest satisfied with 'vague'
class-names, like 'fear,' 'anger,' 'curiosity,' but must attempt
to determine what precise situation produces each particular
reaction.

Take fear. "The inner perturbation which we call the
emotion of fear, running, crouching, clinging, starting, trembling, remaining stock-still, screaming, covering the eyes, opening

the mouth and eyes, a temporary cessation followed by an acceleration of the heart-beat, difficulty in breathing and paleness, sweating and erection of the hair, are responses of which certain ones seem bound, apart from training, to certain situations, such as sudden loud noises or clutches, the sudden appearance of strange objects, thunder and lightning, loneliness, and the dark[1]."

If the emotion or 'perturbation' is essentially the same in all cases of different responses, that at least shows that the responses belong together in some way. But possibly Thorndike would not acknowledge that the emotion is the same. Taking, then, the other responses which he specifies, we find that they can be classified into different groups. Some of them belong to the 'organic resonance' of the emotion, and will therefore show themselves whenever the fear reaches a certain intensity, be the situation which arouses the fear what it may. Take for example the erection of the hair. This indeed is so little a specific response, that it is, in various animals, both a symptom of fear and a symptom of anger[2]. Darwin holds that it is, in fear, more or less "an incidental result," rather than a biologically useful reaction, comparable with "the profuse sweating from an agony of pain or terror[3]." The other phenomena mentioned by Thorndike are real responses, and these belong to one of two groups—responses which represent 'flight' in one form or another, and responses which represent 'concealment.'

Shand[4] would distinguish four varieties of fear according to the different reactions in each case, where the reaction is flight, where it is concealment, where it is silence and immobility, and where it is keeping close to some one or something for protection. Of these reactions the second, third, and fourth are apparently all varieties of a single type of reaction. Shand indeed enumerates five further varieties of instinctive fear, where the reaction is shrinking or starting back, where it is paralysis or immobility, where it is crying for help or protection, where it is aggressive action as of an animal at bay, and disinterested fear for young, where the safety of the young

---

[1] Thorndike, *Educational Psychology, Briefer Course*, p. 20.
[2] Darwin, *Expression of the Emotions*, chap. IV.
[3] Op. cit., p. 102.   [4] *Foundations of Character*, p. 201.

is first secured. Three of these are very ambiguous, and suggest something more than fear, while the other two do not seem to be more than varieties or phases of the first and second. It must be noted that Shand, though apparently agreeing with Thorndike, recognizes all these varieties of instinctive behaviour as belonging to a definite system, of which the emotion is a more or less constant characteristic. The primary emotion is, for Shand, always such a system.

The one great difficulty for Thorndike's view, that there are very many fear instincts, is, as we have already indicated, the emotion itself, which is always, as far as human experience goes, characteristically the same emotion, whatever the particular response may be. Not only so, but the particular response does not of itself serve to satisfy or remove the emotion. The emotion only disappears when the response has secured its end— the avoidance of the danger. Shand is perfectly clear on this point. But it explains another fact, which on Thorndike's view is very difficult of explanation, the fact that all the different responses may be tried in turn to escape any given danger.

Moreover, with the human being at least, it is impossible to say beforehand what the response to a given situation will be, that is, whether it will be of the 'flight' or of the 'concealment' type. Thorndike controverts this view[1], maintaining that the sight of a large animal coming towards us will, as a rule, be responded to by running away, rather than by hiding, whereas a violent thunderstorm will be responded to by hiding, rather than by running away[2]. This is very plausible reasoning, and, at a first glance, appears sound. But further reflection will convince us that it is not sound. Behaviour will be largely determined, first of all, by the circumstances of the case, by what kind of response will best secure safety. It will be determined, in the second place, by the intensity of the fear aroused, and two individuals may behave in two entirely different ways, in response to the same situation, according to the degree of fear aroused. One may escape by climbing a tree, jumping into a river, or running away, while the other stands rooted to the spot, unable to move hand or foot.

[1] Thorndike, *Briefer Course*, p. 21.   [2] Op. cit., p. 22.

If for the human being 'running away' is normally the instinctive response to the situation 'large animal approaching,' and 'hiding' to the situation 'thunder and lightning,' it is somewhat remarkable that some animals, even better fitted for running away than the human being, will seek 'concealment' in the former case, and other animals—for example horses, and domestic animals generally—respond with 'flight' to the latter.   The writer once possessed a Labrador retriever dog, which was very much afraid of thunder.   On one occasion, he was walking with the dog a mile or so from home, when there came a loud peal of thunder.   The dog dashed off in terror, ignoring whistles and calls.   It turned out later that he must have made straight for home, for, a few minutes afterwards— as was discovered by comparing times—he was found crouching upon the doorstep, trembling in every limb.   At the place where the dog took flight there was ample opportunity for concealment, but the instinctive response was nevertheless flight.   When the dog was at home, and a thunder-storm came on, he usually crawled under a bed, or into some dark cupboard.

We do not think the case is essentially different with the human being.   'Flight' and 'concealment' are alternative responses to the same situation.   If there is a place of refuge and concealment at hand, the human being may conceal himself, in place of running away from a large animal; if he is out in the open, he may take flight from a thunderstorm.

Thorndike even goes so far as to throw doubt upon the reality of the emotion, as an essential accompaniment of the various fear responses.   "It is probable further that an impartial survey of human behaviour, unprejudiced by the superstition that a magic state of consciousness, 'fear,' is aroused by 'danger,' and then creates flight and other symptoms of itself, would show that pursuit and capture may produce distinctive responses, whether or no the peculiar inner trepidation, which introspection knows, is present[1]."

Now it is undeniable, as many writers have pointed out that instinctive response to a situation, rousing the 'fear' instinct, may take place without our experiencing the emotion,

[1] *Briefer Course*, p. 22.

except retrospectively. We may, that is to say, apprehend the 'danger,' and immediately make the necessary effective response, without feeling any emotion of fear at the time. There are also cases—for example Livingstone's experience when seized by a lion—where the response is not effective, and yet no fear emotion is experienced. But we should maintain that such cases are exceptional, and cases of the first kind, at any rate, merely confirm our position, that the emotion is not, as such, an essential accompaniment of any instinct.

Of course it is obvious, that we may easily, by "an impartial survey of human behaviour" alone, reach any conclusion we please, as to the presence or absence of an element in the accompanying experience, which nothing but introspection is competent to study; but such a conclusion can hardly be regarded as anything but highly unsatisfactory by the psychologist. When we examine our own experiences of 'danger' situations, they tell a very different story.

It must also be granted, that it is hardly psychologically the truth to assert that 'fear' creates 'flight.' But no psychologist, least of all McDougall, would maintain that it does. 'Flight' is an instinctive response to a perceptual situation, and the perceptual experience is normally also emotional with the 'fear' emotion. There are other instinctive responses to the same or similar perceptual situations, the perceptual experience in each case being coloured with the same emotion. From the observed facts two inferences seem legitimate. In the first place, the emotion 'fear' is integrally connected with the instinctive responses to a 'danger' situation. In the second place, though originally in the history of the race these responses may have represented specific responses to specific perceived situations, and therefore separate instincts, in the human being, and in the higher animals, they represent the multiple response of a single instinct, which is quite properly called fear, and which is normally, or usually, emotional, just because of the multiple response.

The illusory character of the definiteness, which Thorndike's view would impart to all instinctive behaviour of the human being, is even better seen in the case of the 'anger' or 'fighting'

instinct. While Thorndike succeeds in enumerating seven
distinct instincts, which McDougall's 'instinct of pugnacity'
would apparently cover, he is compelled, in the case of several
of the seven, to allow for a variety of instinctive response.
Thus he distinguishes the 'instinct of escape from restraint,'
the 'instinct of overcoming a moving obstacle,' the 'instinct
of counterattack,' the 'instinct of irrational response to pain,'
the 'instinct of combat in rivalry,' the instinct of attack on
other males during courtship, the instinct of attack upon any
obstacle thwarting any other instinctive response[1]. If we take
the first of these, we find that it is the instinct aroused by the
situation "being interfered with in any bodily movements
which the individual is impelled by its own constitution to
make, the interference consisting in holding the individual."
The responses are, in the case of a little child, "stiffening,
writhing, and throwing back the head and shoulders," these
being replaced or supplemented, in the case of an older child,
by "kicking, pushing, slapping, scratching, and biting[2]." We
find the same kind of thing in most of the others, and, not only
so, but the same responses. It is difficult to see where any
advantage derived from the classification comes in, if the
responses are practically as complex and varied as ever.

We are compelled, therefore, to reject Thorndike's view,
that all the instincts of Man can be reduced to, or derived from,
instinctive tendencies of the simple or 'pure' type, and to
recognize, with McDougall, that some of the most important
instincts of the human being, as well as of the higher animals,
are of the 'emotional' type, that is to say, are not merely of
the nature of specific responses to specific situations, but
specific only as to the kind of situation, the emotional accompaniment, and the end secured by the response, and, as regards
the first and third of these, specific in varying degrees. In any
case, alike for 'pure' and for 'emotional' instinct, Thorndike's
ignoring of the affective or interest factor cannot be defended.

We have thus two groups of instinctive tendencies in Man,
which we can distinguish from one another on a psychological
basis, the one group characterized by specific responses to

[1] *Briefer Course*, pp. 23–26. [2] Op. cit., p. 23.

specific situations, like sucking, biting an object placed in the mouth, and the like[1], which are as a rule very difficult to distinguish from reflexes, the other group consisting of tendencies specific in varying degrees as regards situation and response, but always quite specific as regards the accompanying emotion, when that emotion is aroused.   But we cannot stop here.   We must recognize still another group of innate tendencies, which can hardly be said to be specific at all, as regards either situation or response, and which have associated with them no specific emotion, a group to which would belong such tendencies as play, imitation, and the like.   It is obvious that such tendencies can be classified with neither sucking nor fear, and yet they are quite as undoubtedly instinctive.

This third group of instinctive tendencies is also of great psychological interest.   Though play, imitation, and the like, certainly represent instinctive tendencies, they are as far removed from the 'pure' instincts as they could well be. Biologically they may be regarded as the means of supplementing the 'unlearned reactions' of 'pure' instinct.   They do not normally determine specific ends or interests, but attach themselves, as it were, to the ends and interests determined by the specific tendencies, more especially those of the 'emotional' group.   This explains the fact that they have no accompanying specific emotion.   But although there is no specific emotion, the usual instinct-interest may be, and perhaps generally is, present.   This is best seen in the case of play.   In a hunting game, for example, there is, in addition to the specific interest, developing it may be into emotion, of the hunting instinct, the play interest itself, which, while it never can itself become emotional, yet modifies throughout both the emotion and the behaviour of the hunting instinct.

Our psychological classification of the original tendencies of Man is not yet complete.   We may take as a further basis of classification, the fact that some tendencies appear to be determined by some feeling of uneasiness, which we should describe as prior to the impulse, but for the suggestion of

[1] See James, *Principles of Psychology*, vol. II, p. 404. Also Thorndike, *Notes on Child Study*.

relative time order, which the word 'prior' conveys. There is no conclusive evidence, as we have already seen, that the feeling of uneasiness is prior in time to the impulse which it determines. Nevertheless there appears to be in some sense an experienced 'priority,' which quite clearly distinguishes such original tendencies from other tendencies not characterized by this priority of feeling. These two groups we may call respectively the group of 'Appetite' and the group of 'Instinct' proper. Theoretically the distinction between them seems valid; practically it is not without its difficulties.

In the 'Appetite' group we can distinguish the specific from the general tendencies, as in the 'Instinct proper' group. The general 'Appetite' tendencies are two, the tendency to avoid or get away from unpleasant experiences, and the tendency to seek or maintain pleasant experiences. We call these general, because the tendencies are determined by nothing specific in any experience, except its pleasantness or its unpleasantness. The specific 'Appetite' tendencies, most easily recognized and identified, are the four appetites determined by hunger, thirst, need of sleep, and sex. We should, however, be inclined to add to these at least one tendency of an opposite kind—unfortunately there is no definite term to denote this, except aversion, and that will not suit here—the tendency which we call nausea, or primitive disgust.

Our whole classification of Man's original, innate, or instinctive tendencies, with the chief individual tendencies provisionally placed in each class, may be shown schematically as on page 169.

This classification, though it is more fully wrought out, is on the same general lines as McDougall's, from which it differs merely as regards details, some of these being nevertheless not unimportant. The chief differences are:—(a) the classifying of both sex impulse and primitive disgust with the 'Appetite' tendencies, rather than with the 'Instinct' tendencies, (b) the addition of experimentation to the general 'Instinct' tendencies, which is really equivalent to the transferring of 'constructiveness' from the specific to the general, since that is one way in which this general tendency manifests itself, (c) the definite adding of the gregarious instinct, the courtship

Innate Tendencies

'Appetite' Tendencies			'Instinct' Tendencies
General (Seeking of Pleasure Avoidance of Pain)	Specific (Hunger Thirst Sleep Sex Nausea)		General (Play Experimentation Imitation Sympathy Suggestibility)

Specific

'Pure'
(Probably numerous though difficult to dis-
tinguish from reflexes and may perhaps
be classified as:
Reactions of Adjustment and Attention
    ,,   Prehension
    ,,   Locomotion
    ,,   Vocalization)
	'Emotional'
	(Fear
	Anger
	Hunting
	Acquisitive
	Curiosity
	Gregarious
	Courtship
	Self-display
	Self-abasement
	Parental)

tendency, the hunting instinct, and the acquisitive tendency to the specific 'Instinct' tendencies, and therefore to the group of tendencies, in connection with which we must expect to find an interest, which, under certain conditions, develops into a specific primary emotion.

The obvious advantage of such a classification is that it is psychological, and is therefore in place in a psychological discussion of Instinct. Except for the classifications of some of the older psychologists, and of McDougall, most classifications of human instinctive tendencies have been in more or less objective terms, that is, from the point of view of the instinctive response, or the end towards which it is directed.

Thus Thorndike[1] divides the tendencies into two main groups, individual and social. Under the former head he classifies "original attentiveness," "gross bodily control," "food-getting," "protective responses," "anger," and under the second head, that is "responses to the behaviour of other human beings," "motherly behaviour," "responses to the

---

[1] *Briefer Course*, chaps. II and III.

presence, approval, and scorn of men," "mastering and sub-
missive behaviour," "other social instincts," "imitation."

Rutgers Marshall classifies the tendencies, professedly from
"an objective point of view[1]," into "three grand divisions
determined by the laws of organic development," the divisions
being:—

(1) "Instincts which function to the preservation of the
individual organic life";

(2) "Instincts which function to the preservation of the
species to which the individual life belongs";

(3) "Instincts which function to the preservation of those
social groups which we discover amongst many species of animals,
and which appear most markedly in the highest animal—man[2]."

If this distinction between individual and social tendencies
is considered desirable or important, it can quite easily, in
our classification, be applied to the 'Instinct' tendencies, both
general and specific. That is to say, these groups are capable of being further subdivided into tendencies, which we
may call individual, and tendencies, which are social, or at
least necessarily imply or involve relation or interaction
between an individual and other individuals. Thus imitation,
sympathy, suggestibility, the gregarious instinct, the acquisitive
tendency, the courtship tendency, the parental instinct, are all
social in this sense, and to a less extent perhaps, but still unmistakably, the two self-tendencies, while play, experimentation,
anger, fear, the hunting instinct, curiosity, do not necessarily
involve any such social reference, and may therefore be classed
as individual. The 'Appetite' tendencies must all be regarded,
psychologically at any rate, as essentially individual.

We must now take a closer survey of the various tendencies,
and more particularly those which are important from the point
of view of education. Seeing that the 'Appetite' tendencies
present somewhat special and complex problems, their discussion had better be postponed. We shall begin therefore with the
'Instinct' tendencies, and with the specific 'emotional' group.

---

[1] *Instinct and Reason*, p. 102.
[2] *Instinct and Reason*, p. 103. Stout's fourfold classification in the recent
edition of the *Manual* (1913) is on somewhat similar lines.

CHAPTER VIII

THE SPECIFIC 'INSTINCT' TENDENCIES

McDougall has pointed out with great clearness and truth, that, while all the specific 'Instinct' tendencies are characterized by cognition of a more or less specific kind of object, behaviour of a more or less specific character, and an emotional experience of a quite specific quality, it is the third factor that is characteristic and constant. It is true that certain expressive signs of an emotion are almost as specific as the emotion itself. But apart from this, the behaviour, due to any of the 'emotional' specific tendencies may show considerable variation, and is also highly modifiable as a result of education. So is it also with the cognitive factor. We shall see presently that it is only in one or two of the 'emotional' instincts that the impulse is aroused, prior to experience, by specific objects. Generally the instinctive impulse is determined by a more or less specific kind of situation, but in the case of curiosity or the acquisitive tendency the situation is specific to a very slight degree. Hence, the emotional factor being the unalterable and relatively permanent element, it is very fittingly chosen, wherever possible, as the basis of identification and naming in each case.

These facts to some extent explain the difficulty which psychologists experience in determining exactly the instinctive, as distinguished from the derived, impulses and tendencies of the human being, belonging to this category. McDougall suggests, that, in seeking to decide whether any "human emotion or impulse" should be considered "a primary emotion or simple instinctive impulse," we may employ two criteria:—
(1) the display of a similar emotion and impulse in the higher

animals, and (2) the appearance of the emotion and impulse in question in an exaggerated or hyper-excitable form under pathological conditions[1].

Neither criterion can be considered as quite satisfactory from the psychological point of view. Both are essentially objective. As regards the first, it is not clear that there might not be primary emotions, characteristic of human nature, which were not to be found in the higher animals at all. But quite apart from that consideration, the emotions and impulses which the psychologist finds in animals are essentially of the nature of *ejects* from his own experience, and it is not very easy to see, how and why the fact that a human being can read his own emotions into the mental life of animals should afford a criterion for determining the primary nature of these emotions and impulses. Romanes, for example, finds 'jealousy' as low down the scale as fishes, 'emulation' and 'pride' in birds, 'grief,' 'hate,' 'cruelty' in carnivora, rodents, and ruminants, 'revenge' in monkeys and elephants, 'shame' and 'remorse' in anthropoid apes[2]. It is equally difficult to see how and why the second criterion affords a basis for such a decision; at all events, it is not clear *a priori* why a complex and secondary emotion may not appear in an exaggerated form under pathological conditions, as, in fact, it frequently does, in the case of both 'emotions of sentiment,' and 'emotions of desire.'

It cannot be denied that McDougall's criteria are useful to the psychologist by way of confirmatory evidence. But the psychologist has other, and more purely psychological, criteria available. Shand offers us four tests, one of which is practically identical with McDougall's first:—(1) the manifestation of the impulse and emotion early in child life, (2) the wide diffusion of the impulse and emotion in the animal world, (3) irreducibility in introspective analysis, (4) manifestation in genuinely instinctive behaviour[3]. These criteria are also open to objection, but we can at least extract from them three tests, which with McDougall's two will yield us altogether five.

---

[1] *Social Psychology*, p. 48.
[2] *Mental Evolution in Animals*, chap. xx, and Plate.
[3] *Foundations of Character*, p. 219.

These five tests, in what seems to be their order of psychological importance, are:—

(1) Irreducibility by introspective analysis to simpler components.

(2) Arousal of impulse and emotion, with its specific and unmistakable expressive signs, by specific objects or specific kinds of objects, prior to individual experience of these objects.

(3) Manifestation in the early months of child life.

(4) Wide diffusion in the animal world.

(5) Occurrence in exaggerated form under pathological conditions.

Six of the ten tendencies we have named satisfy all these tests—anger, fear, the two self-tendencies, the gregarious instinct, and the acquisitive tendency. It is not quite certain whether curiosity and the hunting instinct satisfy the fifth, and the parental instinct, and the courtship tendency, for an obvious reason, do not satisfy the third.

Surprise appears to be the only other 'emotional' tendency of the human being, on behalf of which a serious claim to be included in this group can be advanced. The reason for excluding surprise is the doubt whether there is any corresponding instinctive impulse. Both McDougall and Shand accept Adam Smith's account of the nature of surprise[1]. According to Adam Smith's account, "surprise is not to be regarded as an original emotion of a species distinct from all others. The violent and sudden change produced upon the mind, when an emotion of any kind is brought suddenly upon it, constitutes the whole nature of surprise." McDougall's account is in slightly different terms. Surprise, he says, "is produced by an impression, which is contrary to anticipation, and to which, therefore, we cannot immediately adjust ourselves, which does not evoke at once an appropriate emotional and conative response." There does not seem any sufficient ground for denying the emotional nature of surprise. It is the emotional response to unexpectedness, and it is unique only in that the emotional response to the *quale* of the impression supervenes,

---

[1] Adam Smith, *The Principles which lead and direct Philosophical Enquiries, as illustrated by the History of Astronomy*, sect. I. McDougall, *Social Psychology*, p. 157. Shand, *Foundations of Character*, p. 421.

so that surprise is always merely a momentary emotion. Its impulse and expression, simply as surprise, do not appear to be very significant, but we should be quite prepared to admit it as another 'emotional' tendency belonging to this group.

Educationally the most important fact to keep in mind with regard to these specific 'emotional' tendencies is, that in them we have—apart from the 'Appetite' tendencies, to which we shall advert later—the original, and ultimately the sole important, motive forces determining an individual's behaviour, the sole original determinants of the ends he will seek to attain, as of the interests which crave satisfaction[1]. To escape from 'danger,' to meet hindrances, obstacles, and hostility with active aggression, to acquire 'property,' to secure the favourable notice of the chosen one of the opposite sex, to protect offspring, to obtain the praise and avoid the blame of superiors or equals, to escape the loneliness of isolation from one's fellows, these, however disguised, developed, or complicated, they may be, apart, as we have said, from the 'Appetite' tendencies, are instances of the chief ultimate forces which control the actions of humanity.

We must now consider briefly some of the more interesting and significant features of the various tendencies individually, and more especially the nature of the situations which determine them, the kind of behaviour in which they issue, the modifications produced by and in experience, and their general operation and function in education and social development.

Fear. McDougall, Ribot, James, and others have already discussed fear so fully from the psychological, and Darwin and others from the expression, behaviour, and biological points of view, that there is little left for us to do in this case, except to supplement the parts of their descriptions which are germane to our present purpose, so far as we can, and to draw such conclusions as seem to us deserving of particular note.

In the human being the fear instinct is specialized, at the outset, for comparatively few, if for any, particular objects. Evidence with regard to the instinctive fears of childhood is,

---

[1] This may possibly need qualification, but we shall consider this point in connection with the general tendencies.

as a rule, not too reliable, the source of the unreliability being more or less general, as far as the primary emotions are concerned.   The general tendency we call 'sympathy'—McDougall's 'primitive passive sympathy'—operates, as we shall see, in such a way as to cause an individual to experience an emotion, when he perceives the signs expressive of that emotion in another individual, or other individuals, towards whom his attention is directed.   Now this tendency undoubtedly operates in a child from a very early age.   Hence many apparently instinctive fears may be derived through sympathy, and not really 'instinctive.'   That is to say, a child may derive fear for a specific object through sympathy, from another person, who is really afraid, or who successfully pretends fear, and the result is a fear, which, without knowledge of the circumstances—and such knowledge is apt to be very elusive—we tend to classify as 'instinctive.'

For example, it is said that children have an instinctive fear of dead things.   Not one of the writer's children has shown the slightest sign of such.   Yet one of them, when aged about five, showed an intense fear of death—he said he could not 'get it out of his head'—when his mother, on one occasion, told him 'he would get his death of cold' by going about with his shoes off, as he had been doing against orders.   This was the first occasion on which we had known him to exhibit fear of death.   We cannot trace its origin, but we are quite satisfied that its origin was either sympathetic, or that he had been told something from which the fear had developed.

We have had an analogous experience with fear of the dark. Of three children, aged from two to five, not one showed the least fear of the dark, until suddenly one evening fear of going out into a dark lobby was manifested, and by all three.   Of the origin of the fear, we are quite ignorant, but it was certainly not instinctive in all three cases, and probably not in any.

If there is doubt about fear being aroused by specific objects or situations, there is no doubt about its being aroused by specific kinds of objects or situations, prior to individual experience of such.   Loud noises, but not all loud noises, strange faces, but not all strange faces, a threatening aspect in human beings or animals—and this seems to be instinctively apprehended, probably through the operation of something akin to sympathy —high places, and any risk of falling, anything "violently opposed to the accustomed and familiar[1]," but only in a certain way, these are the kinds of situations which arouse instinctive fear. The general formula would appear to be "anything that threatens 'danger'." And this formula applies, not merely at the perceptual level, but at all levels. It is usually the threatened 'danger' in loud noises, like the roar of a lion, the loud bark of a dog, that stimulates fear. A loud noise like thunder may apparently, in the majority of children, produce a similar effect at the first experience, but it must be remembered that such an experience is or may be intensely disagreeable, merely as loud noise; the same kind of effect is produced by the horn of a steamer close at hand, but in our own case the sensation is, not only highly disagreeable, but positively painful, and fear produced in such circumstances may be produced by the experienced pain, and is therefore not prior to experience.

The notion of 'danger,' as the only way in which we can express the origin of fear, as well as explain its characteristics in all cases, has hitherto very strangely failed to attract the careful notice and investigation of the psychologist. Shand comes upon it in his search for a general law, which will express and include all forms of the fear behaviour, but, though it is the only notion that could have guided him aright, he has passed it over, to formulate a law which is manifestly false, or at least partial and one-sided[2].

'Danger' may be generally interpreted as the 'promise of pain, injury, or loss to the Self.' The general law of the behaviour of fear, which Shand sought, may be expressed in the form: 'Fear in all its varieties strives to escape danger.' At the purely instinctive level, and at the perceptual level generally, the danger is, in the main, physical danger to the individual or his offspring. At the higher levels, it may be as frequently danger that threatens any part of the 'Self,' and it must be

---

[1] McDougall, *Social Psychology*, p. 54.
[2] *Foundations of Character*, p. 217. His 'law' is: "Fear throughout its varieties strives to avoid aggressive behaviour."

remembered that an individual's sentiments, ends, ideals, purposes, are at these levels parts of the Self.

This notion of 'danger' also enables us to give a satisfactory account of the modifications of which this instinct is capable, as a result of experience, and with the higher degrees of 'psychical integration.' The evolution of the race has secured that certain 'dangers' should be apprehended prior to individual experience. After our discussion of the cognitive element in instinct-experience in Chapter IV, the sense in which we use 'apprehend' will not be misunderstood. Learning at the perceptual level will take place, when pain, injury, or loss is experienced in association with any perceptual situation, and the result may be fear at the moment—or anger, as we shall see— and fear of such a situation for the future. Similarly at the ideational and rational levels. The experienced results of situations, experienced, that is to say, by ourselves or by others within our knowledge, will lead to such situations being labelled as 'dangerous.' Whether the crude instinctive behaviour of fear will manifest itself or not, will depend on a variety of circumstances, but, in any case, fear as a motive will always play its part in determining the behaviour.

McDougall has emphasized, and rightly emphasized, the fact that fear is the great 'inhibitor of all action,' and, as such, is in primitive societies the "great agent of social discipline[1]." But, as McDougall has also more than once pointed out, inhibition is but one aspect of a process, of which reinforcement is the other aspect, and it is sometimes well to look at this other aspect. So long as the fear is not of a paralyzing degree, it directs all our energies towards escape from 'danger.' At the higher levels, when it is one element in a complex emotional state, it is generally most significant when regarded as a reinforcing, rather than as an inhibiting, agent. The individual, who is striving to gain a prize, redoubles his efforts, when he sees the danger of losing it to another. And so is it always, when fear is associated with almost any motive that animates the human being, at least if it is essentially selfish in its tendency, provided, as we have said, the fear does not reach the paralyzing degree.

[1] *Social Psychology*, p. 55.

In connection with the effect of fear in experience, there is one other point deserving of some notice. That is its 'haunting' character. Of all the emotions, fear probably makes the deepest and most permanent impression upon the mind. McDougall has related this fact to the inhibitory effect of fear by pointing out, that, along with the inhibition of other mental activity, there is a 'riveting' of the attention on the object feared "to the exclusion of all others[1]." We cannot 'get it out of our minds.' In other words, the 'haunting' is the result of the inhibiting and reinforcing influence of fear, which, especially when it is experienced in a high degree, not only keeps the attention fixed upon the object or event feared, but persists in memory, to an extent that very frequently becomes morbid.

Even fear experienced in dreams has this effect. We have known individuals, who for years avoided certain streets and street-crossings, because these were associated in a dream with a terrifying experience. They confessed that their action was irrational, and could by a strong effort of will pass through the dreaded zone, but the fear remained. The same kind of thing is notably a phenomenon of children's fears. Fortunately most of these fears are outgrown, but in some cases they are not. How many of the neuroses, the origin of which the Freudians ascribe to instincts of sex, are not due rather to the equally powerful, and at an early age far more manifest, instinct of fear? There seems good reason to believe that many of them are[2].

Anger and the Hunting Instinct. We shall discuss these two instincts, the fighting instinct and the hunting instinct, together, because in many cases they are not easily separable in their effects, as far as human behaviour is concerned. The hunting instinct has been rather strangely ignored by McDougall. It would deserve notice, if only for the part it plays in determining some of the favourite amusements of both young and adult human beings. In this respect at least, the two tendencies are very fittingly bracketed together. But they are not less

---

[1] *Social Psychology*, p. 55.
[2] See Morton Prince, *The Unconscious*, Lect. XIII.

closely associated as regards nearly all the kinds of behaviour they determine.

With respect to the perceptual situation, towards which it is the instinctive response, anger is more closely associated with fear. McDougall thinks that anger "occupies a peculiar position in relation to the other instincts," because "it has no specific object or objects, the perception of which constitutes the initial stage of the instinctive process[1]." But in this respect it does not seem to differ from curiosity, from the acquisitive instinct, or, in our opinion, from fear. For, whether the exceedingly doubtful cases of the determination of fear by specific objects be accepted or not, it remains true that the great majority of instinctive fears, and by far the most important, are determined by specific kinds of situations, rather than by specific objects. Moreover James has pointed out[2] that the situations which produce fear produce also anger. After all it does not seem to be of much consequence whether an instinct is determined by a specific *quale* of situations, or by a specific object.

In the cases where, according to James, fear and anger are both produced by the same situation, though the two impulses are antagonistic, one does not destroy the other, but merely suspends it, and the two emotions may coexist. There is therefore no need to assume a special differentiation of fear, as Shand, for example, does[3], to account for the fighting of the animal which turns at bay. This phenomenon can be much more simply accounted for. On the one hand, there is anger present all along, its impulse being merely suspended. On the other hand, one of the most characteristic forms of anger is that aroused against any hindrance to, or interference with, the impulse of another instinctive tendency. This will be a reinforcement to the anger already involved, and hence, with the baulking of the impulse to escape, the animal or human being will turn in desperation, and with the most furious rage, upon the pursuer.

The situation of the animal at bay presents several very interesting psychological phenomena. In the first place, it

[1] *Social Psychology*, p. 59.   [2] *Principles of Psychology*, vol. ii, p. 415.
[3] *Foundations of Character*, pp. 202-3

illustrates the fact, that the stronger the impulse which meets a check, the fiercer as a rule is the anger aroused. This is also instanced in the anger aroused by sexual rivalry. In the second place, and in explanation of this fact, it must be noted, that it is almost quite generally characteristic of our emotional life, that the motive which finally determines action may draw a large part of its driving force from emotions experienced simultaneously, or so short a time previously, that the emotional disturbance has not had time to subside—emotions, which do not themselves issue in action at all, but which thus lend their force to an impulse, sometimes of a totally different kind. Some instances of the 'sublimation[1]' of the Freudians may be regarded as additional examples of this, but the sexual instincts are not by any means unique in producing such a result.

To return to the situations which arouse anger and the fighting impulse. In the case of the human being, any agent threatening 'danger,' and therefore evoking fear, may also evoke instinctive anger, any agent causing pain, injury, or loss to the 'self,' in its narrow as in its widest sense, any agent obstructing an impulse, or hindering the realization of an end. The instinct may therefore be said to have two main functions. Like fear, but not to the same extent, it is protective; like fear, but to a much greater extent, it is reinforcing. 'Anything that threatens or obstructs' would thus appear to be the general formula for the situations producing anger and its impulse.

What of the situations determining the hunting instinct? This question is a good deal more difficult to answer. Generally it seems that all objects which show the fear or flight impulse tend to arouse the hunting instinct. Hence it is evoked, not only by the fleeing enemy, but also by anything small, timid, or weak. At the same time it must be recognized that there are notable exceptions, due to the operation of other powerful impulses, and chiefly the parental instinct and sympathy. Most frequently, perhaps, the hunting instinct is enlisted in the service of some other instinct or appetite, more especially anger or hunger.

[1] See Jones, "Psycho-analysis and Education," *Journal of Educational Psychology*, pp. 241–256. 1912. Also references.

The cooperation of anger and the hunting instinct has been admirably described by James[1], but before going on to emphasize the psychologically important phenomena of this cooperation, there is one noteworthy fact in connection with anger, which is worth indicating.   The expressive signs of anger, when it is acting in cooperation with the hunting instinct, are usually very different from its expressive signs, as described by Darwin and others[2].   Or rather, some of the expressive signs of anger, which we generally regard as most typical, and which are so regarded by Darwin, and also by McDougall[3], would appear to be the signs, not of anger, as such, but rather of anger associated with a little fear, at all events of anger in its protective function. One anger is noisy, ferocious in aspect, as if to strike terror to the heart of the enemy, and so remove some part of the fear from its own; the other anger is stern, silent, and remorseless, pursuing its enemy, not frightening him away.   If the expressive signs of an emotion are constant in anything like the degree in which the quality of the emotion itself is constant, and there is good reason to believe that they are, then we can only count as expressive signs of anger those signs which are common in the two phases.   An anger that is complicated by fear, or by the hunting instinct, or an anger that has been baulked, and, because it has been baulked, has become a mad rage, cannot be taken as typical.

James, in our opinion rightly, explains many of the less amiable characteristics of the human being under certain circumstances, as due to the cooperation of the fighting and hunting instincts.   Of the ferocity and lust of blood, which may occasionally animate men, who normally are ordinary, law-abiding citizens, we find illustrations throughout history, and none more striking than in our own times, and among our own highly civilized peoples.   Such phenomena are most easily explicable, when we consider them as due, in the main, to this cooperation, especially when contagion has roused to a high pitch the emotional accompaniments of the two tendencies.

[1] *Principles of Psychology*, vol. II, pp. 411–415.
[2] See Darwin, *Expression of the Emotions*, pp. 240–253.   1872.
[3] *Social Psychology*, p. 61.

A great part of the disinterested 'cruelty' of children James would apparently explain in a similar way[1]. But 'cruelty' presents a rather complex problem. Some of the disinterested 'cruelty' of children, as, for example, the pulling off the wings and legs of insects, may have its source merely in curiosity, or the tendency to experiment, though the catching of the insect is undoubtedly due to the hunting instinct. The disinterested 'cruelty,' which kills all helpless creatures, is probably, in most cases, due to the hunting instinct pure and simple. But disinterested 'cruelty,' strictly so called, is quite cold-blooded. On the other hand, real cruelty is generally accompanied by a spasm of quite irrational and instinctive anger, and therefore passes easily over into the ferocity based upon the cooperation of anger and the hunting instinct.

It is thus necessary to discriminate. James quotes with approval in a footnote[2] a passage from Schneider. In Schneider's opinion, the curiosity itself is merely a manifestation of the hunting instinct, or of its impulse, after the prey is captured, and represents the tearing to pieces in order to devour, which naturally follows the chase with those animals which hunt their prey in order to satisfy their hunger[3]. We do not know that this will account for the phenomena in every case. There is good reason to think that a real and not apparent curiosity, and a real tendency to experiment, are involved in many cases.

[1] *Principles of Psychology*, vol. ii, p. 412.
[2] Op. cit., vol. ii, p. 411.
[3] Schneider, *Der menschliche Wille*, pp. 224–7. The chief points of the argument are: "Es ist Jedermann bekannt, welches Gefallen ein Knabe bei dem Anblick eines Schmetterlinges, Fisches, Krebses, oder eines anderen Thieres, und eines Vogelnestes empfindet, und welch starken Trieb er zum Zerzupfen, Erbrechen, Auseinanderlegen und Zerstören aller zusammengesetzten Gegenstände hat, welches Vergnügen er daran findet, einer Fliege Beine und Flügel auszurupfen oder irgend welche Thiere in anderer Weise zu quälen.... In vielen Fällen wird man sagen, dass der Knabe die Dinge aus Neugierde zerlege. Das ist richtig; aber woher kommt diese Neugierde?...Hier handelt es sich um vererbte Triebe, die selbst so stark sind, dass alle Ermahnungen und Strafen dagegen wenig ausrichten....Der blosse Jagdtrieb unterdrückt jede ihm entgegenstehende Regung, der Wahrnehmungstrieb, der ja immer stärker ist als der Vorstellungstrieb, siegt über letzteren, und die Jagd beginnt.... Unsere Vorfahren...haben an dem Verzehren der Beutethiere im rohen Zustande einen thatsächlichen Essgenuss gehabt....Jetzt hat der junge Mensch nicht mehr den Essgenuss...aber die causale Beziehung zwischen der Wahrnehmung dieser Dinge...und dem Jagdtrieb ist geblieben," etc.

The 'cruelty,' which arises from the hunting instinct alone, or from the hunting instinct supplemented by curiosity or experimentation, would seem to be comparatively harmless, and in normal children yields easily to the proper treatment. The 'cruelty' arising from the cooperation of the hunting instinct and an irrational, instinctive anger, is apparently in a different category, and a more serious matter. In extreme cases this may be a premonitory symptom of the maniacal thirst for blood, which has not infrequently shown itself in our midst, and which finds a ghoulish delight in murders of the most fiendish description. In all cases it presents a most difficult problem to the educator.

The emotional accompaniment of the hunting instinct has received no specific name. The probable explanation of this fact is, that the emotional accompaniment of the hunting instinct is so frequently associated with anger, and passes so easily into anger owing to the baulking of the impulse, which, from the nature of the case, must be the normal course of events, that it has never been popularly distinguished as a separate emotion. Nevertheless there can be no doubt whatsoever that there is such an emotion. It can be introspectively recognized, and it finds its purest expression in the realm of sport.

Both the fighting and the hunting instinct afford some confirmation to the view that at least one of the biological functions of play is its cathartic function. This is a modification of Stanley Hall's well-known recapitulation theory of play, due to Carr[1]. It seems as if the hunting instinct at least finds its necessary outlet in games and sport, is, as it were, canalized in such manner as to attain the satisfaction of its impulse under the conditions of modern civilized life, and consistently with these conditions, in the activities of the playground, the moor, and the hunting-field. It also illustrates very well James's principle of the 'transitoriness of instincts[2],' though it is very questionable if the result of non-satisfaction of an instinct at the proper time is ever mere atrophy of that instinct.

[1] Carr, *The Survival Values of Play.* University of Colorado Psychological Investigations. 1902.

[2] See Claparède, *Psychologie de l'Enfant*, p. 90, 3rd ed. 1909.

As for the fighting instinct, that finds numerous outlets in civilized life, far removed from the crude instinctive behaviour in which it originally issues. As a reinforcing agent, when difficulties have to be faced and overcome, its value, both to the individual and to society, is incalculable. Weaklings are what they are, as often through lack of anger in their constitution, or of its developed forms as organized forces in their character, as through excess of fear. By lack of anger we mean, not so much lack of the emotion, which is rather rare, as weakness in the instinctive driving force, the fighting instinct itself, of which anger is merely the emotional manifestation. To some extent the hunting instinct functions in a way similar to the fighting instinct in this respect. Under certain conditions, though not so frequently occurring conditions, it is also capable of acting as a reinforcing agent. In both cases we can get, in the life of the civilized and educated adult of the twentieth century, admirable instances of Freudian 'sublimation.'

The Gregarious Instinct. As we have seen, gregariousness has long been recognized as instinctive in Man. The classic description of the instinct, in the opinion of McDougall at least, is that given by Galton. Speaking of the wild ox of Damara-land, he says:—"Yet although the ox has so little affection for, or individual interest in, his fellows, he cannot endure even a momentary severance from his herd. If he be separated from it by stratagem or force, he exhibits every sign of mental agony; he strives with all his might to get back again, and when he succeeds, he plunges into its middle to bathe his whole body with the comfort of closest companionship[1]."

The perceptual situation, which determines this instinct, appears to be simply separation from 'kind,' and its interest is satisfied in being with the others. That it has operated on a very large scale, and in a very important way, in the evolution of societies, is indubitable. McDougall seems right in assigning to it also a large share in the sum total of influences, which have led to the rise and development of modern cities, and the

---

[1] Galton, *Enquiries into Human Faculty*, p. 49 (Everyman Edition).

depopulation of rural districts[1]. No doubt too, as he shows, it operates widely in bringing crowds together in the lecture-hall, theatre, or picture-house, to watch a procession, a race, or a football match.

To describe the instinctive impulse, as McDougall does, as arising out of the uneasiness felt at isolation from our fellows[2], is rather misleading. The instinct-impulse is the cause, not the effect, of the uneasiness. In fact the peculiar 'uneasiness' may be regarded as the emotional manifestation of this instinct. As an emotion it is not usually of sufficiently high intensity to have secured it a definite name, but it cannot be doubted that the more or less vague 'restlessness' is emotional.

It is perhaps a little unjust to McDougall to attribute to him the view that the gregarious impulse is determined by a prior 'uneasiness'; for his whole teaching is contrary to this view, and the only passage where it seems to occur is in the single sentence referred to. Nevertheless there is in the instinct itself something which suggests such a view, something which might even lead the psychologist to maintain that it belongs rather to the 'Appetite' group in our system of classification, an opinion to which Galton's description would lend some support. There is indeed something primordial about the whole experience involved in the operation of the gregarious instinct. Marshall holds that the 'social' instincts represent the latest stratum of instinctive development[3]. This, the 'mother tendency' of the 'social' instincts, as such, the 'social,' that is, as distinct from the 'family' instincts, bears all the psychological marks of a very ancient tendency. It is perhaps a matter for the biologist, rather than the psychologist, to decide, but, if the biologist should come to the conclusion that the gregarious instinct is indeed very ancient, the psychologist could not refuse him full support.

Gregariousness is as variable in different individuals as any instinctive tendency, but it is probably less modifiable than any, in this respect also resembling the 'Appetites.' But it

---

[1] *Social Psychology*, chap. XII.   [2] Op. cit., p. 84.
[3] *Instinct and Reason*, p. 173 ff.

would be a mistake to consider it entirely unmodifiable, for in the highly intellectualized human being its impulse seems to be directed to means of satisfaction quite different from those of the crude instinct, though, even in this case, the original impulse now and again may reassert itself.

The chief educational interest of the gregarious instinct arises from the fact, that, at the human level of development, its impulse takes the form which McDougall has called 'active sympathy[1].' The name is not without its disadvantages. It suggests a close relation to, and indeed dependence on, 'primitive passive sympathy,' to which suggestion McDougall himself appears to have yielded. There is really no reason to suppose that the relation to 'primitive passive sympathy' is anything more than incidental to the conditions under which, in this case, the gregarious impulse manifests itself. By saying that 'primitive passive sympathy' is incidental we mean that the sense of isolation is, in this case, produced by refusing or repressing any signs of sharing the individual's feelings. Nevertheless 'active sympathy' is itself the impulse of the gregarious instinct, and, in its pure state, of that alone.

The instinct is also educationally important, as the primary basis of the natural groupings of children in and out of school, and as furnishing, therefore, the original opportunity, outside the family, for the operation of the general social tendencies, imitation, sympathy, and suggestibility, determining that development of the individual as a social individual so carefully described by Royce, Baldwin, and others. Of course it is only the primary basis. It determines the formation of the group, but the organization of the group, without which even the gregarious instinct could not hold it together for long, depends on quite other conditions, for the operation of some of which the mere grouping affords, as we have said, the necessary opportunity.

We must not, therefore, attach too much importance to the gregarious instinct. It may lead to the formation of a group, and attract individuals to a group which has been formed, but, in maintaining the group, other factors are even more important.

[1] *Social Psychology*, p. 168.

These factors will depend on the nature of the group. On the lowest plane we have the crowd swayed by the same emotions, and while so swayed, having the same interests and aims. The larger the crowd, the more it attracts the individual, and the more completely it dominates the individual personality. The attraction and the dominancy are, however, not due to the gregarious instinct alone, but to the emotional satisfaction as a whole which the situation affords. There is a kind of intoxication by emotions. But strong emotions, by their urgency, attain their ends forthwith, or exhaust themselves by their own violence, and then the crowd, in spite of the operation of the gregarious impulse, gradually falls apart into the individuals composing it. On the highest plane we have the organized 'community,' with common interests and ends, not welded together by emotion, but held together by these common interests and ends, and therefore depending little upon the operation of the gregarious instinct.

In refusing to recognize the 'consciousness of kind,' alleged as the basis of the gregarious instinct and allied phenomena by Giddings, we are also inclined to agree with McDougall[1]. If by 'consciousness of kind' is meant some kind of instinctive or innate knowledge, then, as we have already seen, there is nothing in instinctive activity which requires us to postulate such a knowledge, and it creates more difficulties than it solves.

The Acquisitive Tendency. In spite of the numerous studies of the 'collecting' instinct, or habit, in children, there is, so far as we know, no good systematic psychological discussion of the instinct itself. McDougall has treated it very summarily. James has devoted to it a little more attention, but has given it by no means adequate treatment. Other psychologists have either ignored it altogether, or avoided the real psychological problems which it presents.

This is rather strange in view of the fact that no instinct, with perhaps one solitary exception, presents more and greater difficulties in its psychology, few present difficulties of which

[1] *Social Psychology,* p. 298.

the psychological solution is more interesting, and few play so prominent a part in the ordinary, everyday life of Man. There is no strong or exalted emotion, it is true, but the impulse to appropriate and possess is powerful in the adult, as in the child, in the civilized man, as in the savage.

The greatest psychological difficulty, which the instinct presents for our solution, is probably as regards the kind of perceptual situation which evokes it. It is almost impossible to make any statement, that it is evoked by this or that situation, without coming upon some manifestations of the instinct, which cannot be reconciled with the statement. If we say the instinct is determined by the perception of objects which give pleasure to the eye, the ear, or to any of the senses, we are faced with the numerous instances where worthless odds and ends, from which no sense-pleasure whatsoever can be derived, are appropriated and hoarded. If we suggest that rare objects evoke it, we are met with the cases of the misers who have hoarded old newspapers[1]. The miscellaneous collection in a schoolboy's pocket seems to defy any general formula, and, were a general formula found to cover all these objects, would it explain the case of the man who stole his own silver spoons from his own dining-room, to hoard them in his barn[2]?

A great part of this difficulty seems to arise from the fact that the tendency, if it is ever specific as regards its object, can easily attach itself to practically any object, and thus becomes almost 'general,' on what McDougall has called the 'afferent' side. This fact might even lead us to classify it among the general tendencies, were it not that the behaviour is always more or less specific, and generally highly specific. The emotional accompaniment too, though it has no definite name in popular speech, unless we take the word 'greed' to signify it, is unmistakably specific in quality.

If we attempt careful analysis, we shall probably come to the conclusion, that primarily any small object, which attracts the attention and pleases, evokes the acquisitive tendency; but, as we find it in Man, it is in the main determined by objects

---

[1] James, *Principles of Psychology*, vol. II, p. 425.
[2] James, op. cit., vol. II, p. 426.

apprehended as 'valuable,' and the attaching of 'value' to the object is largely, though not entirely, a social process. For that reason we classified the tendency as 'social.' We want to possess what others possess and prize, or what others would prize, if they possessed it. The objects sought will thus fall into two categories, and both categories, but especially the second, afford scope for almost infinite variety.

This relation to others seems to indicate that the self-tendencies are cooperating factors. The satisfaction in possession is not in the mere possessing, as it would be if the acquisitive tendency alone were operative, but in the effect of this possession on our relations with our fellows, an effect which may be either real or merely imagined. But, though this would possibly account for most of the phenomena, there are other phenomena which indicate that other tendencies may also cooperate—and almost any other tendency—in giving the 'value.'

Educationally the acquisitive tendency is significant in several ways, but there are two main points which deserve notice. The first is that it may be used as a source of interest both direct and indirect. What is a prized possession has already an interest, which may be utilized in the development of further interest; what would be prized as a possession has an interest, which will be transferred to the means which secure its possession.

The second is in connection with the development of the distinction between *meum* and *tuum*, not merely in theory but in practice. Though social in its origin, the desire to possess is, in the first instance, anti-social in its tendency. It is thus the cause of childish misdemeanours and crimes, which often give the parent and teacher much concern. In dealing with this problem, the principle to be kept in view is, that the recognition in act of the distinction between *meum* and *tuum* must be developed without the unnecessary weakening of a natural impulse, which, normally developed, contributes not a little to strength of purpose, will, and character in adult life.

Two courses may be followed, both of which are inconsistent with this principle, and both of which are unwise. On the one hand, we may attempt direct repression of the acquisitive tendency, and especially of illegitimate manifestations. This will rarely give more than apparent success, and is very likely to cause more evils than it cures. On the other hand we may attempt to weaken the impulse indirectly by developing 'giving' as a habit. To call this the development of generosity, is, in our opinion, to take an entirely wrong view of what is happening. Generosity is of course a valuable quality, but let us not be slaves to words. If the habit of giving away toys, for example, is developed in such a manner as to make the feeling of possession, and the pleasure in possession, practically non-existent, such generosity as results can be of very little moral value, and it has been obtained at a very heavy price[1].

Courtship and the Self-Tendencies. One reason for recognizing the courtship tendency as an original tendency, which may be distinguished from the sex 'appetite,' is that we do not think the latter alone can ever account for the facts of love between the sexes in developed human life; our reason for associating it with the self-tendencies is that, in the behaviour which it determines, it is almost inseparable from these. That we must recognize the impulse of sex on the two levels, the level of 'appetite,' and the level of 'instinct,' seems indubitable. Mating, even as low down as the birds, is not a matter of the sex 'appetite' alone. Some of the phenomena might be explained by James's principle of the 'inhibition of instincts by habits[2],' if we accept that principle, but there are phenomena which such a principle cannot explain. We do not, however, intend to discuss the courtship tendency at present, and have merely mentioned it for the sake of completeness, and because of its relation, as regards behaviour, to the self-tendencies, with which we are mainly concerned.

The self-tendencies, Ribot's 'positive' and 'negative self-feeling[3],' McDougall's 'self-display' and 'self-abasement,' or, as emotions, 'elation' and 'subjection[4]', have only recently

Cf. France and Kline, *The Psychology of Ownership*, Pedagogical Seminary, vol. VI, 1899, p. 455. Also Thorndike, *Educational Psychology, Briefer Course*, chap. IX.   [2] *Principles of Psychology*, vol. II, p. 394.   [3] *Psychology of the Emotions*, p. 240.   [4] *Social Psychology*, p. 62.

been adequately recognized in the psychology of motives.   One
or two of the earlier psychologists, as we have seen, recognized
some of their manifestations, but even James has missed them,
and, more strangely still, Shand, writing with the work of Ribot
and McDougall before him, has apparently chosen to ignore this
part of their work altogether, harking back to an older and
imperfect classification of the primary emotions[1]. On the
biological side, Darwin has given a very full treatment of
'self-display,' regarding it as a manifestation of the courtship
tendency[2], so that the psychologist must, in this case, grant to
the biologist the credit for calling attention to these tendencies,
before psychological analysis was able to discover them in their
purity.

The perceptual situation, which originally determines the
instinct of self-display, is the presence of another, and in some
way inferior, individual of the same 'kind,' that is, apart from
its manifestation under the influence of the courtship tendency,
while the perceptual situation, which determines the instinct
of self-abasement, is the presence of another, and in some way
superior, individual of the same 'kind.'   In the one case there
is perceptual consciousness of superiority, in the other of
inferiority, and probably in the most primitive manifestations
of the two tendencies the superiority or inferiority is nearly
always in size or strength.

The characteristic behaviour of the two instincts has been
admirably described by McDougall in the two words, 'strutting'
and 'slinking[3].' The accompanying consciousness, manifesting
itself in this behaviour, may be described as the 'am I not a
wonder?' consciousness, and the 'please don't notice me' consciousness.   The impulse attains its satisfaction, in each case,
when the other shows the opposite impulse and behaviour.

There are some difficulties with regard to the corresponding
emotions, which are not nearly so well defined as McDougall
would have us believe.   The tendencies are partly satisfied in
their own feelings, but the real satisfaction is nevertheless in
the signs in others of the opposite feelings, 'negative' with

---

[1] *The Foundations of Character*, book II.
[2] *The Descent of Man*, 2nd ed. pp. 394 ff.   [3] *Social Psychology*, p. 64.

'positive,' and 'positive' with 'negative.' If these signs fail
to be forthcoming, the impulse fails to find its satisfaction,
and this is the point at which we should, on analogy, expect
the emotional excitement to show itself, which, if the tendency
continued to be baulked, should ultimately give way to anger.
But—confining ourselves to the instinct of self-display, where
the emotional phenomena are more definite—we find that, in
this case of the checking of the impulse through failure to
elicit the appropriate signs from others, if there is any emotion
at all aroused, prior to anger, it is not 'elation' but the opposite
emotion. 'Elation,' and the corresponding triumphant air,
are really produced when the impulse has attained its end.

These phenomena—and the parental instinct exhibits
apparently phenomena of a similar or analogous nature—
appear to be fatal to McDougall's theory of the instinct-
emotions, but they seem to be equally fatal to our view. Is
it possible to retain our view of the nature of emotion, and
its relation to instinct-interest, at the same time explaining
these emotional phenomena? The solution we would offer is
this: In what we should call the 'joy' emotions, the emotional
'tension' may arise under conditions exactly the reverse of
those under which emotional 'tension' ordinarily arises. In
the ordinary case there is 'tension' because the satisfaction
of the interest lags behind the impulse. In the case of the
'joy' emotions, there may also be 'tension,' because the satisfaction of the interest outstrips action, because action cannot
follow with sufficient rapidity an impulse stimulated by the
satisfaction already attained, which, from the nature of the
case, is always of the stimulating order. When an attempt
is made to interpret either 'elation,' or some of the emotional
accompaniments of parental affection, anger, and several other
instinct-emotions, in a way consistent with McDougall's position,
the denial of the emotional character of 'joy[1]' seems to make
the attempt quite hopeless.

The difficulties are by no means surmounted by considering
'elation' in connection with the self-tendencies alone. Consider the fighting instinct. There is sometimes in the operation

---

[1] *Social Psychology*, p. 149 ff.

of this instinct a 'joy' or 'elation,' which is quite independent of the satisfaction of the impulse, so far as that consists in the destruction of an enemy, and which cannot be considered to arise from anger at all. For some natures merely to fight is "to drink delight of battle," the delight being in the struggle itself, not in its successful issue. This is the kind of fighting instinct which has characterized the great warriors of all ages. In other spheres of action it has also characterized the great sailors, explorers, even reformers. It is *par excellence* the characteristic of a warlike race, and, because of this, the warlike races are nearly always capable, on occasion, of the highest chivalry, for, when they fight, they are inspired by the joy of battle, not by hate of the enemy. The hunting instinct and the acquisitive tendency often exhibit analogous phenomena.

How can we account for such phenomena? One way of accounting for them is by an appeal to the play impulse. But, as we shall see when we come to discuss play, this will not account for the facts. The battle which is a joy is not play, but the grimmest reality; if it were play, the joy would disappear, or at least be radically altered in quality. The real explanation is to be found rather in the cooperation of the 'positive' self-tendency, in the feeling of strength and power developed when we assert our superiority to circumstances, and confidently face a difficult or dangerous situation. This seems to be the only way in which we can explain the joyful emotion, which appears to be quite different in quality from the normal anger of the fighting instinct. We must take into account, as before, the exhilarating character of the 'positive' self-feeling itself, which, stimulating the impulse, develops 'tension' by outstripping the possibilities of action. So is it always in the intoxication of joy, the 'tension,' in the extreme case, being relieved by an emotional 'storm,' usually what we call 'laughter,' the 'sudden glory' of Hobbes, but often by the opposite kind of emotional 'storm,' 'weeping,' and sometimes by a mixture or alternation of the two.

Ribot[1] meets the difficulty of explaining 'joy,' by contending, like McDougall, that we cannot consider 'joy' emotional,

---

[1] *Psychology of the Emotions*, p. 15.

since it is not really separable from sense-pleasure, and therefore belongs with pleasure and pain, as a general characteristic of emotional experience. We have already suggested that pain may be emotional. Where sense-pleasure or any pleasure passes beyond the mere 'satisfyingness,' which we have already discussed, and involves 'tension,' as described, there seems no reason to deny to it also emotional character. So too with grief or sorrow. It is not the case that joy and grief are characteristic of all emotional experience. They are specific, 'joy,' we believe, to the 'positive' self-tendency, with the possible exception that parental affection may sometimes involve an independent 'joy,' 'grief' to the parental instinct, with the possible exception that 'subjection' may sometimes involve an independent 'grief,' but in both cases we doubt the real independence[1].

Very considerable light is thrown upon these phenomena by the fact that the self-tendencies occupy an anomalous position in another respect. In their case it is only in the very young child that the pure instincts, operating at the perceptual level, make up any significant proportion of the total manifestations of the instincts. As soon as the idea of self emerges, a self-sentiment is formed, and, thenceforward, they operate mainly in relation to this sentiment. In this connection we shall have to consider their operation later. In the meantime it is merely necessary to point out that the formation of the self-sentiment inevitably changes the relation of these tendencies to all other instinctive tendencies. Their operation may come, as it were, to cover the whole field. What I think, what I feel, what I do, so far as these come under the observation of other people, are parts of the 'self,' with reference to which the self-tendencies may operate. My sentiments, my opinions, my emotions, my beliefs, my actions, my habits, are all parts of ME, and 'positive' self-feeling is experienced, whenever these meet the approving regards of other people, 'negative' self-feeling, whenever they are disapproved. This is really the primary fact to keep in view in connection with the social and educational significance of the self-tendencies.

[1] See Appendix III.

At the purely instinctive level, however, and apart from their relations through the self-sentiment, these tendencies exert their characteristic moulding influence on the behaviour of individuals, which makes them at all levels so important socially and educationally, a moulding influence, because they necessarily imply a relation to others, and the recognition of the superiority or inferiority of others. Self-display will not repeat that behaviour which fails to procure its satisfaction. 'Negative' self-feeling will open the door wide for the operation of the general tendencies of imitation and suggestibility. Thus, at the purely perceptual level, these tendencies operate, with the gregarious instinct, and its impulse, in assimilating to one another the individuals of a society, in opinion, feeling, and action.

The Parental Instinct. In the parental instinct, with its emotion, we have another tendency, which, in its developed form in the human being, reaches a high degree of complexity, and which presents some of the same psychological difficulties as the self-tendencies. Its importance is also at least equal to theirs. As one main source, perhaps the only source of altruistic conduct, it is probably more important from the social point of view than even the self-tendencies, and certainly deserves the very careful attention of the moralist.

In man the instinct itself, as McDougall has very clearly shown[1], is practically altruistic, for, though phylogenetically based on the instinct of the mother, it has become the instinct of male and female alike, but perhaps not normally to the same extent, and, as impulse and emotion, it has expanded far beyond the perceptual situation which originally evoked it. In man the impulse is not necessarily confined to the individual's own offspring, but may take within its range all children, even all the weak, helpless, and suffering. It may develop, indeed, so as to cover all humanity, and every living creature. In crude instinctive human life, we may regard the parental instinct as the counterpoise to the hunting instinct; in developed human life it may become the counterpoise to all the selfish tendencies.

[1] *Social Psychology*, pp. 69–71, 73–79.

Primarily the perceptual situation which evokes the instinct is the need or distress of the individual's offspring, expressing itself in the characteristic cry. Even at this stage the impulse is altruistic. Normally, in the human being, the instinct is aroused by the cry of any child, in need, helpless, or distressed. The impulse is always to protect and relieve. In this instance simple statements like these tend to be misleading, owing to the very great complexity of the instinct in man, and the variety of situations which may evoke it, the complexity and variety being the result of a long process of evolution, both individual and social. The mere sight of weakness and help-lessness, without any need or distress, much less any cry of distress, is generally sufficient to determine the impulse and its appropriate emotion, while a child's cry of distress arouses the emotion in such intensity, that it passes almost immediately into anger at the cause of the distress.

When we consider the emotional accompaniments of the instinct, we meet difficulties analogous to those we have already met in the case of the self-tendencies. The instinct-emotion itself McDougall, following Ribot[1], calls 'tender emotion.' The name is not very satisfactory, but it is difficult to suggest a better. 'Love' is more appropriately applied to the sentiment, and to apply it also to the primary emotion is simply to create confusion; 'affection' might be used, but this also suggests a sentiment; 'kindly feeling' does not sufficiently express the emotional character, nor does 'tenderness.' We seem, therefore, almost compelled to accept Ribot's term.

Shand denies that 'tender emotion' is primary, and would substitute 'pity' as the primary emotion[2]. Possibly this is a mere matter of terminology, but it indicates a real and important underlying difference and difficulty. 'Pity,' as popularly used, names an emotion which is certainly not primary. Starting from this popular sense of 'pity,' Shand maintains, that we may have 'pity,' which does not involve sympathy, and in that case we have a real primary emotion, a "kind of sorrow[3]." It must

---

[1] *Psychology of the Emotions*, p. 233.
[2] Stout, *Groundwork of Psychology*, chap. XVI, p. 202.
[3] *Foundations of Character*, p. 203.

be remembered, however, that Shand takes a view similar to ours with regard to the nature of emotion, holding that it is always due to some checking of an impulse, some delay of action.

McDougall agrees with Shand in analysing 'pity,' as popularly understood, into the two elements, sympathetic pain, and his primary, 'tender emotion[1],' while he maintains that 'sorrow' is more complex, since it involves a sentiment of love or affection, whereas 'pity' may be felt, when there is no such sentiment[2]. And McDougall holds, in opposition to Shand's view, that the primary 'tender emotion' is always "pleasantly toned, save at its highest intensity[3]." At the same time, one cannot help feeling that McDougall's whole description of 'tender emotion,' and the situations which evoke it, is inconsistent with this contention that it is always pleasantly toned. Thus he says: "the impulse is primarily to afford physical protection to the child[4]," and the original "provocative of tender emotion is not the child itself, but the child's expression of pain, fear, or distress of any kind[5]." Again, he points out that "there are women, who cannot sit still, or pursue any occupation, within sound of the distressed cry of a child; if circumstances compel them to restrain their impulse to run to its relief, they yet cannot withdraw their attention from the sound, but continue to listen in *painful agitation*[6]."

The conclusion, that is forced upon us even by McDougall's own description of the phenomena, is that to say it is always pleasantly toned is to contradict some of the main facts brought forward in the description. It must be remembered that, in so far as any impulse attains its end, there is pleasure as 'satisfyingness.' If the intensity of the emotion varies with the 'satisfyingness,' we appear to have a case similar to 'positive' self-feeling, already discussed. If not, that is, if the emotion varies with the 'tension,' in the more usual sense of the satisfaction of the impulse being delayed or suspended, Shand is not far wrong, in finding in this primary emotion—whether we call it 'tender emotion' or 'pity'—the germ of 'sorrow.'

---

[1] McDougall, *Social Psychology*, p. 253.   [2] Op. cit., loc. cit.
[3] Op. cit., p. 150.   [4] Op. cit., p. 72.   [5] Op. cit., p. 73.
[6] Op. cit., p. 73. The italics are ours.

Hence, the solution of the difficulty is, we believe, to be found in recognizing that the 'tender emotion' is a 'joy' emotion, and, next to the emotion of 'elation' itself, *the* 'joy' emotion. It may be that the 'tender emotion' alone, without the cooperation of 'positive' self-feeling, gives a 'joy' of its own, qualitatively different from any other emotion, and primary, but we do not think this is a true description of the phenomena. We must clearly recognize, that, where 'tender emotion' becomes 'joy,' it is always developed in relation to a sentiment of love or affection. From the very nature of affection, the object of affection becomes, in a very real sense, a part of the 'self.' We should therefore interpret the 'joy' of 'tender emotion' in the same way as we interpreted the 'joy' of anger, as due to a fusion of 'tender emotion' with 'elation,' in presence of a sentiment of love for the object.

If we employ the term 'tender emotion' in a more restricted sense, to denote the primary emotion corresponding to the parental instinct, when aroused under the ordinary conditions of 'tension,' and recognize that, as emotion, it is tinged with pain or 'sorrow,' as Shand suggests, then we have an emotion corresponding to 'subjection,' which is not unlike 'subjection' in some respects, and which will readily fuse with it. We may call this 'tender sorrow,' but there is no 'sorrow' in a strict sense. 'Sorrow' or 'grief,' in the strict and purest sense, is probably best interpreted as a fusion, in presence of a sentiment of love, of the two emotions 'subjection,' and 'tender emotion,' and that which is most characteristic of it is the latter.

This interpretation of the facts seems to involve a recognition of, not one, but two primary emotions, corresponding to the parental instinct. It may be that this is necessary. We are, however, inclined rather to the view, that there is only the one primary emotion, as such, the second, and that, in the first case, 'tender emotion' is not present as emotion, just as anger is not present as anger in the joy of battle. This is our real position, though, in describing the phenomena just now, we have perhaps been unconsciously influenced by McDougall's view of the nature of emotion, and have employed language, which may be a little ambiguous.

Curiosity. Several of the older psychologists, as we have seen, from Descartes to Dugald Stewart, gave particular notice to 'curiosity,' as an instinctive tendency, and Adam Smith[1] has discussed carefully and at length the allied emotions. In modern times Karl Groos has discussed curiosity as a form of play[2], and most biologists and comparative psychologists have noted instances of the tendency in the animal world. The fullest treatment in recent psychology is that of Shand[3]. McDougall's treatment is brief, and contains little of interest. He uses the word 'curiosity' to name the instinct, attaching to it the primary emotion 'wonder.' But, in this case at least, the one term can very well be employed for both instinctive tendency and emotion. Not only so, but something of the nature of emotion is, in this instance, probably felt whenever the instinctive tendency is operating. This view Shand apparently would not accept, for he maintains that curiosity is 'impulse' rather than 'emotion[4],' but surely it is not the impulse that we primarily call 'curiosity.'

The instinctive tendency is easily described. The determining perceptual situation is anything which is new or, within limits, strange. The impulse is to examine, and, if necessary, approach, and handle, for purposes of examination, the novel object.

If 'curiosity' is to be regarded as an emotion, as well as an instinct, it becomes necessary to give some account and explanation of 'wonder.' Probably few psychologists would agree with McDougall[5], in any case, in holding that 'wonder' can legitimately be used to express the primary emotion, corresponding to the instinct of curiosity, although apparently Shand does agree[6], and even goes farther, implying that this use is quite in keeping with the ordinary use of the word. Except in the not infrequent use of 'wonder' as a verb, in such expressions as: "I wonder if so-and-so has happened,"

---

[1] *History of Astronomy.*
[2] *Die Spiele der Tiere*, p. 238 ff.   English translation, p. 214.
[3] *Foundations of Character*, book II, chap. XVII.
[4] Op. cit., p. 441.
[5] *Social Psychology*, pp. 58–9.
[6] *Foundations of Character*, p. 442 ff.   It must be remembered however that Shand regards emotion as due to 'arrested impulse.'

and the like, "wonder," as ordinarily used, always implies
more than curiosity, and even in the case of the verb, which
is most usually only another way of expressing a question,
the interest which prompts the question is not necessarily a
'curious' interest. Most psychologists would agree that
'wonder' is baffled curiosity, but beyond that it would be
difficult to find agreement. The fact is, that 'wonder' is used
very loosely in popular speech; sometimes it is equivalent to
surprise, sometimes to curiosity, sometimes to a fusion of the
two, and sometimes to a fusion of curiosity, surprise, and
'negative' self-feeling.

The main psychological problem, in this connection, appears
to be the mutual relations of surprise, curiosity, and wonder.
Surprise, as we have already indicated, is the emotional response
to 'unexpectedness,' and passes into curiosity, when the situation is not calculated to arouse fear, anger, or some such emotion,
but continues to present a question, that is, when the 'unexpected,' which is always allied to the 'novel,' becomes the
'novel,' which, as 'novel,' arouses the enquiring impulse.
Wonder is developed as the consciousness of a baffled enquiring
impulse developes, but curiosity still persists in wonder, until
the wonder passes into blank astonishment, or, in the extreme
case, amazement. According to this view, there is the question,
the striving to answer the question, the baffled striving still
continuing, the 'giving it up,' corresponding to the 'unexpected,'
the 'novel,' the 'wonderful,' and the 'amazing.'

This appears to be the simplest account and explanation
of the various emotions, and, as such, ought to determine the
psychological use of the various terms. If this view is accepted,
'wonder,' in its simplest and most elementary form, is baffled
curiosity, with perhaps a return of some of the original surprise[1].
It is therefore hardly to be regarded as a primary emotion in
the strict sense.

There are perhaps two objections to this view. In the
first place, it may be argued, that we have already defined
emotion as 'tension,' due to the checking of impulse. If the

---

[1] Shand, *Foundations of Character*, p. 444 f. Bain, *The Emotions and the Will*, chap. IV.

emotion 'curiosity' already involves the checking of impulse, how is a further checking, and a new and different emotion arising therefrom, possible?   The answer is, that we must take the facts as we find them, and suit our explanation to the facts, not attempt to make 'facts' to fit our explanation.   If it is of the nature of this particular impulse 'to know,' that it should always be accompanied, as we maintain that it always is accompanied, by the experienced 'tension' we call the emotion 'curiosity,' we must just accept the fact; if the baffling of the impulse 'to know' always gives rise to a new emotional experience, which we agree to call 'wonder' in the strict sense, then we must also accept this second fact.

In the second place, it may be argued, that in every other case an instinct has associated with it, and characteristic of it, one, and only one, emotion, while, in this case, we appear to have three or four.   Again, if the facts compel us to take such a view, there does not seem to be any escape from it. But the facts do not really force us to go so far.   Surprise may require to be regarded as a primary emotion, but the primary emotion, corresponding to the instinct of curiosity, is the emotion of curiosity; the others are secondary, not primary. That curiosity should, under certain conditions, pass over into wonder, is at any rate not more peculiar than that fear should, under certain conditions, pass into anger, or that 'tender emotion' should pass into sorrow.

The importance of curiosity and wonder, as the basis of that 'intellectual curiosity' and disinterested love of the truth, which furnish the driving power in scientific research, and philosophical investigation and speculation, has been sufficiently emphasized in the past, and by many writers of all shades of opinion.   Perhaps it has been over-emphasized.   In education, at all events, the tendency has been to interpret that interest which the teacher must utilize and guide, in order that successful school work may go on, almost solely in terms of curiosity. This involves two educational errors.   The one lies in ignoring, or belittling, practical interests, which are sometimes more valuable, and often more fruitful, than theoretical interest. The other is what amounts to an assumption, that theoretical interest is always reducible to curiosity.   To interpret curiosity vaguely as the impulse, or desire, 'to know' amounts to a suggestion that the questioning attitude always involves curiosity, when, as a matter of fact, it frequently does not involve curiosity at all, or only to an insignificant extent. A gap in my knowledge may be theoretically of no significance, I may not even be conscious of it as a gap, while practically it may mean the difference between success and failure in something I wish to do. In such a case—and in everyday life there are scores of them—it is some other impulse, not curiosity, that makes me conscious of the gap, that gives it significance, that furnishes the motive force inducing me to strive to fill it up, that gives, in other words, the desire 'to know.' The other side of the story has been so often emphasized, that there seems little danger in occasionally emphasizing this side.

Many other tendencies, apparently belonging to this group, have been claimed as simple and instinctive by various writers, but in practically every case these can be clearly shown to be either complex, or manifestations of one or other of the tendencies we have discussed. Thus James would recognize 'sociability' and 'shyness[1],' 'secretiveness[2],' 'cleanliness[3],' 'modesty' and 'shame[4],' 'love[5],' 'jealousy[6].' Some of these are merely alternative names for tendencies we have discussed. 'Secretiveness' is the only one which offers any difficulty, and that seems to be, not a single tendency, but the manifestation, under certain conditions, of several, as, for example, fear, acquisition, self-abasement. The others are obviously either derived or complex, and some can be shown to involve sentiments, which we shall proceed to discuss immediately.

Shand, in his *Foundations of Character*, sets himself the problem of discovering and formulating the fundamental principles of human character. Working over only part of the ground, for he announces another similar work on the 'sentiments,' he has succeeded in formulating as laws one hundred and forty-four such principles. The psychologist can only regard this formidable total with dismay. If this is to be taken as the only possible kind of formulation of the laws

[1] *Principles of Psychology*, vol. II, p. 430.   [2] Op. cit., vol. II, p. 432.
[3] Op. cit., vol. II, p. 434.   [4] Op. cit., vol. II, p. 435.
[5] Op. cit., vol. II, p. 437.   [6] Op. cit., vol. II, p. 439.

of character, a science of character, in any real sense, must be regarded as unattainable.

Nevertheless it is undoubtedly possible to formulate laws, applicable to the emotional 'instinct' tendencies, which will be fundamental, general, and few, and such laws may justifiably be regarded as the fundamental laws of human character, to the extent that these tendencies form its basis. Of laws of this kind there appear to be at least five, if we include two, for which James is responsible, and these laws may be called: the *law of transference of impulse*, the *law of fusion of emotions*, the *law of complication of behaviour*, the *law of inhibition by habit*, and the *law of transiency*.

(1) The law of *transference of impulse* may be expressed in the form: as a result of experience, and under certain more or less definite conditions, the instinctive impulse may come to be evoked in connection with objects or situations, different from those which originally evoke it.

This law was recognized by Spinoza and Malebranche, Hutcheson, Hume, and Adam Smith, and great stress was laid upon it by the English Associationists. McDougall has also treated it in some detail[1]. In human life, the most important case of 'transference' is probably from the end to the means for attaining that end. But similarity also determines 'transference,' and likewise association by contiguity in space or in time, as McDougall very clearly shows. At the same time we must be very cautious in ascribing to mere contiguity a result, which, in this as in other cases, is really due to the fact that the part-experience gains significance from the whole of which it is a part. In other words, we may classify the case of 'transference,' as due to association by contiguity, but it is explicable only in terms of meaning. Curiosity may afford an exception to this law, if we take it in any strict sense, but it is apparently the only exception.

(2) The law of *fusion of emotions* may be expressed in the form: any primary emotion may fuse with any other primary emotion, with certain possible exceptions, to produce an emotional experience, different from the emotions involved, and *suo genere*, but in general analysable into its elementary components.

---

[1] *Social Psychology*, pp. 34–40.

An exception may be 'positive' and 'negative' self-feeling, which, if McDougall's analysis is right[1], alternate, rather than fuse, to give the complex emotional experience we call 'bashfulness.' It must be noted, however, that the fusion is more or less incomplete in cases where the respective impulses are incompatible, and, in such cases, the component emotions are as a rule easily distinguishable.

(3) The law of *complication of behaviour* follows from the law of *fusion of emotions*, and may be expressed in the form: where different impulses are evoked by the same situation, and different emotions fuse in the resulting experience, the behaviour will at all times be a complication of the behaviours corresponding to the respective impulses; where there is imperfect fusion, owing to the incompatibility of the impulses, the behaviour will show alternation, rather than complication, and occasionally both.

It is perhaps worth remarking, that, in the case of the human being, instinctive behaviour is highly modifiable, but this does not apparently affect the operation of the law.

The next two laws, the law of *inhibition by habit*, and the law of *transiency*, have both been fully discussed by James[2] and we may therefore take his statement of the laws.

(4) "When objects of a certain class elicit from an animal a certain sort of reaction, it often happens that the animal becomes partial to the first specimen of the class on which it has reacted, and will not afterward react on any other specimen[3]."

To a certain extent this may be regarded as a law of the formation of a sentiment, but it also appears to be valid apart from a sentiment, in the usual sense at least. We shall discuss the sentiments presently.

(5) "Many instincts ripen at a certain age and then fade away[4]."

To these five laws we might perhaps add two other fundamental laws of human character, which have a somewhat wider range, but also apply to the instinct tendencies,—the *law of selection by experienced results*, and the *law of development by stimulation*.

The only additional remark we have to make is in connection

---

[1] *Social Psychology*, p. 146.   [2] *Principles of Psychology*, vol. II, pp. 394–402.
[3] *Op. cit.*, p. 394   [4] *Op. cit.*, vol. II, p. 398.

with the fifth law. Whether the law is generally operative or not, it is certain that, in the cases where it is operative, the final result cannot be adequately expressed by the phrase 'fade away,' if that implies no effect left on the nature and character. This is very obvious with some of the more important tendencies, and presumably a similar phenomenon may, on careful investigation, be found in the case of all. Many facts, quite apart from those brought to light and emphasized by psycho-analysts, indicate that there is a process of 'replacement' or 'sublimation,' which may be of the nature of 'transference,' as we have explained it, but often is not, and which may exercise a profound influence upon character and development. This kind of result is most evident, perhaps, in the case of instincts and appetites bearing upon the preservation of the race, but it can be shown to hold of many other instinctive tendencies, and it is important in exact proportion as they are important in 'full,' normal life[1].

The 'Pure' Instincts. The complex emotional instinct tendencies are comparatively easy to specify with more or less correctness, and to describe. It is not so with the simple or 'pure' instinct tendencies, partly because of the fact that the line of demarcation between them and reflexes is very difficult to draw, except theoretically, and partly because they are very early overlaid by numerous 'learned reactions.' Nevertheless it is at least possible to indicate, as we have done, the main groups in which these tendencies may be classified.

There appear to be four such groups. We may speak therefore of instinct reactions of adjustment and attention, instinct reactions of prehension, instinct reactions of locomotion, and instinct reactions of vocalization, giving, in each case, a fairly wide signification to our terms. Some of the reactions which would be included under each head may be reflex, but there cannot be any doubt that many of them are instinctive. Tentatively we should classify under the first head (reactions of adjustment and attention) 'sucking,' 'biting object placed in the mouth,' 'licking,' 'pointing,' and the like; under the second head,

---

[1] See Jones, "Psycho-analysis and Education," in *Journal of Educational Psychology*, vol. I, 1910, p. 498, vol. III, 1912, p. 241.

'clasping object placed in palm of hand,' 'grasping after distant object,' 'carrying object to mouth,' and the like; under the third, 'sitting up,' 'standing,' 'creeping,' 'walking,' 'running,' 'climbing,' or at least the initiatory movements in each; and under the fourth, 'crying,' 'babbling,' 'echolalia.'

Though the psychology of these 'pure' instinct tendencies is naturally simple, the part played by them in the development of the human being is by no means unimportant. Quite the reverse. The 'motor adaptation[1],' through which the child comes to recognize and know his material world, is founded upon and developed out of these unlearned instinct reactions; speech itself, the gateway to the child's social world, is no less founded upon them; and all physical dexterities, in particular, represent chains of activities, the first links of which are always, or almost always, these same simple instinct reactions.

The mode in which these developments take place can also be described in more or less general terms. One of two things may happen in any particular case. On the one hand, a reaction may, owing to circumstances, create a situation which has an interest in relation to some one or other of the complex emotional tendencies, and the course of activity thus initiated is maintained by the interest in question. On the other hand, results produced may be satisfying with reference to an existing instinctive, or more generally appetitive, tendency, and the particular reaction tends thenceforward to be bound up with the particular appetite. The process has been admirably described by Stout[2], except for the fact that Stout largely ignores, or seems to ignore, the instinctive basis of the whole.

Thus, while there is no evidence in the case of the human being of anything approaching the long chains of 'pure' instinct actions, which we find in some of the lower organisms, we can also say that there is no need of, nor any opportunity for, instinct manifestations of this order. Without them the provision of the means of adjustment is complete, and on better lines and after a more efficient model for the particular kind of work in hand.

---

[1] Stout, *Groundwork of Psychology*, p. 91. See also *Manual*.
[2] Op. cit., chap. VIII.

CHAPTER IX

INTERESTS AND SENTIMENTS

We owe to Shand[1] a specialization of the word 'sentiment' for psychological purposes, which almost all the psychologists of the present day adopt. According to this use, a 'sentiment' is defined as "an organized system of emotional tendencies, centred about some object[2]." As Stout[3] puts it, "an object which has been connected with agreeable or disagreeable activities, which has given rise to manifold emotions, which has been the source of various satisfactions or dissatisfactions, becomes valued or the opposite in and for itself," and we call the organized disposition, thus formed, a 'sentiment.'

Theoretically this definite recognition of the 'sentiment,' as an important determining element in human behaviour, seems valuable, and even necessary, for psychology; but practically it involves several difficulties of a more or less serious nature, which psychologists have almost entirely ignored. If we take McDougall's definition, which is probably the clearest and the most concise of the various definitions, our first difficulty arises when we try to attach a fuller meaning to 'organized system of emotional tendencies.' The main questions that face us are: What is organization of emotional tendencies? How many tendencies must be involved before we can speak of an organized system? How is an organized system of emotional tendencies, centred about an object, developed?

Before attempting to answer these questions, we shall postulate that a sentiment is to be regarded, not as innate,

---

[1] Art. "Character and the Emotions," in *Mind*, N. S., vol. v.
[2] McDougall, *Social Psychology*, p. 122.
[3] *The Groundwork of Psychology*, pp. 221-2.

like the instincts, but as a product of experience, and as involving the ideational, as distinct from the perceptual level of intelligence, and therefore a psychical integration that is on a higher plane altogether.

This postulate is inconsistent with Shand's view, that some of the sentiments are innately organized[1]. We can find nothing in the evidence he brings forward in support of this thesis, that cannot be more easily interpreted without assuming innate sentiments. He first of all argues that "all primary emotions and impulses are innately connected with the emotion of anger[2]." So far as this is merely another statement of the fact that interference with the working out of any natural tendency may evoke anger, we of course accept it, but without accepting Shand's view of the primary emotions as 'systems,' thus innately connected with the anger 'system.' When he goes on to argue that the satisfaction of any instinctive impulse involves 'joy,' and its frustration 'sorrow[3],' we are quite unable to agree, without attaching such meanings to 'joy' and 'sorrow,' as to empty them of their whole specific content as emotions.

Hence we are quite unable to accept Shand's conclusion that the primary emotional systems of anger, fear, joy, and sorrow are innately connected with every emotional impulse and with one another[4], in any sense corresponding to the sense in which he understands this connection. It goes without saying, therefore, that we cannot accept the view that this innately organized system of emotional tendencies is also innately connected with certain objects.

The organization of emotional tendencies in the sentiment can only mean for us the association through experience of certain emotional tendencies with an object, or rather idea. This involves that such organization as there is must be looked for in the idea, not in the emotional tendencies themselves. In so far as several emotional tendencies are associated with the idea of an object, so that the emotions tend to be

---

[1] *The Foundations of Character*, book I, chap. IV.
[2] Op. cit., p. 35. [3] Op. cit., p. 36.
[4] Shand, op. cit., p. 37.

readily evoked by the appropriate situations of the object, either perceptually experienced, or ideally represented, the sentiment itself, as a 'disposition,' may be said to be an organized system of tendencies. The first question, therefore, if our postulates are granted, does not present any serious difficulty.

Answering the second question, we may legitimately maintain that a single emotional tendency, with the idea to which it is connected, is an organized system of the kind we call a 'sentiment.' Morton Prince defines a sentiment as "an idea linked with an instinct[1]." And our view practically amounts to this. Any instinct may, in ideational consciousness, pass into a sentiment. If an emotion, say fear, is so strongly associated with a certain object, that, whenever the idea of that object rises in consciousness, the emotion to a greater or a less degree is experienced, there seems no sufficient reason for refusing to recognize this as a sentiment. If we always deal with complex sentiments, we shall always have extreme difficulty in arriving at a real psychological understanding of the character of the system or disposition. It is important that we should recognize the sentiment in this its simplest form[2]. Even in this form it may have considerable complexity, due to the fact that the idea itself has its associations, the idea itself is a centre of relations.

Our third question can now be answered with comparative ease. When any emotion is intensely or frequently excited by any object, the idea of that object, whenever it comes into consciousness, reinstates, or tends to reinstate, the emotion. Thus the simplest kind of sentiment is formed as an 'emotional disposition' in ideational consciousness. Once formed, a sentiment, especially if it is frequently active, tends to develop in strength and in complexity, and it may develop in complexity in two ways. On the one hand, the emotionally tinged idea carries its emotional accompaniment with it, so to speak, into the various ideational complexes into which it enters. On the other hand, the fact that an idea already

---

[1] *The Unconscious*, p. 452.
[2] McDougall also recognizes this. Op. cit., p. 163.

carries with it an emotion tends to cause other emotions to be easily aroused in connection with it, and an emotional complex is therefore formed around the idea in question.

Examples of both kinds of development are by no means rare, either under normal or under pathological conditions. The commonest examples of development in complexity on the idea side are probably those cases, where a concrete particular becomes a concrete general sentiment, as when love for a particular dog develops into love for dogs in general. An example of development on the emotion side is where what begins as a sentiment of fear develops into a sentiment of hate. Thus an individual A is associated in our minds with a terrifying experience or with frequent terrifying experiences. At first the idea of A is merely the centre of a fear sentiment, but the fear sentiment will easily develop into hatred, and, under certain conditions, as, for example, if A belongs to a different town, or, better still, to another nation, it may also become a hatred of all who belong to that town or nation.

Before going on any farther, it is necessary for us to try to determine the exact relation of a sentiment to an instinct. An instinct may also be regarded as a 'disposition,' in virtue of which an individual experiences a certain emotional excitement in presence of a particular object or situation. How does it differ from a sentiment? We might answer by saying that the one is innate, the other acquired as a result of experience. But this difference, however important it may be, does not appear to be the distinction upon which the psychologist ought to lay chief stress. Psychologically the main distinction is that the instinct 'disposition' is perceptual, that is, involves only perceptual consciousness, while the sentiment 'disposition' is ideational, and is a sentiment because it is ideational. This means that the sentiment 'disposition' may become active, and therefore its emotional tendency may be evoked, independently of the perceptual situation which is required to evoke the same emotional tendency in the case of the instinct.

Unless we keep firm hold of this distinction, our recognition of sentiments can only lead to confusion. We have already seen that in Man an instinctive tendency may, as a result of experience, come to be evoked by an object or situation different from that which originally and naturally evokes it, and some of our human instincts are more or less generalized in this respect, apart from experience. At first sight it seems merely an extension of these phenomena, when an instinct, or rather its emotional tendency, becomes associated with the idea of an object or situation, in the case of the human being, or of any animal capable of ideal representation. But it can easily be shown that the formation of a sentiment involves more than the extension of instinct phenomena.

The sentiment provides a setting which controls and limits the activity of the instinct. This is perhaps best seen in the way of repression. In the case of an instinct, as we have seen, the evoking of an emotion by a particular situation does not inhibit the evoking of any other primary emotion at the same time by the same situation. The emotions evoked may show more or less fusion; only their impulses, if antagonistic, tend to inhibit, or inhibit, one another. It may be objected that there are cases where instincts totally inhibit one another, and it must be granted that this may be so in the case of the two self-tendencies, or perhaps anger and the 'tender emotion.' In the latter case, however, it is certain that we may have also emotional fusion of a kind, though the impulses tend to inhibit one another, and at any particular moment only one can operate. Further one and the same object may evoke different instincts with their emotional accompaniments, if presented in different perceptual situations. In both instances the effect of a sentiment is to introduce stability and control, by inhibiting instincts and emotional tendencies which would otherwise be evoked. This repressive function of the sentiment also explains how and why sentiments can, to such an extent, control opinions and beliefs. Its repressive action is by no means confined to perceptual experience, and many of the 'dissociations' of abnormal psychology are also to be explained in this way.

There is another relation of the sentiment which is important psychologically. That is the relation of a sentiment to an acquired interest. This problem has been very much neglected

14—2

by psychologists, and recent psychologists, with the exception of Stout[1], have almost altogether ignored this relation.

The two usages of the word 'interest,' as applied to an experienced feeling, and as applied to that which determines the objects, with regard to which we shall have the feeling, can be at times very confusing. When we speak of 'an interest' or 'interests' in the plural, we are generally using the term in the second sense. Baldwin and Stout suggest[2], that we ought to distinguish between the two meanings, by using a different terminology in each case, and they propose the terms 'actual interest' and 'dispositional interest.' Perhaps it would be better to speak of 'interest experience' and 'interest disposition,' but, at all events, some such distinction would be a psychological convenience.

Now an instinct is an 'interest disposition,' since it determines 'interest experience' in relation to particular objects. We must therefore distinguish further between native and acquired 'interest dispositions.' Are we then to regard a sentiment as simply an acquired 'interest disposition' on the ideational level? If I have an acquired interest in, say, botany, can I call this a sentiment of 'love for botany'? Surely there is some distinction underlying even the loose popular use of the terms, although popular speech often confuses the two. The distinction seems to be, that the activity of a sentiment always involves emotional excitement, whereas the activity of an 'interest disposition' involves merely 'worthwhileness,' 'interest experience.' In a sense the sentiment is merely a particular type of 'interest disposition.' Nevertheless the distinction seems worth drawing and worth adhering to.

This distinction is interesting in view of our refusal to admit McDougall's contention, that the evoking of an instinct necessarily involves an emotional excitement. Acquired 'interest dispositions,' like sentiments, are based upon instincts. Just as the instinct may be active without emotional excitement, so the 'interest disposition' at the higher level, founded upon it and developed out of it, may be active without emotional

[1] See *Groundwork of Psychology*, p. 221.
[2] *Dictionary of Philosophy and Psychology*, s.v. Interest.

disturbance; while, just as the activity of the instinct may, under other conditions, involve emotional excitement, so we have the sentiment founded upon it, and developed out of it, largely through and because of this emotional excitement, involving always in its activity some emotional disturbance.

In the human being, though the acquired 'interest dispositions' and sentiments play an analogous part on the ideational level to the part played by the instincts on the perceptual level, they also involve a synthesis, or an integration, of a higher order. The part played by simple interests and sentiments, corresponding to individual instincts, is comparatively unimportant. In most cases our acquired interests merge in one or other of the great sentiment complexes which are developed. These great sentiment complexes supply, as it were, the final reservoir of energy. Normally the 'interest experience,' determined by an acquired interest, passes into 'satisfyingness' without any emotional excitement. But if there is a check, if some obstacle intervenes, the necessary energy to overcome it is drawn from the appropriate sentiment, and the strength of the impulse seeking satisfaction, and therefore the amount of resistance that will be overcome, depends, in the last resort, on the organized force which the sentiment represents, or at least that part of the organized force, which, in the particular circumstances, can be brought to bear.

In some respects this might be regarded as a repetition of instinct phenomena, for certain instinctive tendencies, as we have seen, are reinforcing agents, but it is a repetition of the phenomena on a higher plane. Organized force, in place of individual force, is evoked, and for that reason the emotional excitement will much more rarely reach the intensity which paralyses action or renders it ineffective.

It must be recollected too that every idea belongs, not merely to a knowledge system, but also to an interest or sentiment system. This we might infer from our previous discussion of 'meaning.' But independent evidence is forthcoming in various phenomena of ideomotor action, of suggestion, and of abnormal conditions of consciousness. On the basis of this fact, an explanation of the affective element in belief may be

obtained.   Belief, in any real sense, is more than mere cognition.
It has relations to feelings and action, which some psychologists
have emphasized as the essential elements of the conscious
state.   Obviously this relation to feeling and to action in the
experience is due to the fact that a belief is either itself an
'interest disposition,' or an element in an 'interest disposition'
or in a sentiment.

Finally we must recognize that, under normal conditions,
there is a 'dispositional whole,' so to speak, which controls
human experience and action.   McDougall has shown that
this 'dispositional whole,' constituted by 'interest dispositions'
and sentiments, presents usually in its arrangement a kind of
hierarchy[1].   There is a relative order of dominance, often with
one single dominant or 'master' sentiment.   Dominance is
determined partly by the original strength of the interests
involved, partly by the organization of the system, and partly
by the frequency with which it has operated in the past.
Hence habit, too, in its wider aspect, habits of thought and
attitude, must be studied in relation to interests and sentiments.
It is unfortunate that this part of psychology should be in so
backward a state, for the importance of the psychology of
habits, interests, and sentiments to the educator can hardly
be overestimated.

We employ the word 'sentimental' to describe two kinds
of character, the character whose actions are swayed by sentiments rather than reasoned principles, and the character of
those people who tend to revel in the emotional excitement
itself, which the activity of a sentiment involves.   The first
of these meanings, at least, leads us to another important
distinction, more particularly as regards the abstract sentiments, that is, the distinction between sentiment and 'ideal.'
Consider, for example, the sentiment 'love of justice' and the
'ideal of justice.'   What is the psychological difference between
the two?   It would appear to be this.   The sentiment 'love
of justice' is a disposition, constituted by certain emotional
tendencies, that is, those characteristic of 'love' sentiments,
associated with the abstract idea of justice.   The 'ideal of

[1] *Social Psychology*, p. 259.

justice,' on the other hand, involves reflection upon the meaning
of 'justice,' and the acceptance of justice as a determining end
of action, that is, recognition by the 'self' of 'justice' as representing *law* for the 'self.'   Thus the ideal, though it is generally
based upon the sentiment, is more than the sentiment, and
involves activity on a yet higher plane, and a yet larger synthesis.   This distinction is obscured in popular usage, but is
worth being adhered to and emphasized in psychology.   Action
determined by sentiment may show all kinds of inconsistencies
and incongruities, owing to two facts, the fact that it is emotionally controlled, and the fact that the ideational consciousness, at the heart of the sentiment, is not rationalized by reflection upon the meanings of the ideas involved and their relations.
Action determined by an ideal is, within the limits of the ideal,
consistent and harmonious.   The ideal therefore represents a
higher level of psychical integration than the sentiment, just
as the sentiment represents a higher level than the instinct.

We have no intention here of entering upon a detailed
discussion of the psychology of ethics, but the points we have
touched upon had to be cleared up for two reasons, in the first
place, in order to show how the instincts of man are involved,
and their operation complicated, in the characteristic processes and dispositions of the human mind, in the second place,
in order to make intelligible some parts of our subsequent
discussion of the general instinct tendencies.

To enumerate the sentiments in any human being is impossible, but it is possible to classify them.   Various schemes of
classification have been proposed.   That which seems most
convenient for psychology is into 'simple,' and 'complex,' on
the emotional side, and then into 'sentiments of love and
hatred' and 'sentiments of value,' under each head.   The
classes 'sentiments of love and hatred' and 'sentiments of
value,' do not appear to be mutually exclusive, and, indeed,
the latter seem to cover the whole field.   This difficulty can
be obviated by explicitly excluding the former, and calling
the class 'sentiments of value, which are not sentiments of love
or hatred.'

A 'simple' sentiment consists of a single emotional tendency, associated with an idea or idea-complex. Such sentiments are numerous, and are very prominent characteristics of various pathological conditions, like the 'phobias.' Under normal conditions, such sentiments play a relatively unimportant part in human behaviour, as compared with the 'complex' sentiments. The 'complex' sentiment consists of more than one emotional tendency, associated with an idea or idea-complex. The great 'complex' sentiments may be exceedingly complex on both sides.

The 'sentiments of love and hatred,' or 'sentiments of attraction and aversion' are those we usually think of when the word 'sentiment' is used. They are numerous, and some of them are of very great importance. The idea at the centre of the sentiment need not be the idea of a person. We have such sentiments as, love of home, love of animals, love of the sea, love of justice, dislike of animals, dislike of traits of character, dislike of material things, belonging to the class of which we usually take affection for friends and hatred of enemies as the typical sentiments. Such sentiments are generally complex on the emotion side, but not often very complex on the idea side. They are relatively simple, compared with some of the great general 'sentiments of value.'

In a sense all sentiments are 'sentiments of value.' We may nevertheless conveniently distinguish by this name sentiments involving primarily neither like nor dislike, neither love nor hatred. These constitute the most important group of all in the normal, developed character, the group to which the great sentiments, like the religious sentiment, the national sentiment, and the personal or 'self' sentiment, belong. These great 'sentiments of value' are in the highest degree complex, both on the emotion side, and on the idea side. This becomes very evident, when we consider the extent to which they tend to 'polarize' words[1]. The religious sentiment best illustrates this effect, and the words, which the followers of certain religions consider it blasphemy to utter, may be regarded as striking instances, though they are extreme cases. The pervasiveness of any sentiment may be judged from its polarization of the

[1] Oliver Wendell Holmes, *The Professor at the Breakfast Table.*

words expressive of ideas belonging to its system. All words, which are significant to any individual, are to a certain extent polarized for that individual, since meaning, as we have seen, is primarily affective. But such polarization is very different from the polarization of a word, which, when uttered, causes emotional reverberations through the whole nature. This effect on words may, therefore, be taken as an index, not only of the extent of the system, but of the strength of the sentiment, the intensity of the emotional tendencies it organizes.

McDougall has traced, carefully and in detail[1], the development of what he calls the 'self-regarding sentiment,' but we prefer to call simply the 'self sentiment,' showing what an important part it plays in the formation of character and the control of behaviour. The 'self sentiment' appears to us to play an even more important part than that assigned to it by McDougall.

The two self-tendencies, very early in life, attach themselves to an 'idea of self,' thus forming a sentiment. From one point of view, this 'idea of self' is almost entirely the idea of a social self from the outset, the idea of a system of relations between the 'self' and other 'selves' being predominant in the sentiment[2]. Just because the self-tendencies necessarily involve a social reference, the development of this aspect of the 'self' will be controlled throughout by the social reference, and the expansion of the 'idea of self' to include all those things, with which the 'self' is identified, which become or may become objects of the "judgments, emotions, and sentiments" of other men[3], family, home, school, church, native town, native land, will depend on the relations of the 'self' with other 'selves.'

But the 'idea of self' develops in a more intimate way, which, though also socially conditioned, is not to the same extent dependent upon this social reference. The 'self,' as it were, extends inwards, as an organizing influence. All sentiments, in so far as they are 'sentiments of value,' become, in proportion to the extent to which they are 'sentiments of value,' integral parts of the 'self.'

[1] *Social Psychology*, chaps VII, VIII, IX.　　　[2] Op. cit., p. 186.
[3] Op. cit., p. 206.

Something in which I am deeply interested, a religious belief, it may be, is spoken of disapprovingly or slightingly. There may be no reflection upon me, either expressed or implied. Yet the sentiment directly involved is not left to fight the battle alone. The fact that the opinion is *my* opinion inevitably involves the 'self sentiment' also. The circumstances may even be such as to favour a cold, dispassionate argument, as to the merits of the case, but nine times out of ten, if there is a strong sentiment involved, the matter is treated as a personal matter, and the emotional tendencies of the 'self sentiment' play their part, sometimes to create lifelong enmity between two people, because of a slight difference of opinion which, on the surface, appears merely intellectual.

If this phenomenon occurs with opinions strongly held, it occurs far more frequently with the sentiments of affection for individual persons. The greater the affection, the more intimate becomes the connection with the 'self,' and the more readily does the 'self sentiment' become involved in the activity of the 'love sentiment.'

Any attempt to interpret such phenomena in terms merely of social reference will inevitably represent only half the truth. Under normal conditions, the 'self sentiment' must be regarded as occupying an unique position among the sentiments, and among the interests, in virtue of which it is an organizing force of the utmost importance.

When the 'self sentiment' is lacking, or weak, or developed in a one-sided way, the whole personality is involved in the weakness or one-sidedness. Overweening self-confidence, lack of self-confidence, pride, servility, vanity, lack of self-respect, are not characteristics of a single sentiment, but of the character as a whole. Further, as McDougall has also very clearly shown, a 'master' sentiment in the hierarchy of sentiments, which takes the place of the 'self sentiment' as the organizing force of character, however powerful it may be, can produce in the character as a whole only the appearance of strength, which may deceive for a time, but ultimately is almost certain to reveal the real weakness in a time of crisis[1].

[1] *Social Psychology*, pp. 260-61.

CHAPTER X

THE GENERAL 'INSTINCT' TENDENCIES

Of the general instinct tendencies, which McDougall terms—in our opinion too widely—'general innate tendencies,' play, imitation, and sympathy are frequently spoken of as instincts. If the difference between such tendencies and instincts is merely the difference between general and specific, which ultimately appears to reduce itself to a difference of degree, then there is little to be said in criticism of such a way of speaking. There is, however, a further distinction to be drawn, as regards the interest or emotional factor involved. When we contrast imitation with anger or fear, it is evident that the emotional factor is a pronounced characteristic in the latter case, but hardly obtrudes itself, even as felt interest, in the former. Even in this respect the distinction does not seem an absolute one. For curiosity does not show any very pronounced emotional tone, and the acquisitive tendency still less, that is to say, under normal conditions. Here too then the difference appears to be merely one of degree between the general and specific tendencies.

So much may be conceded, and yet the classification of the instinct tendencies into general and specific may be none the less convenient, though the line of demarcation between the two groups may, on closer examination, prove to be somewhat arbitrary. All the general tendencies are general, in that their arousal is not dependent upon a specific object, situation, or idea, nor even upon a more or less specific kind of object, situation, or idea, and in that the behaviour to which they lead, their expression, is as little specific. That they involve an affective element, an interest, goes without saying, but this affective element is not of the nature of emotion, nor does it show any tendency to develop into a particular and characteristic emotion in each case. And there is one other distinguishing mark, which might almost be called decisive. Under normal conditions the general instinct tendencies do not determine ends, but rather attach themselves to, and operate in connection with, ends ultimately determined by the specific emotional tendencies. There may be some apparent exceptions to this principle, and particularly in the case of play, but they are exceptions of the kind which 'prove the rule.'

These general instinct tendencies, like the specific tendencies, have all been fully discussed and described by various psychologists, notably by Karl Groos, by Baldwin, and by McDougall. Our purpose here is, as before, to indicate those points which appear to be of educational interest, rather than to traverse ground already traversed.

Play. The classical discussion of the play tendency is that of Karl Groos[1], though the theory of the biological function of play, which is generally associated with his name, can be traced, as we have already seen, to much earlier writers. Groos apparently finds no difficulty in treating play as an instinct, even though he interprets it so widely as to include experimentation, to some extent imitation, and even 'love play' or courtship. We must remember, however, that Groos regards instinct from the purely objective point of view, that, in his opinion, "the idea of consciousness must be rigidly excluded from any definition of instinct which is to be of practical utility[2]."

This wide interpretation of play by Groos tends to obscure his view as to the psychological nature of play, as does his biological conception of instinct. Nevertheless, though it looks like an inconsistency, Groos, unlike many of his successors, examines the psychological aspect of play very carefully. Apparently McDougall, in criticising the theory of play developed

[1] *The Play of Animals*, and *The Play of Man*.
[2] "Der Begriff des Bewusstseins ist vielmehr überhaupt beiseite zu lassen, wenn man den Instinkt in brauchbarer Weise definieren will." *Die Spiele der Tiere*, p. 57. Trans., p. 62. See also McDougall, op. cit., p. 30, footnote.

by Groos, has forgotten this part of his work[1], since he thinks it necessary, in order to account for play, to modify this theory "by the recognition of some special differentiation of the instincts which find expression in playful activity[2]." Undoubtedly this would be necessary, if we were to try to account for certain psychological phenomena of play by any purely biological theory, and, in that case, a biological interpretation of the instincts, differentiated or not, would not carry us very far. But the accusation cannot be justly laid against Groos, that he has neglected these psychological phenomena, for, as we have said, he has discussed the psychological nature of play, as well as its biological function.

Our interest being mainly psychological, our first and chief question is naturally this one regarding the psychological nature of play. In what respects are playful activities differentiated from serious activities, play from work? The first and most easily recognizable psychological mark of play activities is their 'worthwhileness' and 'satisfyingness' in and for themselves. That is to say, the activities are exercised for their own sakes, not for the results which may be obtained through them.

Karl Groos seems to reject the view that this is a mark of play, but on grounds which are entirely insufficient. "It seems a very mistaken proceeding," he says, "to characterize play as aimless activity, carried on simply for its own sake[3]." This conclusion is arrived at in view of the fact that the pleasure afforded by play may be accounted for in other ways, as due to the satisfaction of the instinct involved, or to the pleasure of energetic action, simply as exercise, or to the 'joy in success, in victory,' the satisfaction of that 'striving for supremacy,' which is instinctive.

Groos quotes in support of his conclusion Souriau, Lange, and Grosse, but the gist of his argument, including these quotations, is that in play we always have an end to attain, the

---

[1] *Die Spiele der Tiere*, Chap. v, in English translation.
[2] Op. cit., p. 112.
[3] Op. cit., Eng. trans., p. 291. In his second edition (1907) Karl Groos has made several changes at this point, but the main effect of the argument seems unchanged.

value of which is enhanced by the imagination, that the player always looks to the results of his efforts, and that a game which is not competitive fails to interest.

Now we may grant that all this is true, and yet hold that the play activity, as such, is carried on without any reference beyond itself. In a game the naïve play activity is organized with reference to an end, and there is satisfaction in attaining the end, and also, if it is a competitive game, in beating our opponent, but, even in a game, the activity has a 'worthwhile-ness' and 'satisfyingness' of its own, and the end may some-times be specially created for the sake of that activity. Where play involves exercise, it is true that the exercise, as such, has a stimulating effect on the whole organism, and is felt as exhilara-ting, but this effect can still be distinguished from the enjoyment of the activity as play, and the distinction becomes clearer, when we place exercise, which is taken as exercise, it may be from a due regard to physical health, alongside of exercise which is involved in play.

The statement that in play we always have an end in view, and look always to the results of our activity, will not bear examination, when it is made regarding all play, alike play unorganized, as in day-dreaming, the random running, jump-ing, and the like, of young children, what we call friskiness in many young animals, and play organized in the form of a more or less definite game. Dewey has recorded an observation very much to the point here. "In watching a group of six-year-old children I noticed the following: About half of the children played the game, i.e., they planned their movements to get to the goal first. The other half were carried away with what they were immediately doing; if the one who was 'It' got to running away from the goal, he kept on running, in spite of the fact that others were making for the goal. Their present activity was so immensely satisfying that it was impossible to check and guide it by some result to be reached, even such a simple one as touching the goal first[1]."

The last sentence gives Dewey's interpretation of the obser-vation, and it is also ours. We fail to see that any other

[1] *The School and the Child* (edited by Findlay), pp. 75–6.

interpretation of this, and numberless phenomena of the same kind in children's play, is possible. It might be argued of course that in all such cases the child is following some instinctive line of behaviour. That may be, but at any rate there is no conscious end beyond the activity, no looking for results outside the activity, and that is the essential point which we wish to emphasize.

We may take it then that the first mark of the play activity, as distinguished from serious activity, of play as distinguished from work, is that, in the former case, the activity is pursued for itself without reference to results, in the latter case it exists for the results. For Groos this distinction is obscured by his inclusion of the experimentation tendency under play.

But, since this distinction applies only partially, if even partially, to organized play or games, it is necessary for us to seek a further means of psychologically distinguishing play from the serious occupations of life, or work in a general sense. This second distinction, upon which Groos lays chief stress, and which undoubtedly cuts very deep into our whole mental life, is virtually that between 'belief' and 'make-believe[1].' We may put it this way. A game is play organized with reference to a definite end. The end, as end, has value. But the value of the play end is a 'make-believe' value, that is to say, it does not belong to the systems of ends and values characterizing real life. In the attitude we call 'belief' we are conscious of a 'real,' to which our actions must adjust themselves. This means that, in so far as we feel that our actions are conditioned by a world of reality, over which we have no control, and which exists independently of us, our attitude is that of 'belief,' and this attitude of 'belief' underlies all our serious occupations, not only as regards the conditions to which we must adjust ourselves, but also as regards the ends or values which we seek to attain, as regards the conditions, because they are conditions imposed by the 'real,' as regards the ends or values, because they belong to a world of ends and values, also apprehended as real.

---

[1] See Stout, *Analytic Psychology*, vol. II, chap. XI.

By saying that the end or value sought in a game is a 'make-believe' end or value, we mean that we are conscious of the value as depending upon ourselves, and not as forming part of a real world over which we have no control. We, as it were, make the world of values and conditions for ourselves, and then 'make-believe,' pretend, that it is real, but remain all the while conscious, 'at the back of our minds,' that it is only 'pretend.' This is the source of the feeling which Baldwin calls[1] the 'don't have to' feeling.

Why do we 'make-believe' in this way? Either because the 'make-believe' is itself pleasant or satisfying, because it is itself a play of the imagination, or because we wish to play, and make a 'pretend' end in order to play. In either case this second distinction, however deep it may go, is obviously not the fundamental and ultimate distinction, but is derived from the distinction we have already drawn, the distinction which depends on recognizing play as an activity in and for itself.

This second distinction is not without its psychological difficulties, and the most serious of these arises from the fact that in a game more than mere play is involved. In the first place the choice of end or value is not entirely a choice at random. Only certain 'pretend' values will have an appeal. We must recognize, therefore, that the other instinctive tendencies of the human being will necessarily have a share in determining the ends to be sought in a game, just as they determine the ends sought in a serious occupation. And, as we have already seen, some of our human instincts in the developed civilization of the present day issue mainly in the form of play. In the second place emulation and rivalry exert a considerable influence in most games, and introduce, therefore, another additional factor. The source of this influence must naturally be sought in the self-feelings, and tendencies, which we have already discussed. What is the effect of this influence on a game, as play? It may obviously cause a very considerable complication. For this influence will add to the energy with which the end is sought, and sometimes to such an extent that the other motives—the other instinctive tendencies

[1] *The Play of Animals*, Editor's Preface.

involved with the play motive itself—are almost entirely submerged, and the play motive entirely.   When that takes place, it is very questionable how far we are still entitled to call the game play, and we know that, practically, play may be transformed into earnest quite suddenly.   Theoretically, however, the psychological separation between play and earnest can still be made on the basis of our second distinguishing mark, even when our first distinguishing mark has practically disappeared, for earnest will not supervene on play while the mental background remains that of 'make-believe.'

A third difficulty arises when we consider the professional player of any game.   Does he play, or is he engaged in his serious occupation or work?   As in the case we have just considered, the answer will depend on his psychological condition at any moment.   In so far as he is conscious while 'playing' that he is earning his livelihood, just in so far his mental attitude is 'belief,' and he is working.   But if, and so far as, he forgets all about the world of real things and values—and this must generally, we believe, be the true psychological state, in the great majority of cases—and, remembering only the 'pretend' end of the game, realizes only the pleasure of playing the game, he is really playing.

This 'make-believe' attitude which characterizes organized play may be otherwise described as detachment from the world of real life.   Groos works out a very interesting parallelism between the phenomena of work and play, in this respect, and the phenomena of alternating, dissociated, or multiple personalities[1].   The 'make-believe' in play is, as he points out, of the nature of more or less conscious self-deception.   The deeper we become engrossed in the play activity, the more does the real world recede from consciousness, and also the real self that acts in the real world.   In the extreme case, this detachment of the world of play from the real world, of the self that plays from the self that acts in the real world, may take on a pathological character.   This or an analogous danger has long been recognized as one of the dangers of over stimulating or overindulging the aesthetic imagination of the child.   The danger

---

[1] *The Play of Animals*, English translation, p. 303.

is present in all play, when carried to excess, and is not confined
to the aesthetic imagination as a form of play. There is one
definite group of the derelicts of life, characterized by the fact
that the play world has usurped for them the place of the real
world, and the play personality has become dominant over the
work personality. "All work and no play makes Jack a dull
boy." All play and no work makes the man, that grows out
of the boy Jack, a hopeless inefficient in the world of the
'real.'

Baldwin has indicated another danger, involved in the
'don't have to' feeling, that is characteristic of the 'make-
believe' consciousness[1]. That is the danger which may arise
from a misinterpretation of the freedom of play, leading to a
confusion of such freedom with moral freedom, not so much
on the part of the child, as on the part of those responsible for
the child's education, as the parent, the teacher, or even the
educational theorist who lays down principles for the guidance
of the parent or teacher.

The sense of freedom involved in play may be said to be of
two different kinds. In the first place, there is the sense of
freedom which arises from the fact that the ends which I value
in play are valuable largely because I make them so, and the
conditions to which I adjust myself in attaining these ends are
the conditions of a self-created world. In the second place,
there is the sense of freedom arising from the consciousness
that I can leave off when I want to, that I am under no compulsion to play. The freedom that matters in the game of life
differs essentially from both. The ends and values are not
ends and values because I will them to be such, though I exercise my moral freedom in willing them as ends and values for
me. When I come to a moral crisis in life, it is not open to me
to say "I don't want to play," though the compulsion is an
inner compulsion. That organized games are a valuable moral
influence, cannot be gainsaid, but it must at the same time be
emphatically asserted, that their value in this direction is
strictly limited. A game is a game, the rules of a game after
all are simply rules of a game. But life is real, and the law of life

[1] *The Play of Animals*, Editor's Preface.

a real law. That children should do what they like, when they like, and how they like, in the interests of their moral freedom, is, taken by itself, a very dangerous principle.

There is one other point, in connection with the psychological nature of play, that deserves some little notice. Groos makes play fundamental in the development of the aesthetic consciousness. Now aesthetic creation is undeniably a development of play activity in many cases. But this is not quite the same thing as saying that aesthetic appreciation is derived from the play impulse. A detailed analysis of aesthetic appreciation is quite out of the question here, but certain general and more or less obvious principles may be indicated, upon which its explanation would seem to depend. Partly no doubt aesthetic appreciation depends upon absorption in, and fellow feeling with an object (what German writers have called *Einfühlung* and *Einsfühlung*), but it depends also on pleasure-pain experiences, which are deeper and more fundamental than the play impulse. Absorption in, and fellow feeling with an object depend to some extent on 'make-believe,' and to that extent on what is undoubtedly the play impulse, but they depend also on sympathy, on imitation, and on suggestibility. Hence to derive the aesthetic consciousness entirely or mainly from play, appears to be quite illegitimately narrowing the scope of aesthetics, and the appeal of the aesthetic.

When we consider the biological function of play along with its psychological meaning, we have the key to its educational significance. The theory of the biological function of play, which Karl Groos develops, may be called, as Baldwin suggests, and as Karl Groos himself calls it, the 'exercise theory' of play. According to this theory, activities, which are of service in real life, are developed through play. These activities are of two kinds, corresponding more or less to the two aspects of play we have already considered. On the one hand, there are relatively general activities, involving the development of motor coordination and control, of sensory experience, and of general psychical functions. On the other hand, there are relatively special activities, directed towards the attainment of special ends instinctively determined, developing at one and the same time a fuller consciousness of these ends, and a command over the means necessary for attaining them.

The specific instinctive impulse operating through play is best seen, as far as the human being is concerned, in hunting games or games of combat. But other general tendencies also operate through, or with, play, and this is particularly the case with imitation. Hence, apart from the operation of any special instinct, we may have the development of domestic games and social games, which are of the utmost importance in preparing for the domestic and social activities of adult life.

Experimentation. Very closely associated with the play tendency, and, in its manifestations, very difficult to distinguish from it, is the tendency we have called 'experimentation.' Groos includes it under play. Several other writers include some of its manifestations under play, but assume also an instinctive tendency, which they call 'constructiveness' (e.g., McDougall), and some assume even two specific tendencies, 'constructiveness' and 'destructiveness,' while a few writers recognize all three, experimentation, constructiveness, and destructiveness, as independent of one another and of play.

There seems no good reason for the unnecessary multiplication of instinctive tendencies, and experimentation, as a general tendency, can obviously be made to include both constructiveness and destructiveness, at the same time explaining them, for there is not sufficient evidence to justify us in regarding them as specific instinct tendencies. On the other hand, if we include experimentation under play, we thereby lose to a considerable extent one of our criteria of play. For in play the activity itself, as we have seen, satisfies, while it is of the nature of experimentation that the *results* of the activity should be the source of satisfaction.

The pleasure of 'being a cause[1]' does not quite adequately express or describe the nature of the interest involved in experimentation. If it did, we might perhaps be justified in including experimentation under play. The interest is rather

---

[1] *The Play of Animals* (translation), p. 88.

an interest, not in producing as such, but in what is produced, and in this aspect the tendency is more or less allied to curiosity.

In animals as in young children, this tendency is often very clearly shown. Perhaps the best description of the kind of actions in which it manifests itself is the description by Miss Romanes of the behaviour of a cebus monkey[1]. "To-day he got hold of a wine-glass and an egg-cup. The glass he dashed on the floor with all his might, and of course broke it. Finding however that the egg-cup would not break for being thrown down, he looked round for some hard substance against which to dash it. The post of the brass bedstead appearing to be suitable for the purpose, he raised the egg-cup high over his head and gave it several hard blows. When it was completely smashed he was quite satisfied."

Hobhouse has placed on record his opinion that animals learn more from experimentation than from imitation[2]. Whether the same is true of children or not, it is at least certain that they do learn in this way, and that this tendency plays a very important part in extending their experience, as well as in developing motor control. As regards its biological function, therefore, experimentation may be said to supplement play, and to cooperate with imitation, in preparing the child, both generally and specially, for the activities of adult life.

The most interesting point in connection with experimentation, at least from the standpoint of a psychology of education, has been very little noticed by previous writers. That is its relation to what may be called the 'work' tendency, as opposed to the 'play' tendency. At a certain stage in the development of the child, usually somewhere about the seventh year, there is an important transition from interest in the activity to interest in the result produced, as an *intended* result. This we may call the development of the 'work' tendency, which differs from experimentation, in that the interest in experimentation is satisfied with whatever result emerges, while in the case of 'work' the result which emerges is not satisfactory,

---

[1] Romanes, *Animal Intelligence*, pp. 484–95.
[2] *Mind in Evolution*, p. 204, footnote.

unless it is the result aimed at, or sufficiently approximating to that to be taken for it by the child.

Though the 'work' tendency may, therefore, be distinguished from instinctive experimentation, it may also be regarded as a development from it. And experimentation certainly cooperates in rendering results, of little significance to the child in themselves, sufficiently interesting as results, and as the results intended, to stimulate long and strenuous effort.

Imitation. Like experimentation, imitation has been included under play by Karl Groos. There is no doubt that the three tendencies have a great deal in common. They all involve activity on the part of the individual, generally, though not necessarily in the case of play and experimentation, manifesting itself in outward action. They also combine and cooperate in so many and so intricate ways, that it is often difficult to disentangle the exact share of each in a particular activity, where all are playing their part.

Imitation, however, has one characteristic, which, theoretically at any rate, marks it off unmistakably from the others. It is a social tendency, dependent on the interaction of at least two individuals, and, as a social tendency, it is allied to sympathy and suggestibility, rather than to play and experimentation. Baldwin, indeed, includes sympathy and suggestibility under imitation[1]. Such procedure is more capable of defence than that of Karl Groos, for sympathy can easily be regarded as imitation of feeling or emotion, and suggestibility as imitation of opinion or belief.

It is most convenient to separate these three social tendencies by restricting imitation to the direct copying of behaviour. Theoretically the distinction is sufficiently clear. Practically there is a similar difficulty to that experienced on the other side, as it were, in separating imitation from play. Both sympathy and suggestibility may lead to the same kind of behaviour as would be produced through direct imitation.

---

[1] *Mental Development in the Child and in the Race,* and *Social and Ethical Interpretations of Mental Development.*

Hence, from the objective side, it may be quite impossible to say whether any behaviour is due to imitation, to sympathy, or to suggestibility. The evidence of introspection will, as a rule, serve to distinguish; where this is not available, the distinction must always be more or less hypothetical.

In contrast with those who have endeavoured to explain much of the apparently instinctive behaviour of animals as due to learning, largely through imitation, Thorndike would deny that there is such an instinctive tendency as general imitativeness, at least as a characteristic of the child[1]. The apparent results of such a tendency he would explain as the result of learning from experience, or an illustration of the 'laws of habit[2].' This position, so far as it bears upon the learning of animals, has been very carefully examined by Hobhouse[3]. If it means that animals and young children do not imitate indiscriminately any and every kind of action, that their imitative behaviour is not wholly undetermined by other instinctive factors, we should be inclined to agree. Imitation will certainly depend on 'attentiveness,' and attention will be determined by some interest. Hence imitation will be of behaviour which is interesting, and presumably interesting because of its appeal to specific instinctive tendencies. From this point of view, Thorndike's contention is simply another way of expressing the opinion we have expressed, that ends are determined by the specific tendencies, and that the general tendencies attach themselves, as it were, to ends already determined.

But, even when we consider them objectively, the facts do not warrant Thorndike's conclusion that there is no general instinctive tendency of imitation. He illustrates his position at length by considering the case of language, and he apparently maintains that the child does not learn to speak by imitation, but merely through a process of trial and error. Surely this is largely a quarrel about words. We might reply by asking Thorndike why the child, let it be granted that it cannot at first make sounds at all like the sounds made by the adult to

---

[1] *Educational Psychology, Briefer Course*, p. 41.
[2] Op. cit., p. 42.   [3] *Mind in Evolution*, pp. 142–51.

be imitated, ultimately learns to do so. If he learns by trial and error, what is he trying, and what constitutes error? To explain the whole process as due merely to the original 'attentiveness' of man to the movements of other men, stimulated by the "original satisfyingness of the approval so often got by doing what other men do[1]" is, on the one hand, to ignore many of the facts, and, on the other hand, to admit something very like imitation.

To illustrate by the acquiring of oral speech by the child is itself misleading, for oral speech is a very complex process, and undoubtedly involves, and must involve, more than purely instinctive imitation. Some of the writer's own observations show clearly the variability of children in the acquiring of oral speech, and also phenomena which are with difficulty, if at all, reconcilable with Thorndike's statements in regard to the comparative difficulty of learning one syllable and learning a two or three-syllable series[2]. The writer has sat with a child of two, and flung at him hard words of all kinds from 'hippopotamus' and 'rhinoceros' to 'Nebuchadnezzar' and 'Mahershalalhashbaz,' getting them returned with absolute accuracy every time.

Numerous and well-known facts of animal learning[3] seem to prove beyond any doubt the existence of the general tendency of imitation. In the case of the human being, leaving out of account conscious imitation, which plays a considerable part in the acquirement of speech, we can only account for the acquiring of tones, gestures, accent, which are all picked up in the most amazing way by children, by an imitation which is instinctive.

In dealing with human behaviour, it is necessary for us to distinguish somewhat sharply three distinct types of imitation. These we might call 'perceptual' or purely instinctive imitation, 'ideational' imitation, and 'rational' or 'deliberate' imitation. It would be a great mistake to suppose that imitation, as an instinctive tendency, plays the same kind of part in each case.

[1] *Briefer Course*, p. 45.
[2] See *Journal of Experimental Pedagogy*, vol. III, 1915.
[3] See Romanes, *Mental Evolution in Animals*, chap. XIV.

In the third case, indeed, imitation, as such, is of relatively little importance. This is the 'persistent' imitation of Baldwin, and its characteristic as persistent depends in no way upon the impulse to imitate, but on the value of the end.

Evidences of purely instinctive or 'perceptual' imitation are found far down the animal scale. It is of course very difficult to distinguish such imitation from the imitation of the second type, but theoretically the distinction is easily enough drawn. In the case of 'ideational' imitation, we always have imitation of an action which appeals, because of interest in the actor, in the action itself, or in the result. We have called it 'ideational,' because this appeal seems generally, if not necessarily, to involve ideational consciousness, and may operate in the absence of the action or behaviour on which it is modelled, that is, it is not necessarily imitation at the moment when the action imitated is perceived. This form of imitation is only found in the higher animals and man, though Small found fairly strong evidence of it in rats[1].

Imitation has already been so fully discussed by several writers, that there does not appear to be much new, that can be said about it. One or two phenomena, however, require some emphasizing from our present point of view.

In the first place, imitation is one way in which personal influence acts upon the child, and an important way, if our various sayings like 'example is better than precept' are to be believed. In connection with this the question arises: what factors mainly determine a child's imitation of persons, apart, that is to say, from an interest in an action itself, or in its result, otherwise determined? It is commonly asserted that the child tends to imitate his superiors, rather than his equals or inferiors. This statement requires some qualification. As regards purely instinctive imitation, that appears to be quite independent of the relationship of inferiority and superiority, and, so far as personal influence is felt by the child through the medium of this type of imitation, it will be mainly the influence of those with whom he associates most. As regards the second and third

[1] See Hobhouse, *Mind in Evolution*, p. 150, footnote, or *American Journal of Psychology*, Jan. 1900.

types of imitation, it is unquestionable that the child will tend to imitate his superiors, rather than his inferiors, that 'negative self-feeling' will favour imitativeness, but at the same time it must be remembered that great superiority, the superiority which causes wonder rather than simple admiration, will so far inhibit imitation. It appears to follow from this that the child's behaviour will be modelled rather upon the behaviour of slightly older and bigger children, than upon the behaviour of grown-ups, that is, so far as these types of imitation are concerned.

In the second place, as Baldwin has shown, imitation of all three types plays a very important part in the development of the child's experience, and particularly his knowledge of his social environment and of himself as interacting with his social environment. The three stages in the development of the knowledge of other selves, mediated through imitation, have been called by Baldwin the 'projective,' the 'subjective,' and the 'ejective' stages[1]. It is not quite clear that all three stages are moments of the process of imitation, except of the deliberate kind. But, at all events, by imitating the acts and movements of the persons around him, or those acts which specially interest him, the child gets to know how it feels to do so and so, and his experience of such actions and movements can be, and is, utilized to illumine the actions of other people. Thus the child learns to know himself by means of his social environment, through his own experience secured partly in imitating his social environment, and he learns to know his social environment in terms of his knowledge of 'self.'

In the third place, the development of the child through imitation is not only development as an experiencer, but, in the process, his whole being as a dynamic system is organized. This side of the process has been rather strangely subordinated by most psychologists, owing to their tendency to dwell upon the cognitive side. But it is by no means less important. Through imitation the child learns to attain ends, which are determined by specific tendencies, but provision for the attain-

---

[1] *Social and Ethical Interpretations of Mental Development.* Also Stout, *Manual of Psychology*, p. 542 (1901 ed.).

ment of which is not innately organized. This is especially the case with what Baldwin has called 'persistent,' and we have called 'rational' or 'deliberate' imitation. We might, therefore, say that imitation plays a considerable part, not only in the development of self-knowledge, of the 'idea of self,' but also in the development of self-control, of the dynamic self, understanding self-control, as it ought to be understood, in a wide and positive sense. Self-control has been too often interpreted in terms of mere inhibition. Real self-control is involved in the whole development of the child as a 'doer.'

Sympathy. The most satisfactory treatment of sympathy in modern psychology is probably that of McDougall[1]. He at least tries to get a clear and definite conception of what sympathy is in its primitive form, and then applies this conception consistently in the interpretation of the complex experiences and dispositions in which sympathy is involved. "The fundamental and primitive form of sympathy," he says, "is exactly what the word implies, a suffering with, the experiencing of any feeling or emotion when and because we observe in other persons the expression of that feeling or emotion[2]."

The 'sympathetic induction' of emotion is then, according to McDougall, due to an instinctive tendency, which he elsewhere calls 'primitive passive sympathy' to distinguish it from 'active sympathy,' a manifestation of the gregarious instinct we have already considered. Sympathy, in the ordinary popular sense of the word, is a modification of 'tender emotion' by the sympathetic experiencing of another's pain or sorrow. But there is no psychological need for the word in this sense, and hence we may quite legitimately specialize it for the root sense of 'feeling with.' It by no means follows of course that this 'feeling with,' this 'sympathetic induction of emotion' is due to an original and independent tendency of human and animal nature. We have already seen in our historical sketch what differences of opinion may arise regarding this point, and similar divergence of opinion may be found among present-day psychologists. Tarde and Baldwin explain 'con-

[1] *Social Psychology,* pp. 90–96, 168–173. [2] Op. cit., p. 92.

tagion of feeling,' or the sympathetic induction of emotion, as one of the phenomena of imitation; James speaks of sympathy as an emotion, and Shand apparently takes a similar view; Spencer and some others have taken the view of Mc-Dougall, but few have consistently adhered to it; some have called sympathy an instinct.

This divergence of opinion is not, as a rule, a divergence with respect to the facts, but rather with respect to the interpretation of the facts. Thorndike, however, appears to deny many of the facts. Especially he says that we do not have this sympathetic induction of emotion in two important cases, 'pugnacity—anger' and 'parental instinct—tender emotion[1].' Now it cannot be denied that one of these, at least, presents some difficulty, but it is possible to show, that we have, under appropriate conditions, 'sympathetic induction of emotion,' 'contagion of feeling,' in both.

With anger two results are possible. The anger of A may provoke anger in B, either against A or against the object of A's anger. Thorndike rightly holds that the former cannot be taken as due to 'sympathetic induction.' If the anger of A is directed towards B, the perceptual situation for B is one which rouses instinctive anger against A; similarly, if the object of A's anger is at the same time the object of B's 'tender emotion,' or part of his larger 'self'; not very different is the case where B has a sentiment of dislike for A. On the other hand, where these or analogous conditions are not present, there can be little doubt that anger is contagious, and especially so if opposite conditions are present, if, for example, the object of A's anger also threatens or may threaten B, or is the object of a sentiment of dislike in B, or if A is the object of a sentiment of affection in B. And under any of these circumstances, the anger of B may be due directly to 'sympathetic induction,' because it would not have been aroused had it not been for A's anger. The actor and orator often rely on this 'contagion of feeling' to produce indignation in an audience, not against them, but against the object of their indignation. The facts seem undeniable, the sole difficulty, in the case of anger, being

---

[1] *Briefer Course*, pp. 45–6.

the possibility of arousing an opposing, not a sympathetic anger.

With the 'tender emotion' the facts seem even more clearly against Thorndike and in favour of McDougall. As with imitation, Thorndike bases his argument on complex phenomena, which seem to support it, but only because they are unanalysed. Of course a great deal turns on the exact meaning we assign to 'tender emotion,' and, in the human being, it is very difficult to separate it, as pure emotion, from the sentiment of affection. But the sentiment of affection, on its emotion side, is to begin with 'tender emotion,' and nothing is more certain than that affection begets affection, kindness is reacted to with kindness, not after reflection upon the benefits received, but as an immediate response. Ordinarily, too, we explain the affection of the child for the parent on this basis. It is also undeniable, that, where there is a sentiment of affection between A and B, the manifestation of the 'tender emotion' in A will immediately evoke the 'tender emotion' in B. Thorndike may hold that these instances are not relevant, that they are analogous to the anger of A provoking the anger of B against A. We may even grant this, and it only makes the phenomena of contagion of 'tender emotion' slightly less numerous, and perhaps less striking, but leaves quite sufficient incontestible facts to prove the case against him. Actor and orator rely on being able to produce 'tender emotion' in an audience, not directed towards them, but towards the objects of their 'tender emotion,' and to produce it sympathetically. When your companion puts a penny into the beggar's hat and you follow his example, it may be mere imitation, but, if your companion has shown signs of the 'tender emotion' with his action, in nine cases out of ten you will imitate the feeling as well as the act.

Thorndike is only concerned to deny the phenomena of sympathy (and of imitation) as general. He admits particular cases like "smiling when smiled at, laughing when others laugh, yelling when others yell, looking at what others observe, listening when others listen, running with or after people who are running in the same direction, running from the focus whence others scatter, jabbering when others jabber, and becoming silent as they become silent, crouching when others crouch, chasing, attacking, and rending what others hunt, and seizing whatever objects another seizes," but he admits them as instances of imitating[1].

The interpretation of the facts of 'sympathetic induction' without assuming an instinctive tendency to experience emotion directly, when we observe its expressive signs, is best represented by Adam Smith's account of sympathetic phenomena. Sully has given a somewhat similar account in recent times. The direct communication of feeling by 'contagion' he does not deny, but explains through imitation. Gregarious animals imitate the expressive signs, movements, and sounds, and through these something of the feeling is communicated[2]. But 'sympathy proper' depends, he says, upon a "representative consciousness, sufficiently developed to allow of an apprehension of another sentient creature as such[3]." This he follows by what is practically a restatement of Adam Smith's view. Its plausibility depends on our failing to recognize that it is not the imaginative realization of another's situation, which produces the emotional result, but of that other as experiencing in such a situation certain emotions. The 'contagion of feeling' is direct and immediate, dependent upon our apprehension of the expressive signs of an emotion in another, or our imaginative realization of another as feeling and expressing the emotion, but not upon our imaginatively putting ourselves in the other's place. That may reinforce an emotion, sympathetically originated, or it may originate an emotion, otherwise not experienced, but it can never explain the obvious facts of 'contagion of feeling.'

The 'sympathetic induction' of feeling and emotion plays an exceedingly important part in the development of the child. There is no reason to doubt that the child interprets directly in this way the expressive signs of an emotion, whether it is an emotion he has already himself experienced, or one which he has never before experienced, "provided it is one which he is humanly capable of feeling[4]." In this way the instinctive

[1] *Briefer Course*, p. 47.
[2] *The Human Mind*, vol. II, p. 109.
[3] Op. cit., vol. II, p. 110.
[4] Mellone and Drummond, *Elements of Psychology*, p. 246.

impulses and primary emotions of the child may be extended, independently of his own experience of such objects, to objects which evoke definite primary emotions in the people around him. Thus we may have, as we have already seen, all the signs of an instinctive response, with appropriate emotion, to definite perceptual situations, which, without knowledge of all the circumstances, we are quite unable to distinguish from an original manifestation of the instinct in question.

But these phenomena are not by any means confined to what we may call the simulation of a purely instinctive response. All the emotional attitudes of the persons with whom the child comes frequently in contact may become characteristic also of him. In this way the sentiments and interests characteristic of the family circle become the sentiments and interests of the child. In this way, when he becomes a member of a wider social circle, or of different social groups, a school, a church, a club, a profession, the sentiments, characteristic of such social circle or social group, tend to be adopted, so far at least as the sentiments of the various groups are not inconsistent with one another.

As between two individuals, there are certain circumstances which favour, and other circumstances which hinder, the 'sympathetic induction' of feeling and emotion. A sentiment of friendship favours, a sentiment of antipathy hinders it, apparently quite generally; a feeling of the superiority of the inducing source favours, a feeling of the inferiority hinders, again quite generally. Excessive violence in the manifestation of some emotions, especially anger, may also hinder, and at all times an induced emotion may be favoured by the state of interest or feeling at the time.

As one of the main avenues of personal influence, sympathy, in the sense of 'primitive passive sympathy,' is of enormous importance in the education of the child. It is a positive and direct factor in the development of the child's emotional experience. Where circumstances are favourable, and especially where there is a sentiment of affection on the part of the child for the individual, say the teacher, who is the source of the influence, 'active sympathy' cooperates strongly with 'primitive passive sympathy' in determining assimilation between the sentiments and interests of the child and those of the teacher. But it must always be recognized that the influence of 'active sympathy' is primarily negative, that is, in the direction of control, and only indirectly positive, that is, in the direction of development.

To limit the operation of sympathy to the child's emotions and sentiments is to narrow unnecessarily the scope of the tendency. Wherever a teacher has a real interest in, a real enthusiasm for, his subject, the children in the class will normally be inspired with the same interest and enthusiasm. But it is perhaps in the sphere of the moral sentiments that sympathy is most important. It is not a matter of great difficulty to get a child, say of nine or ten, to understand what honesty, or fairness, or punctuality is, by a process of intellectual instruction, proceeding in the usual way from the simple to the complex, from the concrete to the abstract. But such ideas may not be in the least degree determinants of conduct; an idea, as such, has no motive force. The sentiments of love of honesty, love of fairness, and the like, represent something more than this, and that something more is the emotional factor, which gives the idea motive force. This emotional factor will be conveyed to the child through the 'sympathetic induction' of the teacher's emotion. The teacher who has no real love of fairness or honesty cannot inspire the child with these sentiments, though he may give the child a perfect know-ledge of what these ideas 'honesty' and 'fairness' mean intel lectually. It is also notorious, that emotion, which is merely pretended, in such cases rarely, if ever, establishes itself through sympathetic induction in the child, and this would seem to be further evidence, if that is necessary, of the instinctive character of the sympathetic tendency.

Suggestibility. McDougall defines suggestion as "a process of communication resulting in the acceptance with conviction of the communicated proposition in the absence of logically adequate grounds for its acceptance[1]." Accepting in the mean-time this point of view we should define suggestibility as the

---

[1] *Social Psychology*, p 97.

tendency, under certain circumstances, to accept or act upon the opinions and beliefs of another person, or opinions and beliefs another person would have us accept and act upon, without ourselves having adequate logical grounds for accepting them.

The claim of this tendency to be regarded as an instinctive tendency is rather doubtful. In the first place it seems almost necessarily to involve the ideational level. In the second place, even though we waive this objection, the phenomena of suggestion may be explicable as manifestations of other and really instinctive tendencies, and therefore, even if instinctive, do not imply an independent instinctive tendency.

A review of the conditions under which suggestibility shows itself will lead us to suspect that it depends to a very considerable extent on the attitude involved in 'negative self-feeling.' If we could show that it depends wholly on 'negative self-feeling,' then we should merely recognize its phenomena as manifestations of this tendency on the ideational level. These conditions are of two kinds, subjective and objective, dependent, that is to say, on the individual who is suggestible, or on the source from which, or circumstances in which, the suggestion is given.

The chief subjective conditions favouring suggestion are: (a) youth, (b) inexperience, (c) lack of knowledge of the topic in connection with which the suggestion is given, (d) low vitality through fatigue, sickness, or the like, (e) individual disposition favourable to suggestion, (f) abnormal conditions, artificially induced, as in hypnotism, or pathological. All these are conditions under which 'negative self-feeling' would tend to be evoked. In suggestion, however, the emotion itself does not appear to be evoked, or evoked only in low intensity, but with our view of the relation of emotion to instinctive tendency this objection cannot carry much weight.

The objective conditions fall into three subdivisions, (a) conditions affecting the source from which the suggestion comes, (b) conditions affecting the manner in which it is given, (c) conditions affecting the circumstances under which it is given. The conditions affecting the source are quite generally all conditions which give the source authority or prestige. This authority or prestige may be due to recognized personal superiority in some or all respects, or it may be merely the authority of numbers. The conditions affecting the manner in which a suggestion is given are all conditions which give it vividness, impressiveness, or authoritativeness, independently of conditions affecting the source. The conditions affecting the circumstances are all conditions which tend to create in the mind of the 'patient' a context into which the suggestion fits.

It is not quite clear how these objective conditions, except the first group, can evoke the 'negative' self-tendency. We must therefore give them somewhat closer attention, and the result may be the throwing of some light also on the operation of the subjective conditions. Speaking generally, we may say that suggestion will be favoured, that is, beliefs and opinions will be accepted, in so far as the rousing, by association or otherwise, of ideas which would oppose the acceptance of such beliefs and opinions can be in any way inhibited. As far as the first group is concerned, this is effected by the prestige of the source. In the case of the last group, the mental attitude at the time, or the whole complex, into which the suggested belief or opinion is incorporated, may be regarded as effecting the inhibition. In the case of the second group, the idea itself is made, as it were, to force its way against all opposition.

We have so far been using the kind of language which is generally used with regard to suggestion, but without any intention of committing ourselves to the view of suggestion which such language implies. In the case of the second group of objective conditions, at least, some explanation seems to be required, of how an idea, even if unopposed, becomes a belief, and is acted upon as a belief.

McDougall declines to admit the propriety of speaking about 'suggestive ideas,' or of 'ideas working suggestively in the mind,' holding that such expressions imply that "such ideas and such working have some peculiar potency, a potency that would seem to be almost of a magical character[1]." For him the essential thing is that the idea should occupy consciousness unopposed. If it issues in action we merely have ideomotor action. Thus, in another connection, we are told

[1] *Social Psychology*, p. 101.

that, if we have an idea of a bodily movement in the focus of consciousness, "the movement follows immediately upon the idea, in virtue of that mysterious connection between them, of which we know nothing beyond the fact that it obtains[1]." Hence the acting upon a suggested idea, if it is an idea of action, involves for him no additional mystery, and a 'suggestive idea' is not different from any other idea. Similarly, if the idea is a belief, which, from the nature of the case, cannot immediately issue in action, its potency is due merely to the fact that it is 'accepted with conviction,' and it is on the same footing, therefore, with the idea accepted with conviction on logical grounds[2].

In both cases, McDougall appears to ignore a very real difficulty, in the latter case the psychological difficulty involved in the experience of 'conviction,' in the former the psychological difficulty involved in the issue in action of a mere idea. Is it certain that movement follows immediately on the idea of movement, that the phenomena of 'ideomotor action' have not been misinterpreted by Bain[3], James[4], Stout[5], McDougall, and others? "An idea which is only an idea, a simple fact of knowledge, produces nothing and does nothing[6]."

Thorndike emphatically denies that the idea, as such, acts itself out, apart, that is to say, from the effect of exercise and habit[7]. The effect of habit involves psychological problems, with which we have no intention of dealing at present, but there is no evidence that habit is itself the source of underived motive force, and we should, therefore, regard the motive force of an idea, derived from habit, as derived by habit from some previous source. Setting habit aside, then, we find that Thorndike's view is that "the connection, whereby the idea of a movement could, in and of itself, produce that movement,... does not exist[8]." The opposite view would appear to be equivalent to the recognition of an idea as itself a motive force, the view that "the tendency of an idea to become the reality is a distinct source of active impulses in the mind[9]."

---

[1] *Social Psychology*, p. 242.   [2] *Op. cit.*, p. 101.
[3] *The Senses and the Intellect*, 4th ed., p. 358.
[4] *Principles of Psychology*, vol. II, p. 522.   [5] *Manual of Psychology*, p. 486.
[6] Ribot, *Psychology of the Emotions*, p. 19.
[7] *Educational Psychology, Briefer Course*, chap. VI.
[8] *Op. cit.*, p. 83.   [9] Bain, op. cit., p. 360.

This matter is of very considerable psychological importance.
Either ideas, as such, have motive force, or they have no motive
force. If they have motive force, it does seem absurd, as
McDougall holds, to speak of 'suggestive ideas.' If of themselves they have no motive force, it is difficult to see why any
absurdity or impropriety is involved. But has any evidence
ever been brought forward to show that ideas, as mere cognition,
have any motive power whatsoever? We should of course
hold that the idea which is mere cognition does not exist, is a
mere psychological abstraction. In order that there should
be an idea at all, there must be 'meaning,' and 'meaning'
always involves more than mere cognition. Here we seem to
have the key to the solution of the difficulty.

Apart from the operation of habit, an idea will have motive
force in proportion to the impulsive force of the affective factor
in its 'meaning,' which implies, that it will have motive force,
dependent upon, and in proportion to, the motive force of the
'interest disposition' it arouses, or the emotional tendency it
evokes. A 'suggestive idea' will therefore be 'suggestive,'
because, and in so far as, the 'interest disposition' it arouses,
or the emotional tendency it evokes, can inhibit or repress any
tendencies, which would counteract its being realized, as action,
or as belief. In our opinion belief itself has its source in the
working out of the instinctive interest of a perceptual situation,
so that it involves no factor essentially different from the factors
involved in the suggestion issuing in action.

Applying these results to suggestibility, and the whole process of suggestion, we are forced to conclude that no idea can
be suggested, unless it can be, as it were, linked on to a habit,
'interest disposition,' sentiment, or emotional tendency. When
so linked, it will have the potency for belief, or for action, of the
habit, 'interest disposition,' sentiment, or emotional tendency
in question. This conclusion appears to be confirmed by some
of the most recent work in abnormal psychology, where, if
anywhere, emphasis has always hitherto been laid upon suggestion and suggestibility, to the ignoring of their relation to
feeling. Thus Morton Prince holds that the "linking of an
affect to an idea is one of the foundation stones of the pathology

of the psycho-neuroses," and of their treatment, that "upon it 'hangs all the law and the prophets'[1]."

Are we to hold then that there is no independent general tendency, which can be called suggestibility, least of all an innate or instinctive tendency, and that all the phenomena of suggestion can be otherwise explained? It is very difficult to say. After we have taken full account of 'negative self-feeling,' and the various habits, 'interest dispositions,' sentiments, and instincts, which are appealed to in the process of suggestion, and which determine the suggestibility of an individual, there may be a remainder that can only be explained by an innate general tendency. In the present state of our knowledge we should prefer not to hazard an opinion.

Whatever ultimate view we adopt regarding the psychological character of suggestion and suggestibility, the educational importance of the phenomena is not materially affected. Like sympathy, suggestibility is a condition determining the assimilation of the interests and sentiments of the child to those of the social *milieu* in which he lives. Sympathy affects only the emotional or feeling factors in these interests and sentiments. The transmission of the intellectual factors, the ideas, the opinions, the beliefs, round which the feelings and emotions are associated and developed, is the work of suggestion. If we consider once more an abstract sentiment like 'love of fairness,' we shall see more clearly the part suggestion plays. 'Love of fairness' involves an idea that certain things are 'fair' and other things 'unfair,' and the opinion or belief that 'fairness' is right. The belief is both intellectual and emotional, as we have seen. We may, however, regard the transmission to the child of this opinion or belief regarding fairness, so far as it is intellectual, as well as the opinion that certain things are 'fair,' as the work of suggestion, just as the transmission of the emotional tendencies, which make the sentiment an effective control of action, is the work of 'primitive passive sympathy.' In the opinion or belief, that is not properly a sentiment, the work of suggestion may be practically everything.

---

[1] *The Unconscious*, p. 449, et passim.

CHAPTER XI

THE 'APPETITE' TENDENCIES

When we come to consider the 'appetite' tendencies, we are immediately faced with new and difficult problems, the general nature of which has already been indicated in our discussion of 'pain sensations.' While we have no intention at present of entering upon a full and detailed treatment of these 'appetite' tendencies, there are certain important points, which require to be brought out and emphasized for the sake of completeness. At the same time we might suggest, that no really satisfactory psychological study of the appetites is hitherto available, and that there is here a department of human experience which requires and demands careful exploration by the psychologist.

First of all let us see how the 'appetite' tendencies are distinguished from the 'instinct' tendencies, strictly so called. According to Baldwin's *Dictionary*, the distinction of 'appetite' from 'instinct' depends upon the fact, that 'appetite' "shows itself at first in connection with the life of the organism, and does not wait for an external stimulus, but appears and craves satisfaction." The internal stimulus arises as a "state of vague unrest, involving, when extreme and when satisfaction is denied, painful sensations of definite quality and location[1]."

Reid[2], and, as we have seen, Dugald Stewart also[3], took as the characteristic marks of 'appetite': (*a*) that it depends on states of the body, (*b*) that it is accompanied by 'uneasy sensations,' (*c*) that it is not constant in its operation, but periodical (Dugald Stewart prefers to say 'occasional'). Bain's

[1] Art. "Appetite," signed by Baldwin and Stout.
[2] *Active Powers* (*Works*, p. 551).
[3] *Active and Moral Powers of Man*, vol. I, p. 6.

account of 'appetite' is in these terms: "Certain wants of the
system lead to a condition of pain, with the natural urgency
to work for its abatement or removal. The conscious relief
from pain is followed by an accession of positive pleasure,
which provides an additional motive, so long as the increase
continues. The measure of the voluntary prompting is the
measure of the painful and pleasurable feelings involved in the
case[1]." Finally Sully defines the 'appetites' as "periodic
organically-conditioned cravings[2]."

All these different accounts are in substantial agreement as
to the facts, that is, that there is an 'uneasiness,' which may
become pain, arising from recurring organic needs, and determining a 'craving.' Bain very rightly lays stress upon the
fact that the satisfaction of the 'appetite' involves 'positive
pleasure.' Thus we have the three phases of the 'appetite'—
'uneasiness' or pain, 'craving,' positive pleasure in removal of
'uneasiness.' Dugald Stewart emphatically asserts that, in the
case of hunger, and presumably the same kind of statement
would hold of the other 'appetites,' the 'craving' or desire is
not for happiness, that is, the removal of the 'uneasiness' and
the accompanying satisfaction, but for food[3]. If this is more
than a mere quarrel about words, the psychological analysis
of the pure 'appetite' does not seem to lend the statement
much support. If this difficulty may in the meantime be set
aside, we can, in view of the generally accepted opinions regarding the nature of 'appetite,' distinguish the 'appetite'
tendencies as those in which the impulse, as 'craving,' seems
to arise from organic 'uneasiness,' or more. generally 'pain,'
the 'instinct' tendencies as those in which the impulse seems
to arise from a presented perceptual situation, determining instinctive interest.

It must be observed, however, that it is possible to consider
many of the specific instinct tendencies of animals as determined, in a certain sense, by an 'uneasiness.' For certain
instincts are only evoked under certain conditions of the organism. These conditions make the original setting, ·which may

---

[1] *The Senses and the Intellect*, p. 260.   [2] *The Human Mind*, vol. ii, p. 17.
[3] *Outlines of Moral Philosophy*, p. 32.   Also op. cit., loc. cit.

be represented vaguely in consciousness by what we called in a previous chapter the 'underlying impulse.' Not all the instinctive tendencies are conditioned in this way, at any rate in the human being. Fear and anger, for example, are certainly not determined by a prior 'uneasiness.' Nevertheless a certain 'setting' of the organism may, and does, predispose to either.

This leads us to consider the relation, if any relation can be established, between the 'instinct' tendencies and the 'appetite' tendencies. Baldwin and Stout point out that the movements by which an 'appetite' is satisfied are mostly reflex and instinctive[1]. They instance the 'instinct of sucking' to satisfy the 'appetite for food.' This is a very interesting relation, if it holds as a general relation between the simple and 'pure' instinct tendencies of the human being and the 'appetites.' More psychological work is necessary here, but there are at least strong grounds for the belief that some such relation does exist in the case of the majority of these simple instincts. Bain is also apparently awake to this relation, when he finds in it the germ of volition. "To bring together and make to unite the sensation of the appeasing of hunger with the acts of sucking, prehension, masticating, and swallowing, is perhaps the earliest link of volition established in the animal system[2]."

But this relation merely serves to bring into relief the difficulty, to which we have already alluded, of making any psychological account of the 'appetite' tendencies conform to the general account we have given of Instinct. That difficulty, we believe, can only be surmounted by considering the 'appetites' as representing an earlier stage of conscious life, which, in the human being and the higher animals, is overlaid by the stage to which the development of the specific 'instinct' tendencies belongs. At the earliest stage of conscious life, the stage, shall we say, of the amoeba, the taking of food—Jennings' 'food reaction'—would not normally involve any experience of the kind we have in connection with the hunger 'appetite.' The reaction of the organism to the 'food situation' would be of

---

[1] Baldwin's *Dictionary*, loc. cit.
[2] *The Senses and the Intellect*, p. 263. See also Wundt, *Human and Animal Psychology*, lect. XXVI.

the general nature of 'instinct' behaviour, perception of object, interest in object, specific response to object, all of course presenting a more or less rudimentary aspect, in keeping with the rudimentary conscious life. So far as 'uneasiness' or 'pain' was developed, it would be developed as 'tension,' and would be, therefore, of the nature of 'emotion,' corresponding to this earliest stage of conscious life, the resulting behaviour being of the kind, which Jennings has described as characterizing such organisms, when the usual responses fail of 'success,' and danger to the life of the organism is imminent[1]. If, then, we may take this view, we can regard the 'appetite' tendencies in the human being and the higher animals, as representing the 'instinct' tendencies of a more primitive conscious life, in the condition of 'tension' owing to a submerging of primitive cognition, and therefore involving also the emotions of this lowest stratum of consciousness. The theoretical difficulty would disappear with the disappearance of the gap between 'instinct' and 'appetite.'

The specific 'appetite' tendencies are specific in very much the same way as the specific 'instinct' tendencies. Their enumeration is not free from difficulty, but practically all psychologists are agreed as to hunger, thirst, and sex 'appetites,' while the 'appetite' for sleep or rest (either one or two tendencies), and the 'appetite' for exercise or activity have been added by several[2]. We have added 'nausea' or 'primitive disgust,' and, if James is right as regards the innateness of what he calls the 'instinct of personal isolation[3],' that also might apparently claim inclusion.

We do not intend to discuss in detail these specific 'appetite' tendencies, but, at the same time, it would seem necessary that we explain why we classify 'disgust' here, especially since it would not come under 'appetite' in the ordinary sense, and since McDougall and others have classified it among the specific 'instinct' tendencies. The principle we have applied in the classification is the principle we have just enunciated. When,

[1] *The Behaviour of Lower Organisms,* "Trial and Error." See also Washburn, *The Animal Mind,* chap. III.
[2] E.g., Reid, *Works,* p. 553.
[3] *Principles of Psychology,* vol. II, p. 437.

and so far as, specific impulse is determined by logically prior specific 'uneasiness,' disagreeableness, or pain, we have to do with an 'appetite,' not with an 'instinct,' and it does not matter whether the impulse is 'to'-wards or 'from'-wards.

The best recent discussion of 'disgust' is that of Shand[1]. He distinguishes two types of primitive 'disgust': (a) the more familiar type, where the stimulus seems to be due to taste or smell sensations, determining nausea, and (b) the 'disgust' aroused by the touch of clammy or slimy objects, such as snails, worms, and the like. He also notices a third type, which may not be primitive, and which shows itself in the pushing away, or turning the eyes and head away from, an object which is merely perceived visually, and which is not in contact with the body. We are not convinced that there is sufficient evidence to justify our considering even the second type as primitive, while some of the phenomena ascribed to it, and to the third type, may be accounted for by James's 'instinct of personal isolation.' In any case the first type is simple and primitive, and it is this type that our classification includes.

Our reason, then, for classifying this 'disgust,' which is undoubtedly primitive, and which, we believe, underlies all other forms, with the 'appetites,' although it is perhaps more properly an 'aversion,' is that the phenomena, characteristic of its manifestation, conform to our description of the 'appetite' tendencies, rather than the 'instinct' tendencies. The impulse is determined primarily, not by perception of an object or situation, but by a specific kind of disagreeableness or 'uneasiness' in sensation, which, on being experienced, may determine perception of an object or situation as 'disgusting,' but is, logically at least, prior to such perception.

It must be confessed that this classification of 'disgust' is not without its difficulties. Setting aside the difficulty that 'disgust' differs from most other 'appetites' in the absence of that pleasure in gratification, which is a general characteristic, and the 'craving' which it determines, on the plea that we cannot expect the same kind of pleasure, or the same kind of 'craving,' in the case of an 'aversion,' which may yet be truly

[1] *Foundations of Character*, book II, chap. XIV.

an 'appetite' in the technical sense, we are faced with the further difficulty that a primary emotion, or something very similar to a primary emotion, is evoked in connection with this tendency, just as in connection with the specific emotional 'instinct' tendencies, and that it also, like them, enters into the formation of complex emotions and sentiments. It might even be objected that 'disgust' shows none of the periodicity characteristic of other specific 'appetite' tendencies, but such an objection can only carry weight if we limit very rigidly the 'appetite' tendencies to three or four.

In the light of these difficulties, it must be acknowledged that a strong case can be made for including 'disgust' among the 'instinct' tendencies, and that no serious exception can be taken to classifying it in this way. At the same time, if 'appetites' are marked off from 'instincts' by the characteristic we have selected, and we believe this to be the most fundamental distinction that can be drawn, 'disgust' must be placed where we have placed it. We noticed an analogous difficulty on the other side in discussing the gregarious instinct. Such difficulties are a further indication of the need for regarding 'appetites' and 'instincts' as, in a sense, continuous with one another.

In virtue of the 'craving' characteristic of, and developed in connection with, so many of the 'appetites,' which might almost have been taken as the 'appetite' mark, these tendencies seem to bear somewhat the same relation to 'desire,' as the 'instinct' tendencies bear to 'sentiment.' From this point of view the simplest form of 'desire' is an 'appetite' tendency associated with the idea of an object. By the older psychologists the term 'desire' was used in a very general and indefinite sense; even now its meaning is not at all clearly defined. We believe it would be well, in the interests of a scientific terminology, to restrict the application of the term to the ideational level. This would save us from the very serious confusion of 'desire' with 'purpose' or 'aim.' It is true that an 'end' may be 'desired,' but, as 'end,' it is 'purposed.' 'Desire,' as such, does not seem to imply the rational level at all; purpose, aim, end, ideal, do. This usage would also prevent the tendency to confuse the 'object desired' with the source of the impelling force of the desire. To say that the 'object desired' is not the real 'object of desire' no longer appears paradoxical when we restrict 'desire' in the way suggested, for it is obvious that the real object of 'desire,' in this restricted sense, is always some pleasure, or the satisfaction of relief from some 'uneasiness' or pain, or, we might say, is in an experience, not in the attainment of an end, as such.

Some of the most important ethical controversies of modern times appear to be due to the fact, that one set of thinkers have based their account of motives on 'desire,' the other on 'purpose,' one on 'appetite,' the other on 'instinct.' It is evident that both kinds of motive force must be recognized, and apparently both are psychologically ultimate in the human being. Though 'purpose' may always involve 'desire,' they are psychologically distinct, and 'desire' is closely related to, and of the type of, 'appetite.'

Still another point is worth noting. In addition to the two classes of emotion, which McDougall recognizes, the 'emotions of instinct' and the 'emotions of sentiment,' Shand recognizes a third class, the 'emotions of desire[1].' In this Shand appears to be right. The emotions, hope, despondency, despair, differ from the emotions belonging to either of the other classes, and they differ in respect of a prospective reference, which is the prospective reference of 'desire.' The older psychologists classified 'desire' itself as an emotion, but it is rather the general characteristic of a group of 'appetitive' and emotional tendencies.

The mention of 'desire' leads us to the consideration of the general 'appetite' tendencies. Of these there are two, the tendency to seek pleasure, and the tendency to avoid pain. These tendencies manifest themselves in connection with the specific 'appetite' tendencies, but they also manifest themselves independently. Their primary 'appetite' form is best seen in the sense 'feelings,' or rather the impulses arising from them, which, as Stout has very forcibly pointed out[2], are always

---

[1] *Foundations of Character*, book III.
[2] *Manual of Psychology*, book II, chap. VIII (2nd ed.). Also *Analytic Psychology*, vol. II, chap. XII.

involved in the feelings. That is, as original 'appetites,' the one tendency is the tendency to seek or to maintain sense pleasure, the other the tendency to avoid or escape from sense pain.

On the lowest level, what we may call the 'appetite' level itself, the importance of these general tendencies depends on the fact that they determine the formation of acquired 'appetites' on the sense level, which may play a very great part in the life of an individual. We speak of the 'smoking habit,' the 'drinking habit,' the 'drug habit,' though the important factor is not the 'habit,' but the 'appetite,' which has been acquired. It may be maintained that habit itself can give rise to an acquired 'appetite.' That is probably true, but, in the acquired habits we have named, and in others of the same type, more is involved than what we may call the 'appetite of habit' or of 'routine[1].'

The most usual acquired 'appetites' are developed in close dependence upon the pleasures, associated with the satisfaction of natural 'appetites,' and normally manifest themselves as 'cravings' for these pleasures. Probably in most cases organic changes are also produced, which cause recurring organic conditions, determining the acquired 'appetites' in the same way as naturally recurring organic conditions determine most of the natural 'appetites.'

Very important facts come into view when we consider the interaction of these general 'appetite' tendencies with the 'instinct' tendencies, or tendencies derived therefrom. It is neither true to say that "directly or indirectly, the instincts are the prime movers of all human activity," that "the instinctive impulses supply the driving power, by which all mental activities are sustained[2]," if we use 'instinct' in anything but the widest sense, nor is it true to say that "the effort to hold fast pleasure, or to regain it, and to avoid pain, are the only springs of all practical activity[3]." The truth is that, in the human being, both sets of forces are ultimate motive forces,

---

[1] Cf. Bain, *The Senses and the Intellect*, p. 264.
[2] McDougall, *Social Psychology*, p. 44.
[3] Lotze, *Microcosmus* (trans. Hamilton and Jones), I, p. 688.

and a knowledge of the phenomena and laws of their interaction is of the utmost importance.

The simplest case of interaction, and the most frequent, is the operation of what has been called the 'general law of selection in mental life.' Any activity, instinctive or otherwise, which constantly leads to disagreeable or painful results, tends to be discontinued; any activity, which leads to satisfaction, or involves agreeable results, tends to be continued and strengthened. In this way modification of instinctive behaviour becomes possible through and by means of the general 'appetite' tendencies.

But the satisfaction, which attends the successful operation of an instinct, as pleasant, may itself become the object of 'desire.' In this case an acquired 'appetite' on the ideational level can be formed in connection with instinctive activity. Normally the function of this pleasure is to "contribute to the practical efficiency" of the instinctive impulse, or of the end which it determines on the rational level[1], that is, to act as a reinforcing motive. So long as 'worthwhileness' passes into 'satisfyingness' in the ordinary way, through the effort to attain the end, the accompanying pleasure is fulfilling its proper function. Where the acquired 'appetite' generally arises is where the mere excitation of the feeling or emotion becomes the object of 'desire.' The sentimentalist, who revels in the mere emotional experience, as such, is a case in point. The normal function of emotion, like the normal function of pleasure, is to reinforce effort for an end. In the case of the sentimentalist, the emotion itself becomes the end, or rather the object of 'desire,' the effort, which it ought to stimulate, being aborted or absent.

The formation of these acquired 'appetites' is educationally very significant on account of their bearing upon the 'doctrine of interest.' We may consider acquired 'appetites' of the two kinds mentioned, as well as 'desire,' as representing what might be called 'interest dispositions of the appetite order.' Interest-experience, as 'worthwhileness,' is associated with the

---

[1] Dewey, "Interest in relation to the Training of the Will," in *Educational Essays*, ed. by Findlay, p. 108.

'appetite' tendencies, as with the 'instinct' tendencies. But the interest disposition, built up on the model of the 'appetite,' if we may so speak, is very different from the interest disposition, built up on the model of the 'instinct.'

Though the commonest form of 'interest dispositions of the appetite order' is probably that developed in connection with specific 'appetite' tendencies, or with its basis in the pleasures of sense generally, nevertheless the interest disposition with its basis in the pleasures of emotional excitement, or analogous pleasures, is by no means rare. Apparently the excitement of any of the primary emotions is capable, under certain conditions, of affording pleasure, and the sentimentalist can therefore revel in all sorts of emotional satisfaction, though the 'interest dispositions of the appetite order,' belonging to this class, develop specially in connection with particular instinctive tendencies, as, for example, the 'positive' self-tendency, or the gregarious instinct.

All such dispositions represent an altogether lower plane of mental development, as compared with the 'interest dispositions of the instinct order.' The one kind of interest disposition involves the tendency to attach value to the agreeableness of an experience, and the stronger such a tendency, the more does the mere pleasurableness of the experience come to dominate the ends sought by the individual; the other involves the tendency to attach value to objects, and to the activities possible with regard to such objects. Consequently the one tends to narrow the whole outlook, the other to widen it in proportion as the idea of the interesting object or activity can enter into relation with the ideas of other objects or activities. The difference is not only that the one seldom rises above the level of 'desire,' while the other rises to the level of 'purpose,' but rather that the one tends to general retrogression and intellectual degeneration, the other to progress and more complete organization and power.

An example from the school may make this clearer. The teacher who always tries to make school work interesting by effort, on his part, to attract the pupils to attend by means of story, illustration, picture, and, in short, all the tricks of the 'show lesson,' not merely develops mental 'flabbiness' in these pupils, but also develops the 'appetite' for such lessons. Let us say the subject is geography. There is developed in the class an 'interest in geography,' but it is an 'interest disposition of the appetite order.' It fastens upon the pleasant, amusing, and enjoyable parts of the lesson, is impatient of everything not coming under these categories, and ends in a 'craving' for mere amusement, which becomes more and more fastidious and difficult to satisfy, and which is accompanied, on the intellectual side, by a greater and greater tendency towards passivity in the mere enjoyment of the experiences.

The use of other forms of 'indirect' interest in school may produce analogous results. Where prizes and rewards are abused, an acquired 'appetite' of a simple kind may be established. Where emulation is abused, the 'desire of praise' may develop as 'appetite.' The instance we have given shows the development of a disposition, more complex, possibly rarer than, but at least as dangerous as, those developed in either of these ways.

Of course we do not require to go to the school-room for examples of such phenomena. The 'craving' for amusement is a growing evil of our times; and the 'craving' for amusement has precisely the same source, and the same natural history, as the 'interest in geography' we have just mentioned. The picture house of the present day caters almost solely for 'interest dispositions of the appetite order.' It also develops them with enormous rapidity, and often with enormous destructiveness, where there are no counteracting influences.

APPENDIX I

MEANING AS AFFECTIVE

The view that 'Meaning' is originally and primarily affective appears to demand some further elucidation and possibly justification. It goes without saying that, if we restrict the signification of the word 'Meaning' in such a way as to connote only cognitive elements in experience, to assert that primary Meaning is affective is simply to talk nonsense. It is almost equally clear that, if Meaning at any stage in its development is cognitive, and cognitive only, then it must at all stages of its development be cognitive at least in part, but then also there seems to be no room for it at all in the earliest and most rudimentary perceptual experience.

In connection with this problem there are two considerations neither of which must be lost sight of. The first is that the problem is a psychological one, and that, therefore, whatever signification we attach to any term must be a psychological signification, if the term is employed to denote a psychological phenomenon. This is the same point we have had to emphasize in connection with the biological sense of the word 'instinct.' In the present case the danger of confusion of thought arises from the side of logic. The other consideration is that pure cognition is psychologically unintelligible, and that, therefore, Meaning, psychologically regarded, can never be cognitive only, even in its developed form as secondary Meaning. If there is any hesitation or doubt about accepting this conclusion, the doubt will probably be dissipated by the careful examination of a concrete case. I am going, let us say, a boating expedition, and immediately after breakfast glance at the barometer, which is falling rapidly. My immediate cognition is of a column of mercury in a certain position—we may start at this point, though obviously the analysis might begin still farther back—

and this apprehended situation has for me Meaning, both primary and secondary probably, but we are only concerned in the meantime with the secondary. The Meaning may be expressed as 'bad weather coming.' There may or may not be concrete imagery, but the imagery, if it is present, is not the Meaning. Nor is the Meaning a mere conceptual synthesis, eviscerated of everything concrete and particular. Such is perhaps the logical, but not the psychological Meaning. It is concrete and particular by its relation not only to my present cognition, but also—and this is the more important fact—by its relation to my present interest, and it would still be concrete and particular, in the same way and for the same reason, if my interest were to formulate the conceptual principle that a falling barometer portends worse weather.

From this second consideration, then, it follows that there is always an affective element in psychological Meaning. Our contention is that this element is the primary and original factor without which Meaning, as such, could never arise, and which actually, if we may put it in that way, converts the bare sensation into experience.

Let us go back to primary Meaning. Take the apprehension in perceptual experience, and for the first time, of a particular object or situation which determines an instinctive reaction. On the bare cognition side we have certain sense impressions, arising from the qualification of the experience by the nature of the object acting through the sense organs. At best—that is with the minimum of Meaning conceivable—the object would be apprehended as a 'that.' As a matter of fact there is always a certain 'whatness' about the apprehension of any object or situation, however unfamiliar and new. It is this element of 'whatness' we should call Meaning in this case. This 'whatness' appears to be determined by the relation of the object to the instinctive impulse and interest. That is to say, in the case of an apprehended situation or object, with reference to which an animal behaves instinctively, the 'whatness' in the experience can only be described as affective.

The position will perhaps become clearer, if we consider the matter from the point of view of 'Appetite' rather than

'Instinct.' A certain object is apprehended for the first time. It is not an object the apprehension of which determines any specific behaviour prior to individual experience. With the first apprehension of the object, however, the experience is, let us say, markedly disagreeable or unpleasant. Assuming that the experience, apart from this affective element, is a bare 'thatness'—it is doubtful whether it can ever be so in reality for reasons which, however, do not seem to affect our argument —it appears obvious that it is the affective element which gives the experience its primary 'whatness.'

The same conclusion will be arrived at by following another line of thought. The Meaning of a situation is what determines our attitude—that is, in the simplest case, motor attitude— towards that situation. Primarily, and independently of the Meaning which is significance, this can only be the relation of the situation to us, as determined for us in affective experience. To use a term employed by Driesch[1], Meaning is the 'regulating' factor in perceptual experience, and it is the 'regulating' factor just because it is affective in the first instance.

Moreover, in living experience, or from the psychological point of view, Meaning, even in its secondary form as signifi- cance, is, as we have seen, never purely cognitive. The whole process of 'acquirement of meaning,' and acquirement of significance, as described by Stout, depends upon continuity of conative process, but it is impossible to conceive of cognition being influenced in any way by conation except in and through affective experience. Just as the psychologist, for purposes of analysis, may concentrate attention on the cognitive aspect of experience in isolation from the whole to which it belongs, so he may similarly abstract the cognitive aspect of Meaning, as significance, and for the time concentrate attention on the Meaning of logic. Nevertheless he must always be carefully on his guard against the temptation to take this partial aspect for the whole. Otherwise he will, as many psychologists have done, create for himself insoluble difficulties, when he under- takes the task of explaining the origin and development of Meaning as we find it in concrete experience.

[1] *The Science and Philosophy of the Organism*, vol. II, p. 45 *et passim*.

APPENDIX II

DRIESCH'S PHYSIOLOGICAL CRITERIA OF
REFLEX ACTIVITY, INSTINCT, AND 'ACTION'

It is desirable that some notice should be taken of a view and interpretation of Instinct recently submitted by Driesch (*The Science and Philosophy of the Organsim*—Aberdeen Gifford Lectures for 1907–8), more particularly because he indicates a physiological conception of Instinct, which would apparently satisfy the biologist, and which has considerable interest for the psychologist.

Little contribution had been made by physiologists to our conception and knowledge of Instinct, apart from the contributions already noticed, until comparatively recent times. The new movement in physiology—and in biology—of which the view of Driesch is the outcome, began, according to Driesch's account, with Loeb, who, accepting for physiology the position that Instinct is a compound or chain reflex, treated Instinct physiologically from this point of view. Driesch argues that Loeb has assumed as a fact what is really a problem for physiology, and his own contribution is in the attempted physiological solution of this problem.

It must be premised that both Loeb and Driesch when discussing Instinct confine their attention to instinctive behaviour. Driesch again and again asserts that science is concerned only with 'bodies in motion.' But, by considering the behaviour with reference to the stimulus which evokes it, both may be said to cover the whole field of Instinct, so far as it can be covered by the physiologist.

Driesch classifies organic movements into 'single motor acts' and 'coordinated motions.' The elemental 'single motor act' is the 'motion at random[1],' that is "an indefinitely variable motor effect following some sort of stimulus, and having no specific relation to the locality of the latter." Of such original organic movements, there are, he says, two kinds requiring to

---

[1] *The Science and Philosophy of the Organism*, vol. II, p. 20.

be distinguished from one another: those which show an absolute, and those which show a relative, contingency, that is,
those in which any stimulus may be followed by "every possible
movement, in every geometrically possible direction out of a
strictly indefinite number of possibilities," and those in which
possible movements are restricted by a definite 'action system.'

The 'coordinated motions' include 'chain reflexes,' Instinct,
and 'action.' In distinguishing between these Driesch suggests
that the 'chain reflex' is stimulated by the simple and elemental
agents in nature, instincts by specific objects, 'individualized
stimuli,' while in 'action' there is determination both by
'individualised stimuli' and by experience. He further suggests, though this part of his theory is not developed, that we
must assume some kind of innate 'knowledge' in the case of
Instinct, to account for the operation of the 'individualised
stimuli.' It is necessary to give his own words. If we allow
ourselves, he says, "the use of the common pseudo-psychological
terminology, we may say that all cases in which individualised
stimuli were at work would require the assumption of a something that wou'd be nearly related to the 'innate ideas' refuted
by Locke in another sense. Physiologists of the old school of
the German 'Naturphilosophie' often have spoken of a sort of
dreaming as being the foundation of instinctive life. It would
be this sort of dreaming that we should meet here, and the only
difference between the old investigators and ourselves would
be one of terminology: we should not speak of dreaming or of
innate ideas, but, as naturalists arguing from the standpoint
of critical idealism, we should say that an autonomic, an
entelechian natural factor was found to be at work in instinctive
life, as far as the reception of stimuli is concerned[1]."

The view of 'action' appears to be really fundamental.
Trying to avoid the psychological implications of 'experience,'
Driesch suggests the alternative expression 'historical basis.'
'Acting' is then "correspondence between individualised stimuli
and individualised effects occurring on a basis of reaction that
has been created historically from without[2]." To the acting
something—which cannot be a machine—Driesch applies the

[1] pp. 44–5.   [2] p. 80.

term 'psychoid,' thus avoiding once more the use of psychological terms like 'mind,' 'soul,' or 'psyche.' Moreover he also affirms that, though the 'psychoid' may also be the 'basis of instinctive phenomena[1],' in that case we should have to distinguish between the two 'psychoids,' the instinctive 'psychoid' characterized by the absence of 'experience[2],' and the 'action' 'psychoid' characterized by its presence.

To summarize Driesch's views. He distinguishes 'action' from Instinct by the presence of learning in the former and its absence in the latter, for that is what the distinction really amounts to, and he distinguishes Instinct from reflex activity by the 'specificity' of the stimulus in the former and its generality in the latter.

Before criticising this definition of Instinct from the psychological point of view, let us turn to what Driesch has to say regarding learning, the 'historical basis' of 'acting.' His schema for rudimentary 'experience' is simple enough. The 'elemental fact' is the recognition of 'sameness' in an impression to an impression that has gone before. This is one of the two 'immediate functions' of the 'historical basis.' The other is 'association by contiguity.' The fact corresponding to this second function is that "any sensation is not only regarded as the 'same' or 'different,' but that it also awakens the remembrance of other sensations of the past, which were connected with it in time or space upon a former occasion[3]."

Psychological criticism of this is easy. Recognition of 'sameness' and 'association by contiguity' are in no sense elemental, save as modes of explicit remembering. Both depend upon more fundamental psychological functions, without the clear recognition of which the processes are unintelligible and the terms psychologically meaningless. Driesch's reply would probably be that he is not speaking psychologically except for illustrative and descriptive purposes. Hence the psychological criticism appears to miss the mark. Nevertheless it suggests the real line of attack on Driesch's position, and such an answer would merely reinforce the suggestion. The

[1] p. 83.   [2] p. 83.   [3] p. 97.

suggestion is that the physiological account both of 'acting' and of Instinct is necessarily imperfect and incomplete.

Driesch himself is quite aware of this imperfection and incompleteness, and his full discussion of learning is explicitly in psychological terms, though even in this case it is doubtful how far we may take the discussion as really psychological. In fact it is not very clear what Driesch really understands by psychology. He speaks of 'psychology' and of 'pseudo-psychology.' Sometimes the latter opprobrious term is apparently directed against spiritualism and allied developments, but it is impossible to be certain that it is not sometimes directed also against a quite legitimate and scientific psychology.

In any case his psychological description of learning runs somewhat in this way. In order that there may be learning on any considerable scale the power of 'abstraction' must be present, that is to say, the capacity of resolving the sense datum into its elements, and recombining these elements freely (Stout's 'conceptual analysis and synthesis'). The main difference between the learning of man and the learning of animals is due to the operation of this factor[1]. Learning on the lower level depends largely on 'association by contiguity' of unanalysed wholes. The simplest type of learning or remembering is the mere recognition of 'sameness,' but of this by itself we can have no objective evidence in the behaviour of the organism. 'Association by contiguity' is really a second, and higher, stage of remembering. Even this, by itself, though concerned in 'acting' is not 'acting,' and perhaps should not be called 'experience.' 'Association by contiguity' only becomes 'experience,' and becomes 'acting,' when one of the associated elements is "able to call forth liking or to overcome disliking." Such experience is the origin of volition and the basis of 'acting' at the lowest level.

Random movements, "called forth by unknown general causes from without and within," are the starting-point of 'acting.' The effect of each movement may be noted and

---

[1] pp. 107–9.

may determine pleasure or pain. Hence arises desire for certain effects, and desire to avoid other effects. Effects of movements, 'liking' or 'disliking' of these effects, sensations of movement, and stimulations to movement all enter together into the 'historical basis.' We have two cases or types of 'acting.' On the one hand there is acting which starts from chance, and is of the kind we call 'trying.' In this the object is to gain a 'liked' or avoid a 'disliked' experience. On the other hand there is learning by experience that "a simple secondary phenomenon always accompanies the primary one which is the proper motor stimulus of your acting," and then "in response to that secondary or indicating phenomenon" performing the action which originally followed the primary stimulus. The example Driesch gives of this second type of learning is learning to identify different tramway lines by different colours[1].

In the one case, therefore, a stimulus a ('disliked,' say) may call forth in succession reactions A, B, C, A and B failing to abolish the 'disliked' factor, and C proving successful. Then, on a subsequent occasion, the stimulus a calls forth the reaction C at once. This is typical learning by 'trial and error.' In the other case a reaction ('liked,' say) is called forth at first by stimulus a with which b is always associated, and later by stimulus b alone. Both these cases offer examples of the 'historical basis.' "In the first it is not only the former stimuli, but former effects also, that are responsible for the specificity of the reaction; in the second it is former stimuli only[2]."

The psychological defects of this description of the process of learning from experience in its most rudimentary form are very obvious, and have already been indicated in our criticism of Lloyd Morgan's views. But accepting the description as accurate we find the greatest difficulty in understanding why, and on what evidence, Driesch refuses to recognize such learning as a characteristic of Instinct. There is ample evidence that many familiar and commonly recognized instincts are within varying limits modifiable, change their 'specificity,' as a result

[1] pp. 62–4.   [2] pp. 110–3.

of experience. In such cases the behaviour would apparently according to Driesch's schema cease to be instinctive, and would become 'acting,' since it would depend for its 'specificity' partly on an 'historical basis.' Surely this would leave a very narrow field for the operation of Instinct.

Moreover, in the human being at least, all acting does not originate in random movements which have led to 'liked' or 'disliked' experiences, as Driesch seems to assert. This is simply Hobbism and has been refuted time and again. In human behaviour we must take account of 'acting,' and very important kinds of 'acting,' originating in impulses which are prior to, and determine, 'liking' and 'disliking' of reactions and results. And the facts of instinctive behaviour would seem to indicate that the same kind of thing is found, though not on the same scale, in animal life.

On the other hand, the suggestion that 'specificity' of stimulus distinguishes the instinct from the reflex is a very interesting one. But 'specificity' is relative as regards aspects, dependent upon discriminating power, and dependent upon precedent and concomitant stimuli and organic conditions. The reflex itself may depend upon the 'specificity' of the place to which the stimulus from a simple and elemental power of nature is applied, and on the 'specificity' of organic conditions when it is applied. Moreover, at the other extreme, the 'specificity' of reaction seems to tend towards disappearance with the development of general conceptions and a knowledge of general laws in the case of the human being. Hence, though the physiologist may perhaps reasonably look for interesting and valuable results from investigations along the lines suggested by Driesch, his criterion is necessarily suspect from the very outset.

The simple truth appears to be that, as far as our present knowledge will enable us to judge, physiology can never give us an adequate account either of Instinct or of 'acting,' and, so long as we confine our view to the objective study of 'motions of animals,' and the stimuli which produce these motions, we shall give a very incomplete, and in all probability very misleading account of the behaviour of organisms, even when these

organisms are fairly far down the scale.   The introduction of
the conception of a 'psychoid'—if that is legitimate for the
physiologist—merely masks our ignorance, is of no real service,
and tends to obscure rather than clear up our notions regarding
the various phenomena involved.   The same appears to be
true regarding the entelechian factor which takes the place of
'innate ideas,' innate knowledge, or 'clairvoyant intuition,' in
determining the 'specificity' of instinctive action, or rather the
reception of the specific stimulus which evokes it.   Such an
attitude as Driesch adopts seems tantamount to refusing to
accept the assistance of a different science studying the same
facts from another point of view, and taking refuge in mere
meaningless terminology—for these terms are quite meaningless
as far as physiology is concerned—to escape the disagreeableness
of confessing ignorance, of acknowledging that there is a blank
and apparently insurmountable wall across the path.   At present
the only clear and approximately adequate account of all the
phenomena from the point of view of descriptive science is an
account in terms of psychology, and the only satisfactory
attitude is a frank recognition of this fact.

APPENDIX III

THE EMOTIONAL PHASE OF AFFECTIVE EXPERIENCE

The psychology of the affective processes appears to have
arrived at a parting of the ways.   In the one direction lies a
definite scientific psychology with generally accepted principles,
an accepted terminology, a clear, comprehensive, and adequate
classification and interpretation of the facts; in the other
direction lies the confused, arbitrary, unscientific psychology of
the past, with no definite universally accepted body of doctrine,
no agreed terminology, or classification, or interpretation.   If we
follow the one path affective psychology will soon take its place
beside intellectual psychology in the sense of being a scientific

discipline showing the marks and the fruits of a scientific discipline. If we follow the other the hope of a scientific psychology of the affective processes must be abandoned, and the old wilderness of individual opinion and quasi-metaphysical speculation will be the scene of our wanderings for another forty years. That we are in the position of being able to reach a scientific psychology of the affective processes at all must stand to the credit of McDougall. The greatest of all the services rendered to psychology by his *Social Psychology* is to have enabled us to approach and discuss the emotions in a way that has not been possible hitherto, and that, whether we agree with his findings or not. Such being the case, it should surely be within our power to reach at least some agreement as to what ought to be the accepted usage regarding certain terms we employ in connection with our emotional life. As to the facts it will probably be found that there is relatively slight divergence of opinion, once we begin to speak the same language.

The chief words requiring technical fixation are: 'emotion,' 'instinct,' 'desire,' 'sentiment.' With respect to the last it may be taken as certain that Shand's original suggestion regarding it, accepted by Stout and McDougall, and hailed with something approaching enthusiasm by many of the newer school of psychologists, represents in the main the technical meaning of that term for the psychology of the future.

To 'desire' and 'sentiment' we shall return later. As regards 'instinct' we have attempted to show at length that McDougall's use of the word is not merely the only use which has any value in psychology, but is also the traditional use. In the preface to the new edition of his *Social Psychology* McDougall has declined to follow our usage in drawing a somewhat sharp line of distinction between instincts and appetites. He prefers, he says, "to regard instinct as the comprehensive class or genus." We may agree. But that does not appear nevertheless to invalidate the distinction we drew under the more comprehensive head—which it is interesting to note is practically equivalent to the Freudian distinction between the 'pleasure-pain principle' and the 'reality principle.' We are quite prepared to use the term 'instinct' in the most comprehensive sense possible, as covering all the congenital active tendencies of every kind, either in the dispositional aspect or the experience aspect, or both. All the same, there seems to be a valid and important distinction between tendencies evoked by affective experiences and tendencies evoked by perceived situations. This is the distinction between 'appetitive' and what we may now call 'reactive' tendencies. It may be that this distinction breaks down "when we apply it at all rigidly to animal life," but we doubt it. It is true that, as we pass down the animal scale, the distinctions we draw in the case of the human being gradually disappear, that categories become confluent and ultimately coalesce. But that the distinction is a clear and radical one as regards the human being can hardly be denied, and this is all we are really disposed to contend for. We have also distinguished under the head of specific reactive tendencies—the general tendencies do not come into the present discussion—the two groups of simple or pure reactive tendencies and emotional reactive tendencies. Now both of these distinctions appear to be important in connection with the main point on which we are unable to accept McDougall's teaching, viz. the relation of emotion to instinct. If it is to be maintained that the affective element in all instinct experience is of the nature of emotion, the only group of congenital tendencies which might conceivably answer to this description, is the group of emotional reactive tendencies. Hence we must either confine the term 'instinct' to these, or, if we retain its comprehensive use, abandon the view that an emotion as such is an essential element in instinct experience. There does not seem any serious difference between us as regards the facts, and our object at present is to suggest a point of view from which the facts may be most conveniently grouped, and to suggest at the same time a terminology which will best meet the needs of the case.

Let us in the first instance examine the nature and function of affective experience in general. It is possible that the emphasizing of the difference between pleasure-unpleasure and emotion is one main source of the present controversy, and it seems worth while to make an attempt to bring them nearer together, at least so far as affective experience is concerned. Elementary affective experience, if unqualified, can only be described as a kind of subjective excitement, similarly unqualified. Such unqualified subjective excitement, however, would seem to be merely an abstraction. In the concrete the experience is always qualified as either pleasure or unpleasure, satisfaction or dissatisfaction, and this *bipolarity* or *bivalency* is, together with its subjectivity, the most fundamental characteristic of affective experience. In the light of this it is easy to see how the main psychological function of feeling is its regulative function. This regulative function implies a directing influence on the course of psychical or nervous energy. We can best figure this process as inhibition through a drainage, that is either positive or negative, as far as that neural system is concerned, on which we are fixing our attention. This in turn would seem to imply that simple feeling, pleasure-unpleasure or satisfaction-dissatisfaction, is in some sort and sense a source of energy, because no direction of energy can be conceived as taking place without the utilization of energy. But the sense and sort in which it is a source of energy we must leave undetermined. It may be it is a creative source, or a source only in the way in which the turning off and on of a tap is a source.

For analytical psychology the elementary affective experience is thus in the concrete qualified as either pleasure or unpleasure, satisfaction or dissatisfaction. Is it qualified in any other way? Quantitatively, yes; qualitatively, *qua* affective experience—we do not think so, though it is a difficult matter to prove the negative. In our view any further differences, as between one pleasure and another, or between one unpleasure and another, must be regarded as inhering in the aspects of the total experience other than the purely affective. For analytical psychology, the affective, to express our view briefly, is always adjectival, never substantive, and this adjectival may show either of two antagonistic or antipodal qualities, while all other qualitative differences belong to one or other of the substantive elements.

Such a view already involves the rejection of McDougall's view of the primary emotions as the affective elements in instinct experience, since it involves holding that affective elements can show only the two qualities, while emotions are all qualitatively distinct from one another. It involves also the view that emotions do not represent purely affective elements at all, but are complexes of affective with substantive elements, which is indeed in accord with the ordinary meaning we attach to 'emotion,' though that is no argument for retaining that meaning in psychology if convenience should determine otherwise. We ought to banish the word 'emotion' from analytical psychology altogether, though its place in genetic and functional psychology is not in question, and we should speak of 'instinct feeling,' where McDougall uses 'emotion,' to designate the affective element in instinct experience.

Let us now turn for a moment to the consideration of the nature of emotional experience as distinct from elementary affective experience. In the first place, emotions, as we have just said, present a complexity which differentiates them at once from elementary affective experiences. Wherein does this complexity consist? We find by careful examination of experiences which would be universally described as emotional that the complexity arises from two distinct sources. On the one hand, emotions involve conative as well as affective factors. McDougall in a footnote on p. 387 of the new edition of his *Social Psychology*, says: "For purposes of exposition it would usually suffice to treat of the affective and conative parts of the disposition (sex instinct) as forming a functional unit." It is because in his analysis he has not separated these two parts that he finds it possible to regard the primary emotion as the affective element of the instinct. On the other hand, the organic resonance of an emotion gives it a complexity partly affective and partly sensational. Hence even if we restrict the term 'emotional' to the purely affective, we should still be able to maintain that complexity is a differentiating characteristic.

In the second place, another characteristic of emotional experience which differentiates it from non-emotional experience is only exhibited clearly where the emotion is itself well-marked. That is the phenomenon of emotional dissociation, as distinguished from what I have called mere inhibition by drainage. We would emphasize this point as of fundamental importance. The regulative function of simple feeling, carried out through the direction of the flow of nervous energy from one neural system to another by means of drainage, must obviously be distinguished from the monoideistic function of emotional experience, secured by the development of nervous energy in a single neural system in such a way as to dam back for a brief period, or for a long interval of time, the normal currents which carry the mental life. While fully awake to the objections that may be urged against mixing up the psychical and the neural in this way, the writer feels that the use of neural terms at this point makes the meaning he wishes to convey more definite than the use of purely psychical terms could. Probably no one would deny that dissociation is characteristic of violent emotion. But it seems to be really characteristic of all emotions, and we should be inclined to take this as the psychological differentia of emotion, always recognizing, however, that the condition may shade gradually over into simple affective experience. In any case this characteristic, together with complexity due in part to organic resonance, and in part to conative elements, would seem sufficient to mark off what we should call an *emotional phase of affective experience*.

If we turn to the instinct feelings we shall find that they bear the character of simple affective experience in some cases, while in other cases, more especially as regards the emotional reactive tendencies, they appear to be emotional. But even when the instinct feeling is emotional, the relation between instinct and emotion is by no means so simple as that assumed by McDougall. The evoking of the instinct by the presentation of the appropriate situation always indeed involves that kind of subjective excitement which we call affective experience, but this subjective excitement is *bipolar* or *bivalent*, exhibiting one polarity or the other, according as the conative impulse moves freely and rapidly towards its satisfaction, or is retarded or obstructed. In the case of the emotional reactive tendencies the instinct feelings may pass into the emotional phase almost or quite immediately. Even so, the bipolarity characteristic of all affective experience remains, and we have not one but two emotions associated with each individual tendency. This is a second point which appears to be of great importance, so much so that its expansion is desirable.

We have already come to the conclusion that certain instinctive tendencies are capable of yielding what may be designated as 'joy' emotions, in addition to the emotions evoked under the normal condition of delay or obstruction. We are now disposed to go farther and maintain that this is characteristic of all instinctive tendencies, because it is due to the universal character of all affective experience. The writer would now agree with McDougall in holding that joy and sorrow are not individual primary emotions, but the common characters of groups of primary—and other—emotions. He would indeed go farther than McDougall. It appears to him that in joy and sorrow we see the bipolarity of affective experience in its emotional phase, and in laughter and tears we see its extreme manifestation. Take the gregarious instinct. The sorrow of isolation, the joy of bathing in the crowd effect, represent the two poles of feeling, negative and positive, as we may term them. Or take the fighting tendency. The joy of battle, the sorrow or pain of baffled rage are in this case the two poles. And so also of any instinctive tendency we care to select—the acquisitive, the hunting, the parental, the escape or flight tendency. The one difficulty is presented by the self-tendencies, which curiously enough first led the writer to undertake this line of investigation. To these we shall return later.

In order to determine the conditions under which the emotional phase of instinct feeling in either of its polarities may be developed, it will be best to consider in the first instance well-marked cases, cases verging indeed on the extremes of laughter or tears. We have tried to show that there must be a condition of what we have called 'feeling-tension' before we have emotion, and that this 'feeling-tension' may arise either where there is some check, or at least pause, in the attainment of the end or satisfaction of the impulse, or where the end is attained so quickly or abundantly that action cannot keep pace with feeling. It must be admitted that this description is somewhat vague. Let us attempt to make it more detailed and accurate, always premising that we have in view experiences of such a kind that their emotional character is not in doubt.

Consider situation and impulse as linked together, as it were.

Let us represent this schematically in the form $s_1 - i_1$, $s_2 - i_2$ etc. The linkage is a real one in that integration which is consciousness, and it is, as it were, qualified by the instinct feeling which at the same time functions as a regulating factor, securing that the changes of situation-impulse linkages shall pursue their normal course. In the series of situation-impulse linkages constituting a course of instinct experience and behaviour at a relatively low level of development, $s_1 - i_1$ may be followed by $s_2 - i_2$, which we will consider the course towards satisfaction, or $s_1 - i_1$ may be followed by $s' - i_2$, which will represent temporary failure. In the latter case the regulating feeling tends to the substitution of a new impulse i', which we will assume restores the normal course. If there is no structural provision for this simple substitution, or if the simple substitution does not meet the needs of the case, the regulating function of feeling in its simple phase has exhausted its possibilities, and the condition which may be called 'feeling-tension' arises—the emotional phase in its negative form.

Now it may very well be maintained—as McDougall would probably maintain—that with the emotional reactive tendencies this structural provision for simple substitution is absent—that is why the character 'emotional' is present—and therefore the emotional phase develops immediately. We are not concerned at present in maintaining the contrary, though inclined to hold the contrary, for it is a point of minor significance, since there can be no doubt whatever that there may be an almost immediate development of the emotional phase in any case. What we are concerned in maintaining, in the interests of a consistent analytical psychology of the affective processes, is that instinct feeling as such is not necessarily emotional.

What of the positive form of the emotional phase—the joy emotion? In this case a condition which might be described as 'feeling tension' would apparently show itself under either of two sets of circumstances. If the situation develops in the satisfying direction with greater rapidity than might be considered equivalent to the effort put forth by or under the influence of the impulse, there would obviously be what we might call an accumulation of affective energy, seeing that only a portion is required in the maintenance of the activity itself in accordance with the regulating function of the instinct feeling. The same result would be arrived at in the case of a situation being presented, which at one and the same time satisfied the impulse and stimulated to maintain and repeat. Of course both sets of circumstances might be combined, with accelerated production of what we are calling accumulation of affective energy. And such accumulation of affective energy represents 'feeling tension' quite as clearly as in the case of the negative 'feeling tension.' In other words we should have here again the emotional phase of affective experience, this time positive.

A moment's consideration of the biological function of the emotional phase, in both its positive and its negative form, will enable us to understand why human emotions are characterized and attached as they are. The main function appears to be to stimulate, direct, and reinforce special effort. It is perfectly clear, independently of the strongly confirmatory evidence from the line of investigation pursued by Pavlov, Cannon, and others, that this is precisely the part played by the negative form at all events of the emotional phase, as manifested in well-marked emotions like fear, anger, and the like. It is true that the affective disturbance may overshoot the mark, but this overshooting of the mark leads to further problems, biological and psychological, with which we are not for the present concerned. That this is also the part played by the positive form is perhaps not so clear at a first glance, though the assertion that it is does not present any formidable difficulty in the proof. We may take it as a general principle that that kind of behaviour which is successful, or biologically useful, will be precisely the kind of behaviour stimulated and maintained by the regulating function of feeling, that stimulating and maintaining correspond to the positive direction of the feeling, while, just in the same way, discontinuing and inhibiting correspond to the negative direction. Now the emotional phase in the positive form will merely exaggerate the stimulating and maintaining effect, and, if we take the memory function into account, the same effect will be repeated on this new plane. As before there may be an overshooting of the mark, but it is perhaps worth while pointing out, or rather suggesting, that in this case, as in the other, a kind of safety valve is provided in the phenomena of laughter, or of tears, as the case may be.

There is still another point which is perhaps worth noting. Appetites may be developed or acquired for emotional experience of practically any kind. That is to say, the affective experience which is involved in the emotional phase may itself come to determine a new active tendency. As a general rule, perhaps, the biological end of the emotion will thereby fail of attainment, but nevertheless the fact is there. And it is another fact which is significant in connection with the view we are urging. The instinct feeling, as pure feeling, does not in our opinion explain this development of a secondary appetite, the appetite being determined by those elements in the emotional phase which make it emotional. We have said that appetites may be developed for emotional experiences of practically any kind. The fact itself is a very curious one. All sorts of so-called perversion of appetite appear to be possible. Once more we touch ground which Freud and his followers have surveyed from their special point of view. We are indebted to them for many carefully observed facts, facts which are especially significant in relation to any psychological study of the affective processes. But while accepting the facts gratefully, we must be careful to distinguish between facts and theories about the facts, and the sexual explanation, in any ordinary acceptation of the word 'sexual,' is a theory, requiring clearer and more unambiguous evidence than has yet been submitted, since the facts—for example masoschistic manifestations as they are considered by Freudians—can obviously be fitted into theories other than the Freudian, of which the view we are expounding may be regarded as one.

The time has now come to define more clearly the relation of these views to McDougall's theory of instinct and emotion as a whole, and incidentally to Shand's theory. Shand has claimed that the primary emotions represent complex systems which may involve several separate instincts, but he argues that the primary emotions must be distinguished from the instincts, because of the variable as contrasted with invariable type of behaviour they respectively produce, and because, while the instincts are always directed to biological ends, the primary emotions "may create other ends through their organization in sentiments." Or, taking both differences together, primary emotions are not to be regarded as instincts "because of their capacity to vary their means and to vary their ends, because they are not confined to the biological ends of instincts, nor, like each instinct, to one invariable type of behaviour[1]." It is obvious that Shand does not accept McDougall's definition of 'instinct,' but rather Thorndike's. For him human instincts are simple, few, and fragmentary, because the definite reactions which the human being inherits, are few and fragmentary. It is useless for McDougall and Shand to argue any further. They are not speaking the same language. Shand's primary emotion systems are McDougall's 'instincts.' To be quite frank, Shand nowhere brings forward sufficient reasons why the psychologist should abandon the old usage, sanctioned by psychologist after psychologist, through the long record of psychology as a branch of knowledge, for a recent biological usage which is quite valueless for psychological purposes. On this point we are in entire agreement with McDougall. For us, as for him, the primary emotion system— "a superior type of organization to the system of the instinctive impulse," according to Shand—is to be included under the head of instinct. But so far there is no difference between the three of us as to facts, the difference being merely one of terminology. As regards the list of primary emotion systems or emotional reactive tendencies, there is some slight difference as to facts. Shand would place joy and sorrow among them, while we, for reasons already given, would agree with McDougall in rejecting joy and sorrow as primary emotion systems.

From this point the differences between the views begin to make themselves felt, and more particularly the differences between our views and those of McDougall. There are really three differences. The first is, as we have indicated, a relatively minor difference. McDougall holds that emotion is necessarily involved in the functioning of the instinct. As far as the emotional tendencies are concerned, we are willing to concede that it practically amounts to that, though theoretically we are com-

---

[1] *Proc. of Arist. Soc.* vol. xx, 1919–20, "Of Impulse, Emotion, and Instinct."

pelled to hold that even the emotional tendencies may be evoked without the emotion being immediately present, at least in the limiting case. This point is a relatively minor one. We agree with McDougall that the emotion is practically always present. The second difference is of rather greater importance. For us each emotional reactive tendency—McDougall's instinct—involves the possibility of not one but two emotions. But here we do not seem to be using the term 'emotion' in the same sense, and this brings us to the third difference which is the most important of the three. We cannot identify the emotion, as McDougall describes it, with the instinct feeling, because to us the phenomenon he describes appears to include part of the instinct response.

For us the emotional phase of affective experience is what it is, partly at any rate through the organic resonance. This seems to be essentially instinct response, but has obviously its affective aspect as well. For McDougall emotion seems to include not merely these two affective elements, but also the organic response itself in its sensational aspect, and to some extent the generated impulses deriving from affective sources. Practically, all the differences do not amount to very much if we both recognize that in the emotion we have not the elementary, but the complex and secondary, so far as affective experience is concerned. We are not sure that McDougall would agree to this, and hence this important theoretical difference still remains.

As against these differences, we agree that the primary emotions which underlie and constitute practically all the definite emotions in human experience, and in which we must seek one group of the fundamental forces determining human behaviour at all levels, represent the functioning of a highly important class of human instincts, but not that these are the only human instincts. To the question why this particular group of human instincts should have this particular character, we should reply by pointing out that this character is the necessary implication of those very peculiarities which lead Shand to deny the whole group the status of instincts. They have not the definiteness and uniformity or invariability, which he takes as proper to true instincts. Or rather they have and they have not.

The organic resonance, regarded as an instinctive response, is quite definite and uniform over a very wide range among living organisms, the subsequent behaviour is not. Is it not just to secure a kind of behaviour appropriate to the end to be attained that the emotion is there? To hold as Shand does that the primary emotions create new ends which are to be contrasted with the biological ends characteristic of the simple instincts is mere confusion. What does he mean by 'biological ends'? If he means ends which the biologist would recognize and describe in his biological universe of discourse—self-preservation and perpetuation of the species—we fail to see that any valid psychological distinction has been drawn. The laws of transference of impulse, fusion of emotions, and complication of behaviour, which are psychological laws, will easily enable us to trace the new ends, which Shand claims as created, back to the more fundamental biological ends from which they are derived. Apart from the fact that they are derived ends, there does not seem a psychological distinction between the two groups of ends. The formation of the sentiment does not introduce any new forces, but merely organizes those already present. It cannot therefore be properly said to create new ends; here too the apparently new ends can readily be shown to arise out of the old.

The last point to which we may draw attention in this connection is the system of desire, as Shand calls it, and the emotions belonging to this system. The main question is: are the emotional phases of affective experience confined essentially and ultimately to the emotional reactive tendencies? We should reply in the negative and take up the position that the emotional phase is a quite general possibility of all affective experience. As before the outcome of this view involves agreement with McDougall as to general results, though differing from him as regards the nature of the original feeling. For while he holds, as we have seen, that the excitement of any instinct disposition whatever "is accompanied by some subjective excitement or feeling which is of the same nature as the primary emotion," and is compelled by his theory to trace all emotion ultimately back to such, we deny that the instinct feeling is necessarily emotional, but admit that all feelings may exhibit the emotional phase. Now the only case not already considered is the group of emotions classified by Shand as belonging to the 'system of desire.' For Shand the 'system of desire' is a highly complex emotional system including "actually or potentially the six prospective emotions of hope, anxiety, disappointment, despondency, confidence, and despair." Our view seems to clear up the whole situation here. There is some measure of validity in the contention that these prospective emotions are in some instances at least real emotions. How are we to interpret them? Our distinction between appetitive tendencies and reactive tendencies ought to be regarded as a radical distinction separating two different types of instinct disposition at and below the perceptual level, and, when carried over to the level of ideal representation, separating the type of disposition we call a sentiment from the type of disposition conditioning what we call desire. Both these words ought to be specialized for phenomena involving the higher level. Desire would thus designate, not an emotional system or a complex emotion, but appetitive tendency conscious of its object. This suggestion we have already made. Similarly, as regards sentiment, we have argued that sentiment as such necessarily involves the ideational level, if not for its activity, at any rate in its formation. This view of sentiment McDougall declines to accept, but we nevertheless still adhere to it. We cannot recognize purely perceptual sentiments. Such cases as McDougall indicates are explicable either in terms of the law of transference, when it seems merely to invite confusion to apply the term 'sentiment,' or in terms of symbolism, when obviously the original conditioning structure involves or has involved activity at the ideational level. But, quite apart from the definition of these terms, it is obvious that our view that all affective experience whatever may enter on the emotional phase will account satisfactorily for the prospective emotions of desire, as well as the group of primary emotions involved in the activity of the emotional reactive tendencies and the group of more complex emotions involved in the activity of sentiments. That desire is not itself on the same footing as the primary emotions, as McDougall classifies them, is clear. It is also clear that the emotional phase in all cases may take either of two directions, the positive or the negative, and thus joy and sorrow will be characteristic of all the emotions of appetite and of desire, as of all the primary emotions and derived emotions on the reactive side, and of all the emotions of the sentiment.

One topic we left over for discussion later—the self feelings—and we would in conclusion attempt a solution of the difficult problems they involve, difficulties which exist for McDougall's view as well as for the view here maintained. Apparently, in the case of the human being, we start with two tendencies—emotional reactive tendencies, according to my nomenclature, instincts, according to McDougall's—but curiously related to one another as far as the connected emotions are concerned. On the one hand, there is the tendency towards display, evoked by others apprehended as inferior, or ourselves as superior, with the emotion of elation, *so far as the tendency finds its satisfaction* in the exhibition of the expressive signs of the opposite tendency on the part of those others. On the other hand, there is the tendency towards abasement, evoked by others apprehended as superiors or ourselves as inferiors, with the emotion of subjection, presumably again *so far as the tendency finds its satisfaction,* in the manifestation of the opposing tendency by those others. There is however some doubt in this case, for subjection as emotional would appear to be distinctly bipolar. However that may be, it will be acknowledged that the situation as regards the positive tendency at all events is a peculiar one, when it is remembered that the tendency to escape from danger has accompanying it the emotion of fear, *so far as avenues of escape are cut off,* not so far as avenues of escape are opened up. This peculiarity is still more apparent when we note the fact that the display tendency, so far as it is frustrated, will give rise not to its own emotion but to the emotion of the opposing negative tendency, at least if anger is not evoked.

At first sight it would seem as if the solution of the difficulty were easy along the lines of our view of the bipolarity of the emotional phase. But this would imply a single original tendency, and the facts seem to show that there are undeniably two, that the bipolarity is not merely a bipolarity in affective experience, but a bipolarity of original tendency. All the same the two tendencies are without question closely connected with one another, so that there is a suggestion that ultimately but a single complex disposition is involved. It will be remembered that the anger and fear tendencies are also closely connected, as we see evidenced in the behaviour of the animal at bay, but in this instance there is association merely, not identity, while in the case of the self tendencies, positive and negative, we seem to be dealing rather with identity of disposition, and not close association of dispositions.

A speculative solution of the difficulty is all we can offer. Let us assume an original disposition involving in its activity a single emotional reactive tendency, which might be designated either self-security or self-expansion. The instinct feeling, in the emotional phase, would show two polarities, and these two polarities would correspond more or less closely to positive and negative self feeling as we actually know them. This is the starting position, and fundamentally there has been little change. But owing to the exigencies of community life, a second subsidiary reactive tendency has been subsequently developed on the negative side. This would give us the effect of a single complex disposition, with the two tendencies, one secondary and subsidiary, the two marked polarities of feeling, and a third subsidiary polarity, the positive of the subsidiary negative tendency, which is apparently exactly what we do find. Such a theory would seem to fit the facts as we find them. At all events the facts seem fatal to the simple solution proposed by McDougall, and go to confirm the conclusions we have already drawn from other phenomena of emotional experience and instinctive behaviour.

BIBLIOGRAPHY

LIST OF WORKS AND EDITIONS, TO WHICH REFERENCE,
OR OF WHICH USE HAS BEEN MADE

1. ARISTOTLE, Historia Animalium. Berlin, 1831.
2. AVELING, F. Consciousness of the Universal. London, 1913.
3. BAIN, ALEXANDER. The Senses and the Intellect. 4th ed. London, 1894.
4. —— The Emotions and the Will. 2nd ed. London, 1865.
5. —— Mental and Moral Science. 3rd ed. London, 1879.
6. BALDWIN, J. MARK. Mental Development in the Child and the Race. 3rd ed. London, 1906.
7. —— Social and Ethical Interpretations of Mental Development. 4th ed. London, 1907.
8. —— The Individual and Society. London, 1911.
9. —— Preface and Appendix in "The Play of Animals" (Groos). London, 1898.
10. —— Dictionary of Philosophy. 4 vols. London.
11. BELL, SIR CHARLES. The Anatomy and Philosophy of Expression. 6th ed. London, 1872.
12. BERGSON, H. Creative Evolution. Translation by Arthur Mitchell. London, 1913.
13. BOSTOCK, JOHN. An Elementary System of Physiology. 3 vols. London, 1827.
14. BÜCHNER, LUDWIG. Mind in Animals. Translation by Annie Besant. London, 1880.
15. BUTLER, JOSEPH. The Analogy of Religion. 1st ed. 1736.
16. —— The Analogy and Sermons. Ed. Angus. N. D. London (Religious Tract Society).
17. CABANIS, P. J. G. Rapports du Physique et du Moral de l'Homme. 8th ed. Paris, 1844.
18. CAIRD, EDWARD. The Critical Philosophy of Immanuel Kant. 2 vols. Glasgow, 1889.
19. CARPENTER, WILLIAM H. Principles of Human Physiology. 3rd ed. London, 1846.
20. —— Principles of Mental Physiology. London, 1874.
21. CARR, H. WILDON. Instinct and Intelligence. Brit. Journ. of Psychology, vol. III, 1909–10.
22. CLAPARÈDE, ED. Psychologie de l'Enfant et Pédagogie expérimentale. 3rd ed. Geneva, 1909.
23. —— Experimental Pedagogy and the Psychology of the Child. Translation of 4th ed. by Mary Louch and Henry Holman. London, 1911.

24. COLVIN, STEPHEN S. The Learning Process. New York, 1911.

25. COMBE, GEORGE. The Constitution of Man in relation to the Natural Laws. London, 1893.

26. DARWIN, CHARLES. On the Origin of Species. London, 1869.

27. —— The Descent of Man. London, 1888.

28. —— The Expression of the Emotions in Man and Animals. London, 1872.

29. —— Posthumous Essay on Instinct, in Romanes, "Mental Evolution in Animals."

30. DEARBORN, G. V. N. The Emotion of Joy. Psych. Rev. Monograph Supplements, vol. II, no. 5. 1899.

31. DESCARTES. The Philosophical Works of Descartes. Rendered into English by Elizabeth S. Haldane and G. R. T. Ross. 2 vols. Cambridge, 1911–12.

32. —— The Discourse on Method, Meditations, etc. Translation by Veitch. Edinburgh, 1850.

33. DEWEY, J. The School and the Child. Edited by Findlay. London, 1906.

34. —— Educational Essays. Edited by Findlay. London, 1910.

35. DRIESCH, H. The Science and Philosophy of The Organism. 2 vols. Aberdeen, 1908–9.

36. ERDMANN, J. E. A History of Philosophy. Translation by W. S. Hough. 3 vols. London, 1891.

37. FERGUSON, ADAM. An Essay on the History of Civil Society. 3rd ed. London, 1768.

38. GALTON, F. Enquiries into Human Faculty. Everyman Library.

39. GROOS, KARL. Die Spiele der Tiere. 2nd ed. Jena, 1907.

40. —— The Play of Animals. Translation by Elizabeth L. Baldwin. London, 1898.

41. —— The Play of Man. Translation by E. L. Baldwin. London, 1901.

42. HARTMANN, E. VON. Philosophy of the Unconscious. Translation by Coupland. 3 vols. 1884.

43. HERBERT, LORD, OF CHERBURY. De Veritate. London, 1633.

44. HOBBES, T. The English Works, now first collected by Sir W. Molesworth. 11 vols. 1839–45.

45. —— The Leviathan. Everyman Library.

46. HOBHOUSE, L. T. Mind in Evolution. London, 1901.

47. HOLMES, O. W. The Professor at the Breakfast-Table.

48. HUME, D. Philosophical Works. 4 vols. 1825.

49. —— Treatise of Human Nature. 2 vols. Everyman Library.

50. HUTCHESON, F. Nature and Conduct of the Passions. 1728.

51. —— Illustrations upon the Moral Sense. 1728.

52. IRONS, D. A Study of the Psychology of Ethics. Edinburgh, 1903.

53. JAMES, W. The Principles of Psychology. 2 vols. London, 1890.

54. JENNINGS, H. S. Contributions to the Study of the Behaviour of Lower Organisms. Carnegie Institute of Washington Publication No. 16.

55. Jones, E. Psychoanalysis and Education. Journ. of Educ. Psychology, vol. i, 1910.

56. —— Psychoanalysis and Education: The Value of Sublimating Processes for Education and Reeducation. Journ. of Educ. Psychology, vol. iii, 1912.

57. Kirby, W. History, Habits and Instincts of Animals. (Bridgewater Treatise.) 2 vols. London, 1835.

58. —— W., and Spence, W. Introduction to Entomology. 7th ed. London, 1858.

59. Lewes, G. H. A Biographical History of Philosophy. London, 1857.

60. Lotze, H. Microcosmus. An Essay concerning Man and his relation to the World. Translation by Elizabeth Hamilton and E. E. Constance Jones. 2 vols. London, 1885.

61. Martineau, J. Types of Ethical Theory. 2 vols. 3rd ed. Oxford, 1889.

62. McDougall, W. Physiological Psychology. London, 1905.

63. —— An Introduction to Social Psychology. London, 1908.

64. —— Psychology, the Study of Behaviour. London, 1912.

65. —— Body and Mind. London, 1911.

66. —— Instinct and Intelligence. Brit. Journ. of Psych., vol. iii, 1909–10.

67. Magendie, F. Elementary Compendium of Physiology. Translation by E. Milligan. Edinburgh, 1831.

68. Malebranche, N. De la Recherche de la Vérité. Edited by Bouillier. Paris, 1879.

69. —— De Inquirenda Veritate. Geneva, 1691.

70. —— The Search for Truth. English Translation by Taylor. 2nd ed. 1700. (Translated also by Sault, 1694.)

71. Marshall, Henry Rutgers. Instinct and Reason. London, 1898.

72. Martineau, J. A Study of Spinoza. 3rd ed. London, 1895.

73. Mellone, S. H., and Drummond, M. Elements of Psychology. 1907.

74. Mitchell, P. C. Article "Evolution" in Encycl. Brit. 11th ed.

75. Mitchell, W. Structure and Growth of the Mind. London, 1907.

76. Morgan, C. Lloyd. Animal Behaviour. London, 1900.

77. —— Instinct and Experience. London, 1912.

78. —— Introduction to Comparative Psychology. London, 1894.

79. —— The Natural History of Experience. Brit. Journ. of Psych., vol. iii, 1909–10.

80. —— Instinct and Intelligence. Brit. Journ. of Psych., vol. iii, 1909–10.

81. —— Article "Instinct" in Encycl. Brit. 11th ed.

82. Münsterberg, H. Psychology and the Teacher. New York, 1909.

83. Myers, C. S. Instinct and Intelligence. Brit. Journ. of Psych., vol. iii, 1909–10.

84. Newland, C. Bingham. What is Instinct? London, 1916.

85. Peckham, George W., and Elizabeth G. Wasps, Social and Solitary. Westminster, 1905.

86. PREYER, W. Die Seele des Kindes. 4th ed. Leipzig, 1895.
87. PRINCE, MORTON. The Unconscious. New York, 1914.
88. REID, THOMAS. Philosophical Works. Edited by Sir William Hamilton. 5th ed. 1858.
89. RIBOT, TH. Psychology of Attention. Open Court Trans. Chicago, 1911.
90. —— The Psychology of the Emotions. London, 1897.
91. ROMANES, G. J. Animal Intelligence. London, 1882.
92. —— Mental Evolution in Animals. London, 1883.
93. ROUSSEAU, J. J. The Social Contract and Discourses. Everyman-Library.
94. SCHNEIDER, G. H. Der Menschliche Wille, vom Standpunkt der Neueren Entwickelungstheorien. Berlin, 1882.
95. —— Der thierische Wille. Leipzig, 1880.
96. SCHOPENHAUER, A. The World as Will and Idea. Translation by Haldane and Kemp. 3 vols. 1886.
97. SETH (A. S. PRINGLE-PATTISON). Scottish Philosophy. 3rd ed. 1899.
98. —— Hegelianism and Personality. 2nd ed. 1893.
99. SHAFTESBURY, ANTHONY, EARL OF. Characteristics of Men, Manners, etc. 3 vols. 1732.
100. SHAND, A. F. The Foundations of Character. London, 1914.
101. —— Character and the Emotions. Mind, n.s., vol. v.
102. SHERRINGTON, C. S. The Integrative Action of the Nervous System. London, 1906.
103. —— Article "Brain" in Encyc. Brit. 11th ed.
104. SIDGWICK, H. Outlines of the History of Ethics for English Readers. 4th ed. London, 1896.
105. SMITH, ADAM. The Theory of Moral Sentiments. 1757.
106. —— The Principles which lead and direct Philosophical Enquiries, as illustrated by the History of Astronomy.
107. SPENCER, H. Principles of Psychology. 2 vols. 1873.
108. SPINOZA. Ethics. Everyman Library.
109. STANLEY, HIRAM M. Studies in the Evolutionary Psychology of Feeling. London, 1895.
110. STEWART, DUGALD. Philosophy of the Human Mind. 3 vols. 1827.
111. —— Philosophy of the Active and Moral Powers of Man. 2 vols. 1828.
112. —— Outlines of Moral Philosophy. London, 1864.
113. —— Collected Works. Edited by Sir William Hamilton. 11 vols. 1854-60.
114. STOUT, G. F. Analytic Psychology. 2 vols. London, 1896.
115. —— Manual of Psychology. 2nd ed. London, 1901.
116. —— Manual of Psychology. 3rd ed. London, 1913.
117. —— Groundwork of Psychology. London, 1905.
118. —— Instinct and Intelligence. Brit. Journ. of Psych., vol. III, 1909-10.

119. STURT, H. The Principles of Understanding. Cambridge, 1915.
120. SULLY, J. The Human Mind. 2 vols. London, 1892.
121. THORNDIKE, E. L. Educational Psychology. 3 vols. New York, 1912–14.
122. —— Educational Psychology, Briefer Course. New York, 1915.
123. —— Notes on Child Study. New York, 1903.
124. TITCHENER, E. B. Lectures on the Experimental Psychology of the Thought Processes. New York, 1909.
125. VERWORN, M. Allgemeine Physiologie. 1903.
126. WALLACE, A. R. Darwinism. London, 1889.
127. —— Contributions to the Theory of Natural Selection. London, 1870.
128. WARD, J. The Realm of Ends, or Pluralism and Theism. Cambridge, 1911.
129. —— Naturalism and Agnosticism. 4th ed. London, 1915.
130. WASHBURN, M. F. The Animal Mind. New York, 1909.
131. WEISMANN, A. Das Keimplasma. Jena, 1892. (Translation in Contemporary Science Series. London, 1893.)
132. WUNDT, W. Lectures on Human and Animal Psychology. 2nd ed. Leipzig, 1892. Translation by Creighton and Titchener.
133. —— Elemente der Völkerpsychologie. Leipzig, 1913.
134. DREVER, J. A Study of Children's Vocabularies. Journ. of Exp. Pedagogy, vol. III, 1915.
135. SHAND, A. F. Of Impulse, Emotion, and Instinct. Proc. of Aristotelian Society. 1919–20.
136. CANNON, WALTER B. Bodily Changes in Pain, Hunger, Fear, and Rage. New York, 1915.

INDEX

Aberrations of Instinct, 105 f.
Abnormal psychology, 68, 211, 244
  states, 56, 213
Ach, N., 138
Acquired appetites, 52, 253 ff.
  educational significance of, 254 ff.
Acquired characteristics, transmission
  of, 78, 79
Acquirement of meaning, 130, 259
Acquisitive instinct or tendency, 53,
  73, 169, 170, 171, 173, 179, 187 ff.,
  193, 202, 219
  educational significance of, 189
Addison, Joseph, quoted, 77
Admiration, 32, 33, 35, 234
Aesthetic consciousness, 227
'Affections,' 39, 41, 43, 45, 49, 51, 54
Affective aspect, 21, 145, 156, 158, 166
  element or factor, 155, 220, 240, 244,
  259
Altruistic tendencies, 38, 195
Ambition, 53
Ammophila, 92 f., 123, 144
Amoeba, behaviour of, 248 f.
  experience of, 145
Analgesia, natural, 146
Anger, 25, 39, 85, 160, 161, 165 f., 169,
  170, 173, 177, 178 ff., 192, 196,
  198, 200, 208, 211, 219, 236, 248
Animal, at bay, 179 f.
  behaviour, 2, 8, 19, 43, 56, 62, 64, 97
  inclinations or propensities, 23, 50,
  52, 53, 72, 73, 74
  mind, 43, 55, 56, 58, 62 f., 76
  psychology, 42, 72, 76, 172
'Animal spirits,' 25, 33, 34
Ants, observations of, 102, 106
Appetite, 23, 25, 39, 44, 45, 49, 51, 52,
  73, 149, 168, 169, 170, 185, 190,
  205, 246 ff., 267
  general tendencies, 168, 169, 252 f.
  specific tendencies, 168, 169, 249 f.
Aristotle, 56
Association experiments, 138 ff.
  of ideas, 37, 41, 210
Associationism, 8, 21, 42, 118
Associationists, English, 42, 203

Attention and adjustment, reactions of,
  169, 205
Aversion, 23, 40, 41, 44, 103, 168, 216,
  250

Bacon, Francis, 12
Bain, A., 77, 243, 246, 248
Baldwin, J. M., 72, 80, 186, 212, 220,
  226, 227, 230, 233, 234, 235,
  246, 248
Behaviour, 2, 3, 4, 10, 18, 22, 83, 84,
  85, 97, 98, 100, 102, 112 f., 125,
  146, 152, 153, 155, 191, 230
  of human beings, 164, 165, 204,
  207, 232
  of living organisms, 2, 3, 6, 12, 18,
  56, 81, 98, 150, 231, 263, 265
  of lower organisms, 5, 6, 10, 206
  249
Behaviour experience, 103, 116 f., 134,
  137, 141
Belief, 49, 193, 213 f., 233, 243, 244, 245
Bergson, H., 58, 61, 68, 82, 83, 89, 92 ff.,
  98, 100 f., 107 ff.
Biological account, 2, 10, 15, 19, 78 f.,
  86, 126, 141, 152, 191
  view of Instinct, 19, 57, 69, 76, 78 f.,
  81, 94, 110, 112, 119, 122, 124,
  150 f., 220, 257
Biology, 2, 5, 11, 21, 55, 69, 76, 85, 86,
  98, 124, 260
Bipolarity, of cognition, 88
  of experience, 88, 129
Body and mind or soul, 26, 33
Bonnet, C., 69, 72, 76, 131
Bostock, J., 70 (footnote), 75
Brain, localization of functions, 74, 75
  physiological study of, 5, 75
Brehm, A. E., 77
Büchner, L., 77, 78, 105
Buffon, G. L. L., 76
Bühler, K., quoted, 136
Butler, J., 24, 38, 41, 55

Cabanis, P. J. G., 69 ff., 74
Carpenter, W., 75
Carr, H. Wildon, 111, 126